Chris Beswick is District Inspector with responsibility for foreign languages for the City of Manchester. He was previously Head of Modern Languages at Shena Simon Sixth Form College, Manchester and Head of Modern Languages at Wright Robinson High School, Manchester.

Chris Beswick has also been an assistant examiner for the Oxford Local Examinations Delegacy.

Peter Downes was Senior French Master at Manchester Grammar School and Head of Linguistic Studies at Banbury School before becoming Head of Henry Box School, Witney. He is now Head of Hinchingbrooke School, Huntingdon, where he continues an active role in teaching French. He is French Reviser for the Oxford and Cambridge Schools' Examination Board and for the Southern Universities Joint Board. He was Conference Chairman of the Joint Council of Language Associations from 1984–86.

Peter Downes has written and edited over 70 books relating to language teaching and is best known as co-author of *Le Français d'Aujourd'hui* and *French for Today*. His work has been recognized by the conferment by the French Government of the award of Chevalier dans l'Ordre des Palmes Académiques.

Pan Study Aids for GCSE include:

**Accounting**

**Biology**

**Chemistry**

**Commerce**

**Computer Studies**

**Economics**

**English Language**

**French**

**Geography 1**

**Geography 2**

**German**

**History 1: World History since 1914**

**History 2: Britain and Europe since 1700**

**Human Biology**

**Mathematics**

**Physics**

**Sociology**

**Study Skills**

**PAN STUDY AIDS**

# FRENCH

C. Beswick and P. J. Downes

A Pan Original
**Pan Books**  London, Sydney and Auckland

First published 1988 by Pan Books Ltd,
Cavaye Place, London SW10 9PG

9 8 7 6 5 4 3 2 1

© C. Beswick and P. J. Downes 1988

ISBN 0 330 29417 2

Text design by Peter Ward
Photoset by Parker Typesetting Service, Leicester
Printed and bound in Hong Kong

This book is sold subject to the condition that it shall not, by way of trade or otherwise, be lent, re-sold, hired out or otherwise circulated without the publisher's prior consent in any form of binding or cover other than that in which it is published and without a similar condition including this condition being imposed on the subsequent purchaser

# CONTENTS

Acknowledgements 7
The Examination Associations 8
Introduction to GCSE 9
Introduction: To the students 11
How can this book help? 15

**Part One: Vocabulary topics**

1 ▶ **Developing and revising vocabulary**     21

**Part Two: Getting ready for the examination**

2 ▶ **Listening comprehension**     161

3 ▶ **Reading comprehension**     183

4 ▶ **Speaking**     199

5 ▶ **Writing**     217

6 ▶ **Verb tables**     235

Answers     243

Index     295

# ACKNOWLEDGEMENTS

The co-operation of the following examination associations, whose addresses are listed on page 8, for permission to reproduce sample questions is gratefully acknowledged:

Midland Examining Group, Northern Examination Association, Southern Examination Group.

The publishers are also grateful for permission to reproduce questions from the York Level 5 Mode 3 CSE and GCE O Level French Examination July 1985, conducted by the Joint Matriculation Board and the Yorkshire and Humberside Regional Examinations Board.

The suggested answers and methods of working are those of the authors and not necessarily those of the examination associations.

The co-operation of the following organizations in allowing us to reproduce authentic material in the vocabulary topic chapters is also gratefully acknowledged:

**Topic 1**
Cheval Magazine
Larousse

**Topic 3**
Ville de Courtenay
Office de Tourisme, Ville de Gérardmer
Sealink Ferries SNCF

**Topic 4**
SNCF Région d'Amiens
SNCF
Société des Autoroutes Paris Rhin Rhône
Association des Sociétés Françaises d'Autoroute (also Topic 5)

**Topic 5**
Les Cars Simplon
Musée de l'Automobile Française, Reims

**Topic 6**
Fédération Unie des Auberges de Jeunesse
Comité Départemental de Tourisme du Loiret

# Acknowledgements

**Topic 7**
Flunch
Marest
Laiteries Hubert Triballat

**Topic 10**
Volvo France S.A.
Le Parisien
Comité National du Secours Routier Français

**Topic 11**
Radio Magnum
A.R.V.I.F. Laon

**Topic 12**
L'Express International
Le Français dans le Monde

**Topic 13**
Lycée Français Charles de Gaulle

**Topic 14**
Hachette Export Livre

**Topic 15**
Carte Bleue

**Writing section (back of picture postcard of St Claude)**
As de Cœur

Every effort has been made to trace the copyright holders of the numerous items of authentic material in this book. In some cases this has still proved impossible. The publishers would be pleased to hear from holders in those instances where it has not yet been possible to make contact and seek permission.

The authors and publishers would like to thank all those involved in producing the cassette to accompany this book: the BBC for permission to use some of their recordings; Nicole Gore, Guy Rigaud, Françoise Holland and Béatrice Pearson for providing the authentic voices; many others who contributed by their willingness to be interviewed; above all, our thanks go to Peter Dyson, Director of the Language Teaching Centre at Oxford University, for providing some of the material and for producing the master tape.

# THE EXAMINATION ASSOCIATIONS

The addresses given below are those from which copies of syllabuses and past examination papers may be ordered. The abbreviations (MEG, NEA etc.) are those used in this book to identify actual questions.

London and East Anglia Examining Group (LEAG),
c/o University of London School Examinations Board,
London University,
Stewart House,
32 Russell Square,
LONDON WC1B 5DN

Midland Examining Group (MEG),
c/o University of Cambridge Local Examinations Syndicate,
Syndicate Buildings,
1 Hills Road,
Cambridge, CB1 2EU

Northern Examining Association (NEA),
c/o Joint Matriculation Board,
MANCHESTER, M15 6EU

Northern Ireland Schools Examinations Council (NI),
Examinations Office,
Beechill House, Beechill Road,
Belfast BT8 4RS

Southern Examining Group (SEG),
c/o University of Oxford Delegacy of Local Examinations,
Ewert Place, Summertown,
OXFORD OX2 7BZ

Welsh Joint Education Council (WJEC),
245 Western Avenue,
Cardiff CF5 2YX

# INTRODUCTION TO GCSE

From 1988, there is a single system of examining at 16 plus in England and Wales and Northern Ireland. The General Certificate of Secondary Education (GCSE) replaces the General Certificate of Education (GCE) and the Certificate of Secondary Education (CSE). In Scotland candidates will enter for the O grade and Standard Grade examinations leading to the award of the Scottish Certificate of Education (SCE).

The Pan Study Aids GCSE series has been specially written by practising teachers and examiners to enable you to prepare successfully for this new examination.

GCSE introduces several important changes in the way in which you are tested. First, the examinations are structured so that you can show *what* you know rather than what you do *not* know. Second, courses are set and marked by six examining groups instead of the previous twenty GCE/CSE boards. The groups are:

Northern Examining Association (NEA)
Midland Examining Group (MEG)
London and East Anglian Group (LEAG)
Southern Examining Group (SEG)
Welsh Joint Examinations Council (WJEC)
Northern Ireland Schools Examination Council (NISEC)

One of the most useful changes introduced by GCSE is the single award system of grades A–G. This should permit you and future employers more accurately to assess your qualifications.

| GCSE | GCE O Level | CSE |
| --- | --- | --- |
| A | A | – |
| B | B | – |
| C | C | 1 |
| D | D | 2 |
| E | E | 3 |
| F | F | 4 |
| G |   | 5 |

Remember that, whatever examinations you take, the grades you are awarded will be based on how well you have done.

Pan Study Aids are geared for use throughout the duration of your courses. The text layout has been carefully designed to provide all the

## Introduction to GCSE

information and skills you need for GCSE and SCE examinations – please feel free to use the margins for additional notes.

**N.B.** Where questions are drawn from former O level examination papers, the following abbreviations are used to identify the boards:

UCLES (University of Cambridge Local Examinations Syndicate)
AEB (Associated Examining Board)
ULSEB (University of London Schools Examination Board)
SUJB (Southern Universities Joint Board)
O&C (Oxford & Cambridge)
SCE (Scottish Certificate of Education Examination Board)
JMB (Joint Matriculation Board)
SEB (Scottish Examining Board)
ODLE (Oxford Delegacy of Local Examinations)
WJEC (Welsh Joint Examinations Council)

# INTRODUCTION: TO THE STUDENTS

### WHAT DO I NEED TO KNOW ABOUT THE THINKING BEHIND THE EXAMINATION?

GCSE has not only replaced the old GCE and CSE examinations but also caters for a much wider range of students. There is now a single examination system but this does not mean that every student entering for a particular French syllabus takes the same set of papers. Different combinations of papers will be taken, according to the candidate's levels of attainment in the four skill areas of speaking, listening, reading and writing.

The new examination is designed above all else to test whether you have the ability to use French for the purposes of **practical communication**. What you are asked to do in the examination must correspond to the things you would have to deal with in French in **real life**, either on a visit to a French-speaking country or in contact with a French-speaking person visiting Great Britain. The texts, printed or recorded, which feature in the examination, will be real-life ones, rather than being made up for the occasion by an examiner.

### HOW DOES THIS AFFECT ME AS A STUDENT?

If your examination entry is going to be made by a school or college you will need to know from your teacher or tutor exactly which combination of papers you are going to take. Examination associations will have a two-level system of basic and higher tests in the four skills. The combination of papers makes a significant difference to the maximum grade which you can be awarded. It is not possible, for example, to get a grade higher than D if you do not enter at least for the basic writing test.

The minimum number of papers at basic and higher levels which you must take in order to be eligible for the various grades is as follows:

Grades G, F and E: Basic Speaking, Basic Reading, Basic Listening
Grade D: Basic Speaking, Basic Reading, Basic Listening + any one Higher level test OR Basic Writing
Grade C: Basic Speaking, Basic Reading, Basic Listening + Basic Writing + any one Higher level test

## Introduction: To the students

Grade B: Basic Speaking, Basic Reading, Basic Listening + Basic Writing + Higher Writing + any one other Higher level test
Grade A: Basic Speaking, Basic Reading, Basic Listening + Basic Writing + Higher Writing + any two other Higher level tests

**POINTS TO NOTE**

1 Some examination assocations may use different wording for 'basic' and 'higher', e.g. 'general' and 'extended'.
2 As a general rule, you must take the basic paper in a particular skill if you are intending to attempt the higher paper. In the speaking test you can enter for either basic or higher. If you do the longer, higher level test in speaking it will also include within it a basic test, so you will only have the one oral examination paper.
3 There is obviously a difference between **entry requirements** to qualify for certain grades – which are what you have in the table above – and a satisfactory **performance** to score those grades. Entering for the test alone doesn't guarantee you the grade! However, it is important for you to be aware of what is in the table. What it means is that however well you do in Basic Speaking, Basic Reading and Basic Listening, you cannot score higher than a Grade E if you only take those three tests. To be eligible for higher grades you have to show what you can do in additional papers. You might feel that it would be best for you to persuade your teacher/tutor to enter you for all the higher level tests so as to give you a chance of the higher grades. Ultimately you have to rely on the professional advice which is offered to you. If you really have no chance of coping with higher level speaking and writing, for example, there is no real point in your entering. There has to be a happy medium between the two extremes of giving you insufficient challenge – by playing safe and sticking to basic papers – and putting you through an unpleasant ordeal by entering you for higher papers which are far too demanding for your current level of attainment.

If you are a 'private' candidate you will need to obtain full information for yourself on the syllabus and differentiated papers from the appropriate examination associations (see page 8). You may also wish to obtain a copy of The National Criteria for GCSE French from the Department of Education and Science or from the Welsh Office.

### ISN'T GCSE LIKE ANY OTHER EXAMINATION – TRYING TO CATCH ME OUT?

No. GCSE is much more interested in what you **do** know, **can** do and **can** understand. Recognition is given to basic levels of attainment in all the four language skills. Instead of thinking in terms of 'pass' and 'fail' the idea is of a ladder with rungs representing different levels of competence. The lower rungs are felt to represent worthwhile foundation skills, not failure.

There are no 'trade secrets' known only to examiners. The printed

## Introduction: To the students

syllabus tells you exactly what you are expected to know and to revise.

The fact that you are much more in the picture is a great confidence booster. Careful revision will pay dividends because you know you will actually be asked about the things you have revised! It has to be easier aiming for clearly defined targets rather than 'shooting in the dark'.

### WHAT ARE THE DIFFERENCES BETWEEN THE SYLLABUSES?

Because the language tasks and topics set for candidates are rooted firmly in real life this means that there is now a large degree of similarity in the format of the tests in different parts of the country. As a rule of thumb, the listening and reading activities are very similar. There are some variations in the speaking and writing tests. This book tries to cater for the common ground so it can help students whichever area they are from. This makes it important for you to find out the exact details of the syllabus which you will be taking.

### HOW WILL CANDIDATES BE ASSESSED?

The new examination will be **criterion referenced**. If you show your competence in the things asked for in the syllabus for the award of that grade then that grade is yours. What matters is your performance alone. You will not be compared with other candidates in a way which might end up with only a certain percentage getting an A, a certain percentage getting a B and so on.

A good comparison is the driving test. Candidates pass if they show they can do certain things. If everyone taking the test on a particular day drives safely and competently everyone passes. The examiner doesn't compare the different performances and pass a certain percentage only. Nor would you feel that you hadn't taken a 'proper examination' which must have been too easy because lots of other people passed the same day!

You will receive an overall grade for your performance in the examination but you might also be given a profile which will show the level of competence you reached in the different skill areas of speaking, listening, reading and writing. This is not only useful to you, because it tells you where your strengths and weaknesses are, but also to other people (employers, for example) because it tells them **how** you can put to **practical** use the language you've been learning.

# Introduction: To the students

## WHAT ARE THE BENEFITS OF THE COURSE AND THE EXAMINATION?

The best summary can be found in *The National Criteria for French* which lists the following as the desired aims of your course.

1. To develop the ability to use French effectively for purposes of practical communication.

   This was always a **stated** aim but often it was not what the old examinations tested.

2. To form a sound base of the skills, language and attitudes required for further study, work and leisure.

   What you have at the end of course is something you can pursue in later life, at the very least on a holiday level.

3. To offer insights into the culture and civilization of French-speaking countries.

   Learning a language is very much to do with how real people in different countries live.

4. To develop an awareness of the nature of language and language learning.

   Learning one language should make it easier for you to learn other languages which you may find you want or need to learn in later life.

5. To provide enjoyment and intellectual stimulation.

   Yes, even the difficult parts can be enjoyable at times, because of the challenge.

6. To encourage positive attitudes to foreign language learning and to speakers of foreign languages and a sympathetic approach to other cultures and civilizations.

   Perhaps this will improve the terrible reputation which the British have in this area. It could improve our trade balance and even lead to a more harmonious world.

7. To promote learning skills of a more general application (e.g. analysis, memorizing, drawing of inferences)

   Your French course should develop and improve study skills which are helpful in your other subjects and indeed in real life.

# HOW CAN THIS BOOK HELP?

**IT PROVIDES**

(i) Guidance on **what** to revise and **how** to revise, including specific pointers for the different components of the examination.

(ii) Help with revision and practice in vocabulary topic areas, working on authentic materials which reflect a range of difficulty with tasks similar to those you will tackle in GCSE. A good vocabulary is impor-

**IS THE BOOK C...**

...your use of the book even more
...which goes with the book.
...ning activities for which you
...to print the script, you still
...m reading the text. Only the
...e across to **listen to** and **read**
...ities to speak French. There will
...s of the book covering those three

(iii) ...**cise books** and **course books** from your ...nch, if you have been studying in a school or colleg...

(iv) If you feel it would help you, by use of a **dictionary** for occasional use when working on authentic materials for practice. In the examination itself there should be very few words which are not on the syllabus but this will not always be the case with things you may wish to read in French as practice material. Two words of warning, though. Firstly, the dictionary should be your last resort. This book should help you to develop skills in reading comprehension which will make it unnecessary to use a dictionary to look up lots of words which you **thought** you didn't understand. Secondly, there is a whole range of

## How can this book help?

study skills involved in using a dictionary properly. Unless you take steps to acquire those skills (through a study skills course at school/college or from a study skills book) there is little point in spending money on the dictionary.

### HOW TO USE THIS BOOK

You can find detailed advice at the beginning of each major section but here are some general pointers.

(i) The secret of any good revision campaign is proper forward planning. Trying to cram in too much at the last minute simply gives you mental indigestion. Frequent, varied work in regular 'doses' spread over a much longer period of time will be of much more use to you. Short, sharp bursts during which you really concentrate are better than very long sessions where you get bored. In other words, a little, often, can be a good way of working.

(ii) It is important that you cover a wide range of ground rather than spend too much time on certain aspects of the examination to the exclusion of others. Doing really well in just a few areas (say in one skill, like reading, or in just four or five vocabulary topics) will not give you the best chances of getting the grade you want.

(iii) You need to be quite certain about the syllabus content of the examination papers you will be taking (i.e. the vocabulary topic areas, items of grammar and the types of tests) and make sure that revision is covering the different areas in rotation. One way of doing this would be to make a large chart which could go on your wall for you to record the work you do from this book, making a note of the date and the length of time you spent, with a reference to the page number in the book.

(iv) Your chart could have columns for each of the fifteen vocabulary topics and each of the four chapters on the examination skills. You can then see at a glance if there are areas you are over-doing or neglecting.

(v) You are not obliged to work through this book in any particular order once you have read this introduction. The **starting point** for most of your work should be the material in the vocabulary section which is designed to help you acquire and revise words and phrases in real life contexts.

(vi) Sometimes you will make your own decisions which will take you from work on a vocabulary topic to another section of the book. If you find reading comprehension difficult you may decide you want to spend some time on the specific chapter of the book which gives hints on techniques. You may come across a difficult verb which you need to re-memorize from the verb tables. You shouldn't look on the different sections of the book as watertight compartments. They are very much interconnected and quite deliberately so.

## How can this book help?

(vii) Above all else make your revision **active**! There is little point in staring at a page for hours. You need to test yourself – by saying, writing or doing something – or work with someone else, which is the most enjoyable and the only really effective way of practising orally. If you can't find a partner to work with you then some people find it helpful to use a small cassette recorder for recording answers or practising oral work.

# PART ONE

# VOCABULARY TOPICS

CHAPTER ONE

# DEVELOPING AND REVISING VOCABULARY

**CONTENTS**

| | | |
|---|---|---|
| Topic 1 ▶ | Identity – talking about yourself, your family and your friends | 27 |
| Topic 2 ▶ | Home | 33 |
| Topic 3 ▶ | Your surroundings and the weather | 40 |
| Topic 4 ▶ | Travel and transport | 47 |
| Topic 5 ▶ | Holidays | 64 |
| Topic 6 ▶ | Accommodation | 73 |
| Topic 7 ▶ | Eating and drinking | 83 |
| Topic 8 ▶ | Shopping | 94 |
| Topic 9 ▶ | Services – bank, post office, cleaners and repairers | 101 |
| Topic 10 ▶ | Health, safety and welfare | 113 |
| Topic 11 ▶ | Leisure | 124 |

## Contents

| | | |
|---|---|---:|
| Topic 12 ▶ | **Relations with others** | **133** |
| Topic 13 ▶ | **School and career** | **140** |
| Topic 14 ▶ | **Language** | **146** |
| Topic 15 ▶ | **Money** | **152** |

# Developing and revising vocabulary

The syllabuses for the new examination have closely defined vocabulary lists under various topic headings. You **may** find it helpful to get hold of a copy of the one for your particular syllabus, but you could be put off by the length of the lists!

The vocabulary section in this book tries to reflect as closely as possible the topic headings of those published lists, but it cannot guarantee to match **exactly** the requirements of any single one. The basis for the 15 topic headings is in fact the Northern Examination Association syllabus but as much as possible of the content of other syllabuses has been incorporated within this framework.

There are bound to be some words in the practice material in this book which are not in the word lists for any of the syllabuses. This is inevitable because the texts are generally real ones, not ones specially made up for practice using only certain words from a list.

Don't worry about this though. In the first place you can be sure that in the examination you will not need to know any words which are not on the lists in order to answer all questions correctly. If you have done your revision properly you need have nothing to fear. Secondly, this book will give you some tips in the sections on tackling different parts of the examination on how to train yourself into working out the meaning of unknown words (or words on the lists which you forget) in a more scientific way than by haphazard guesswork.

**USING THIS SECTION OF THE BOOK**

It is divided into 15 units or vocabulary topics. You can work on the units in any order you like but don't forget to keep a record of what you do. (See page 16) Leaving things to the last minute is a bad tactic generally for revision. It can have disastrous consequences in the particular case of work on vocabulary. There is simply too much of it and it is too important for all parts of the examination for it to be neglected. So start early!

Each unit will have three sections:

**PART 1**

**Stimulus material** (often in the form of dialogues) which is designed to get you thinking about the sorts of things you will need to say in

# French

French on this topic. Some of the activities may also ask you to jot things down as a way of testing yourself or even to work with a partner if possible on certain tasks.

### PART 2

**A language skills practice** section which offers you authentic materials in French with suggested activities, some easier, some more difficult, involving speaking, reading, writing and listening.

### PART 3

**A summary page** which provides a **check-list** of language tasks for you to work through in the last stages of your revision on the topic. You will be asking yourself, 'Am I able to do these things in French?'

## WHY NOT JUST MEMORIZE A LIST OF WORDS?

Lists are not the best **starting point** for revision. Working on the texts and activities gives you much fuller ideas on the **type** of vocabulary you need. Often what **you** will need to say about yourself is unique to you and may not necessarily be covered by a word list. It could be, for example, that your father is a lighthouse keeper. You need to be aware that you may need to say this. If the word isn't on the syllabus (which it won't be!) you will then need to take steps to find out how to say it.

The work you do on this section of the book is about **acquiring** and **developing** vocabulary, as well as revising it. You should take an **active** role in the process, not a passive one of absorbing the print off the page. It would be helpful if you could buy a loose-leaf folder and set up a section on each of the 15 topics. You may find you need one or two extra headings for topics on your syllabus which you feel are not catered for by the fifteen headings in this book.

In the first part of the section in your loose-leaf folder on each of the 15 topics **collect** words and phrases connected with the topic which you come across in your French course or in the authentic materials in the vocabulary units in this book.

Just as an example, you could read the magazine survey on French holiday habits in Topic 5 (see page 70) and after you've done the activity ask yourself this question, 'What phrases are there in this text which I can use or adapt for **me** to say something in French about **my** holiday habits?'

It may only be a very short sentence which you note down or it could be a longer one but the important thing is that you will have taken the step of taking what someone else has written or said and making a small part of it your own. Working in this way makes your revision more economical because your reading (and listening) practice is actually contributing to your speaking (and writing) skills as well.

# Developing and revising vocabulary

Train yourself to do this with each piece of French you come across in this book and you would come up with a very useful collection. What's even more important is that you are much more likely to remember phrases you have gathered yourself in this way rather than a long list of words which someone else has put in front of you.

In the second part of your own loose-leaf section on each of the topics work through the check-list of language tasks printed in this book and jot down how you would say those things in French. Often you will be able to think of more than one way of saying a particular thing, which is fine.

**USING THE MATERIALS IN PART 2 SKILLS PRACTICE SECTION OF EACH UNIT:**

The majority of the practice materials on each of the 15 topics are 'authentic' French taken from everyday life. Some of the documents are reproduced from sample papers reproduced by kind permission of the examining groups, along with their questions. Others are of a broadly similar type with a variety of activities, many of which will correspond to those you will have to do in the GCSE tests. Some of them may be different from the tasks set in the examinations but the work you do should still be relevant practice. Instructions will be given for each activity, so train yourself into doing what you must do in the examination itself – read them carefully several times!

Some of the activities can only really be done with a partner. This can be a really good way of revising if you can find someone also aiming for GCSE French, preferably with her or his own copy of this book.

Some documents will ask you to practise several skills – you will have to read and understand, say something in connection with them and even write something on occasion. Sometimes a task will involve working on more than one document, as can happen in the examination.

Wherever possible, suggested answers will be given at the back of the book, starting on page 243. Frequently this is not possible because you are asked to answer in a very individual way, giving details about yourself which only you can know. In the case of any sample examination papers which figure in this part of the book, the answers provided are the authors' suggestions, not necessarily approved versions by the Examination Associations themselves.

**SUCCESS OR NOT?**

What if you don't feel your first attempts at the practice material are very successful?

Don't forget in the first place that the material provides a range of practice activities, some easier and others more difficult. You cannot necessarily expect to do well from the word 'go' in all the activities.

We all learn at different rates and in different ways. Some things which are unclear and difficult initially begin to make sense and to stick after three or four attempts. The important thing is that you are sure in your own mind that you really are trying your best.

It could be that you find the techniques demanded by the activity (in speaking, listening, reading or writing) especially difficult. You may therefore like to spend some time working on the appropriate section of the book covering each of those skills in terms of examination techniques. (*Getting ready for the Examination*, beginning page 159).

# TALKING ABOUT YOURSELF, YOUR FAMILY AND YOUR FRIENDS

**A  DIALOGUE AU COMMISSARIAT**

AGENT  *Alors, jeune homme, vous avez vu votre passeport la dernière fois hier en sortant de chez votre correspondant?*
JEUNE HOMME  *Oui, c'est ça monsieur.*
AGENT  *Alors il faut compléter cette déclaration de perte. Vous vous appelez comment?*
JEUNE HOMME  *Choudri.*
AGENT  *Voulez-vous bien épeler ça, s'il vous plaît?*
JEUNE HOMME  *C–H–O–U–D–R–I*
AGENT  *C'est votre nom de famille. Votre prénom?*
JEUNE HOMME  *Kaius – K–A–I–U–S.*
AGENT  *Vous êtes de quelle nationalité?*
JEUNE HOMME  *Britannique.*
AGENT  *Vous êtes né quand et où?*
JEUNE HOMME  *Le 17 mai 1968 à Leicester. L–E–I–C–E–S–T–E–R.*
AGENT  *Votre adresse en Grande-Bretagne?*
JEUNE HOMME  *48 Granby (G–R–A–N–B–Y) Avenue, Leicester.*
AGENT  *Vous êtes chez qui en France?*
JEUNE HOMME  *Chez Lorne (L–O–R–N–E), 11 rue du Bayard, St. Morez.*
AGENT  *Est-ce qu'on peut vous contacter par téléphone?*
JEUNE HOMME  *Oui, monsieur, au 34-98-80.*
AGENT  *Vous êtes étudiant?*
JEUNE HOMME  *Oui, monsieur.*
AGENT  *Vous avez une pièce d'identité, à part votre passeport?*
JEUNE HOMME  *J'ai cette carte bancaire, monsieur.*
AGENT  *Merci. Voulez-vous bien signer ici, s'il vous plaît?*

**Activity**

Work through the dialogue, preferably with a friend. Each take a turn at giving the correct personal details. The dialogue is not complete. Imagine what was said before the first line and how the conversation ended.

If you have a partner to work with, then try the following adaptation. Jot down, without showing your partner, a set of details which you make up, i.e. circumstances in which you lost the passport, name, age, address etc. Your partner then has to write down all the information which you give her or him. Compare notes when you've been through your new dialogue to see how well you've communicated the details in French.

### B  EXTRAIT D'UN ENREGISTREMENT SUR CASSETTE

'... Salut! Je suis ta correspondante française. Je m'appelle Aude Berger. J'ai quinze ans et je suis née au Canada. Je n'ai pas de photo récente de moi. C'est pour ça que je vais te donner quelques détails sur moi et sur ma famille. Je suis de taille plus ou moins moyenne – je mesure 1.50 mètres. Je pèse 49 kilos. J'ai les yeux verts et les cheveux longs, bruns et frisés. J'ai un frère et une sœur. Nous habitons avec notre mère. Nos parents sont divorcés, malheureusement. J'aime bien faire du sport. Je fais partie d'une équipe de gymnastique. Je vais souvent à la piscine et à la patinoire. Nous n'avons pas d'animaux chez nous. J'adore lire et écrire des lettres mais je déteste faire la cuisine...'

**Activity**

Write the script for the reply which you would record on cassette. Add in extra details which will really put the 'tape friend' in the picture, e.g. more on your physical appearance (hair, eyes, whether you wear glasses) and that of members of your family. Are your parents employed? Do you have pets? What are your likes and dislikes? Ask your friend to reply quickly.

### C  FAISONS LA CONNAISSANCE DE...

Nom:                          Prénom:
Date de naissance:
Lieu de naissance:            Pays:
Domicile actuel:
Cheveux:                      Yeux:
Poids:                        Taille:
Situation de famille:         (Marié/Célibataire)
Métier:                       Langues vivantes:
Couleur favorite:             Repas favori:
Qualités:                     Défauts:
Adore:                        Ne peut pas supporter:
Ambition:                     Passetemps:

**Activity**

The table above is the kind of thing which celebrities are often asked to fill in when they are being interviewed by journalists. Can you work out the questions which you need to ask in each case to get the required information? Try your questions out on a partner, getting her or him either to answer as her- or himself or take on the role of

## Talking about yourself, your family and your friends

someone famous and answer as that person! There could be scope for humour – or for a guessing element. See if you can work out the name of the famous person from the answers, in which case you would miss out the first two items on names.

### SKILLS PRACTICE

**1**  **CORRESPONDANCE**
Je recherche une correspondante âgée entre 14 et 16 ans aimant le cinéma, la danse, la musique, la natation, la plage, les fêtes, la mode. Parlant français ou anglais. Joindre photos. J'attends vos lettres. Ecrire à **Séverine Lecacheur, 13, rue Bruyère-sur-le-Coq, Toussaint, 76400 Fécamp.**

Apart from writing to a magazine, Séverine has also written a copy of this letter to your school.

Write a short note in English to insert in the school bulletin, which covers the following points, so that a good 'match' for Séverine can be found: the age range and interests of the pen-friend being sought; whether the letters are to be in French or English; any additional requests.

If you 'fit the bill' and would be a good match, plan and then write out your introductory letter to Séverine.

**2**  **AVIS DE RECHERCHE**
Nous lisons régulièrement OK! et nous trouvons votre journal génial. Nous recherchons Gilbert qui est moniteur de ski à Méandre. Il est brun, a les yeux marron et mesure environ 1m75. Nous étions deux, Christelle, brune aux yeux verts, et Sophie, blonde aux yeux marron. Nous étions dans cette station fin février. On skiait sans bâtons et étions souvent avec Claude un perchman. Si vous le reconnaissez ou s'il se reconnaît, qu'il nous écrive à **Christelle Didelot et Sophie Augendre, 27, rue Joanny-Chamrion, Cercié, 69220 Belleville-sur-Saône.**

In this letter a person is also being sought, but for different reasons from the first letter. Try to complete the table below as a way of finding out how much you've understood. There are bound to be some gaps as the letter does not contain all the information required to complete every column.

| Names of people involved | Colour of hair | Colour of eyes | Height |
|---|---|---|---|
| 1 | | | |
| 2 | | | |
| 3 | | | |
| 4 | | | |

Where they met.
What activity brought them together.
They hope that one of the persons mentioned will perhaps read the letter. Which one?
What is the request to readers of the letters page of the magazine?

3   The British are known for their love of dogs. If you were with non-French-speaking friends on a trip to France and saw these two notices about dogs, could you explain what they meant? The first is at the entrance to a park and the second at a car park.

(a)    PAR MESURE D'HYGIENE L'ACCES DES CHIENS MEME TENUS EN LAISSE EST INTERDIT DANS LE PARC
(b)    PENSEZ A LA CHALEUR! NE LAISSEZ PAS VOTRE CHIEN DANS LA VOITURE

4   Here are some statistics which you come across in a French magazine about pets in France.

Pourcentage des foyers possédant un animal: 55% (ce chiffre représente le pourcentage le plus élevé du monde).
Le hit-parade des animaux: chiens (9 millions); oiseaux (8 millions); chats (7 millions); poissons (5 millions); autres: tortues, hamsters, lapins (2 millions).
Parmi les groupes qui ont le plus d'animaux sont: commerçants et agriculteurs
Parmi les groupes qui ont le moins d'animaux sont: ouvriers et cadres

(a)    Which of the figures quoted represents a world record?
(b)    Which animal is the most popular and which are the least popular?
(c)    Can you name one group of people who fall into the category of most likely pet owners and one group who fall into the category of least likely pet owners?

5   You come across this letter in a magazine which you are leafing through whilst on a trip to a French-speaking country.

**Pas si gros, les Shetlands**

En feuilletant un magazine sur l'Écosse, j'ai trouvé un article sur les îles Shetland. J'ai vu des photos de poneys qui, bien que de la même taille que Snoopy, ne lui ressemblent pas vraiment. Snoopy, mon poney Shetland, est aussi petit mais il est bien plus gros que les poneys de la photo. S'agit-il de la même race?

Ferréol Buvat

En effet, les poneys Shetlands sont bien originaires des îles ... Shetland, situées au nord de l'Écosse. Si Snoopy te paraît bien plus 'rondouillard' que les poneys de la photo, c'est qu'il est sûrement suralimenté. Les Shetlands sont extrêmement rustiques et se contentent largement d'une nourriture sobre. Sur les îles Shetland, l'herbe n'a rien à voir avec celle de nos vertes prairies; elle y est rase et clairsemée. 'Nos' Shetlands sont, bien souvent, excessivement nourris. Il en résulte des poneys énormes, sujets aux fourbures. Si tu veux que ton poney retrouve sa ligne, offre-lui un pré et une nourriture simple.

(a)    What is Ferréol's worry about Snoopy?
(b)    What is the editor's explanation of why the pony looks the way it does?
(c)    What is the suggestion for changing the appearance of the pony?

# Talking about yourself, your family and your friends

**6** **L'adolescence commence plus tôt**
À 13 ans, la plupart des enfants ont une maturité comparable à celle qu'avaient leurs parents à 16 ans. Entre 11 et 14 ans, 78% des enfants vont régulièrement faire des achats dans des magasins; 56% ont en permanence de l'argent sur eux, 47% ont économisé de l'argent pour s'acheter un objet. L'influence de l'environnement est déterminante sur cette évolution. A la télévision, au cinéma ou à la radio, les enfants reçoivent des messages qui ne leur sont pas spécialement destinés. Ils voyagent plus tôt et plus loin, pratiquent plus d'activités, bref accumulent plus rapidement les expériences de la vie.

**Les 8-14 ans et l'avenir.** Les progrès qui les étonnent le plus sont l'ordinateur, les jeux vidéo et électroniques, la navette spatiale, le laser et ... le bébé éprouvette (29% des filles, 8% des garçons). Leurs principales préoccupations sont liées à l'actualité dramatique (les enfants parlent de plus en plus de la guerre). Ils sont généralement hostiles à la 'politique' et envisagent l'avenir sans optimisme mais sans crainte excessive.

(a) Is the left-hand article above about
  (i) pocket money
  (ii) the media
  (iii) children becoming grown-up more quickly nowadays
  (iv) shopping habits?
(b) Can you give two examples of the ways in which children show their *financial* independence?
(c) What two things are said about travel at the end of the article?
(d) Is the right-hand article about
  (i) war
  (ii) politics
  (iii) computers
  (iv) attitudes?
(e) Can you give three examples of technological progress which young people find astounding?
(f) What worries them the most?
(g) Is their attitude to the future
  (i) neither too optimistic nor too pessimistic
  (ii) fearful and pessimistic
  (iii) generally hostile
  (iv) optimistic?

**7** Overleaf is part of the form which you have to fill in if you wish to register with the *Service de la Correspondance Scolaire Internationale* to be matched up with a French-speaking pen-friend. Fill in the details about your school and class plus the personal details about yourself, exactly as requested on the form overleaf. Follow any instructions about using block capitals.

# 32　　　　　　　　　French

*Etablissement:*　　　　　　　　　　　　　　　　　　　　　　　　*Classe*
*Date:*　　　　　　　*Nº du code postal*　　　　　　　　　　　　*Ville*

1 Nom de famille　⎫　　　　　　　　　　　　　　　　　　　　　Langue (s) étrangère (s)
2 Prénom de l'élève　⎬ en lettres d'imprimerie　Sexe　Age　Adresse complète de l'élève　　étudiée (s)
3 Occupation du père　⎭　　　　　　　　　(en lettres d'imprimerie)　　1re ou 2e langue
　　　　　　　　　　　　　　　　　　　　　　　　　　　　　　　　　Goûts dominants

1

2

3

## CHECK-LIST

**Essential language tasks**
To be able to talk about yourself, members of your family and friends covering the following details.
(a)　　name (spelling it out aloud in French when necessary)
(b)　　address (spelling out name of town aloud in French when necessary)
(c)　　phone number
(d)　　nationality
(e)　　age and birthday
(f)　　your position in the family (e.g. youngest, oldest)
(g)　　the jobs people do
(h)　　likes/dislikes
(i)　　descriptions of what people look like or their characters (e.g. married/single; colour of hair; eyes; height; clothes.)
(j)　　family pets (e.g. who owns them/feeds them.)
To be able to find out all the information above from someone else.

# YOUR HOME

**A  DIALOGUE**

*Un jeune Anglais arrive chez son correspondant.*
FRANÇOIS   Alors Peter, je te présente ma mère.
SA MÈRE   Enchantée, Peter. On a déjà beaucoup parlé de vous. Asseyez-vous. Vous voulez prendre quelque chose à boire ou à manger?
PETER   Merci, non. Je n'ai pas tellement faim – mais peut-être quelque chose à boire un petit peu plus tard?
MÈRE   On va vous montrer votre chambre.

Voilà – la salle de bains est à côté. Voici l'armoire. Là-dedans vous avez des cintres. Il y a aussi un oreiller et des couvertures si vous en avez besoin.
PETER   Merci bien. C'est parfait. Est-ce que je peux prendre une douche, s'il vous plaît? Et après, je voudrais me coucher. Je suis fatigué après le voyage.
MÈRE   Bien sûr. Vous voudriez aussi peut-être téléphoner à vos parents? Et on va prendre un petit chocolat chaud. Ça fait dormir.

PETER   Merci bien. C'était du très bon chocolat. Si ça ne vous gêne pas, j'aimerais me coucher maintenant. Un autre soir je vais vous aider à faire la vaisselle.
MÈRE   Mais non! Bonne nuit! A demain et dormez bien!

**Activity**

1. If you were the young person above arriving for a two-week stay with a French family you would also very likely be tired and want to get to bed on the first night. Make a list of questions that you would want to ask the following morning about all the routines in the household. What are the normal times for getting up, eating and going to bed? May you use the telephone? How can you help? Where do you put your clothes etc. and suitcase?
2. Choose a moment when there is no one else in at home and then walk around the flat or house, preferably with a cassette recorder. Try recording a commentary on each of the rooms in French, imagining that you are showing round a French-speaking boy or girl who has just arrived for a stay with your family. Think of helpful information which you could give her or him about each room.

## 34 French

**B  EXTRAIT D'UN ENREGISTREMENT SUR CASSETTE**

'... tu m'as demandé de décrire notre petit appartement. Il est au cinquième étage d'un immeuble. Depuis le balcon on a une très belle vue. On voit une grande rue car le bâtiment est au centre de la ville. Le seul problème, c'est qu'il y a toujours du bruit à cause des voitures qui passent dans la rue ...'

**Activity**

Write down what you would say if you were returning a cassette in French all about your home. Begin as in the extract above by saying something about the location of your home and about the outside. Then go on to describe the rooms inside, your own room in particular. Say how long you've been living there and why you like it or don't like it.

**C  ENQUÊTE SUR L'ÉLECTROMÉNAGER:**

| Appareil | Essentiel | Utile | Assez utile | Inutile |
|---|---|---|---|---|
| brosse à dents électrique | | | | |
| chaîne stéréo | | | | |
| congélateur | | | | |
| four à micro ondes | | | | |
| lave-vaisselle | | | | |
| machine à laver | | | | |
| magnétophone à cassettes | | | | |
| magnétoscope | | | | |
| micro-ordinateur | | | | |
| réfrigérateur (combiné congélateur) | | | | |
| téléviseur noir et blanc | | | | |
| téléviseur couleur | | | | |

# Your home

**Activity**

1. Try the survey above out on your friends. Think of how you would phrase the question in French to find out whether they rate the different appliances as essential, useful etc. What is your rating? Could you say the reasons why in French?
2. Imagine you're talking in French about the appliances you have at home. If you'd forgotten the word for one of them, (and you had no dictionary with you) could you have a go at describing them in French so that the people listening to you would understand what it was you were talking about and then tell you the French word for it! Go through the list and have a go at this for each word. Try your explanation out on someone who speaks French (e.g. someone in your class) and see if they can work out which you're talking about.

## SKILLS PRACTICE

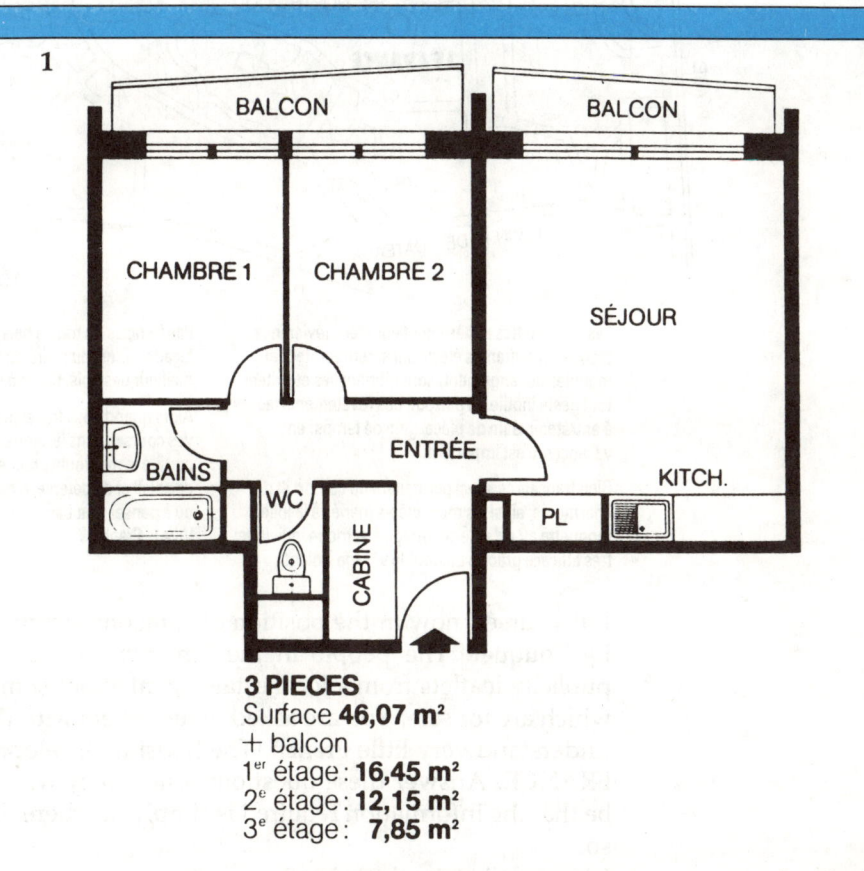

1. 

[Floor plan showing: BALCON, BALCON, CHAMBRE 1, CHAMBRE 2, SÉJOUR, BAINS, WC, CABINE, ENTRÉE, PL, KITCH.]

**3 PIECES**
Surface **46,07 m²**
+ balcon
1$^{er}$ étage : **16,45 m²**
2$^e$ étage : **12,15 m²**
3$^e$ étage : **7,85 m²**

This is a plan of the holiday flat which your family is renting at a French holiday resort. Re-label it in English, so that members of your family who don't understand French can see what is in it. (Here 'cabine' is a small cubicle for two bunk-beds.) Can you work out what PL might stand for, next to the sink? Why are different surface areas in square metres given for the balcony?

# French

**Extension**

(a) Find a partner who understands French and *without showing her/him the drawing in the book* try and communicate, in French only, the lay-out and rooms in the flat. Get her/him to draw it as you explain it. Check her/his drawing with this drawing when you've finished to see how successfully you have communicated.

(b) Imagine you are staying in the flat. Write a short letter to your pen-friend who lives in another part of France telling him/her all about the flat. If you like, wait until you've looked at Item 2 below before you try this activity, as there are further details about the surroundings of the flat which might give you extra things to say.

**2**

Les kitchenettes entièrement équipées (évier inox, plaques chauffantes électriques, réfrigérateur et meubles de rangement) sont rationnelles et évitent tout geste inutile. Et partout, des revêtements faciles à entretenir. Gain de place, gain de temps: en vacances, c'est important.

Bien français ce souci permanent du confort et de l'harmonie, ainsi les murs crépis mariés à la jolie moquette au sol et le chauffage électrique individuel très efficace grâce à un double vitrage isolant.

Pas français du tout le bois qui habille en partie les façades. C'est du cèdre du Canada, le plus beau et le meilleur des bois. Bravo à nos 'cousins' canadiens!

Alors quand vous traverserez les jardins pour faire vos courses dans le centre commercial voisin ou pour partir à la mer toute proche pour une longue journée de soleil et de détente, n'hésitez pas à crier bien haut, ou à penser tout bas:
Vive le France!

Put yourself now in the position of someone staying at a campsite in Le Touquet. The people in the tent next to yours pick up some publicity leaflets from a local estate agent about some holiday homes which are for sale. You are asked to help them with this leaflet as they understand very little French. The housing development is called LE FRANCE. Answer these questions which they want help on. It may be that the information required is simply not there, in which case say so.

(a) What are the prices?
(b) Are there service charges?
(c) What kind of furniture/fittings are included?
(d) Does it say anything about rates?
(e) Do they have gas or electric?
(f) Does it say anything about heating or insulation?

## Your home 37

 (g) What does it say about the outside of the building?
 (h) Is it far from the shops and the beach?
 (i) Is there a sales office on site and where?
 (j) Are any other amenities mentioned in the publicity or marked on the map?

**3**

LECTEUR DE CASSETTE STÉRÉO "Tom Pouce" plus petit qu'une cassette audio, un astucieux tiroir rétractable permet de recevoir celle-ci. Touches : lecture, avance rapide, stop. Alim. 2 piles 1,5 volt R 6 (non fournies). Prise alimentation extérieure. Livré avec casque stéréo. Dim. 6,5 x 10,8 x 3 cm. Garantie 1 an. Prix franco magasin.
Réf. 394.475 . . . . . . . . . . . . . . . . . . . . . . . F 199,00

**199 F**
soit une réduction de **40 F** sur le catalogue

You've heard that some electrical goods are cheaper in France. You need to replace your walkman, so when you see this advert in a mail-order/discount warehouse catalogue whilst staying at your French pen-friend's flat, you are naturally interested. Can you answer the following questions for yourself in order to arrive at a decision whether to purchase or not?

 (a) What does the advert say about the size of the walkman which seems surprising?
 (b) How many function keys has it got and what do they do?
 (c) What details does it give about power supply?
 (d) What kind of guarantee is there?
 (e) Why might it be better to buy it in the warehouse rather than by mail-order?

**Extension**

Write down what you would say in the warehouse if you wanted to buy the walkman. State which model. Ask if the guarantee is valid in the UK.

> **RÉSERVÉ AU VERRE USAGÉ**
>
> VERRE RECYCLÉ · PROPRETÉ · ÉCONOMIE
>
> N'Y JETEZ PAS
>
> COUVERCLES, BOUCHONS, PORCELAINES,
> et autres corps étrangers
> BRIQUES, CAILLOUX, TERRES
>
> **SEULEMENT LE VERRE**
>
> NE DÉPOSEZ PAS D'ORDURES...
> MERCI DE VOTRE PARTICIPATION!
> PAS DE VERRE DANS LES ORDURES MÉNAGÈRES. C'EST UNE MATIÈRE PREMIÈRE

4. You see the notice above on a large metal bin in a supermarket car park. Someone who is with you is curious about what it's for. Could you explain to them the purpose of the bin? What things are you *not* supposed to throw into it?

5. The following is an extract from a letter to a magazine. A teacher, called Jacqueline Blaser, is writing about commercial pressures from banks aimed at getting teenagers to open accounts. Mme Blaser has a 15-year-old son.

> '... Qu'on le veuille ou non, c'est bien dans une société de consommation que nous vivons. Aussi, donner à l'enfant les moyens d'y être préparé le plus tôt possible n'est pas une aberration. Frédéric? L'argent n'a jamais été un problème dans nos relations. Il a en règle générale 50 F d'argent de poche par semaine plus les 'plus'. Cela dit, il a encore le comportement enfant qui consiste à tout dépenser sans jamais rien mettre de côté. Mais il est assez raisonnable...'

(a) What is the one item of fact which we learn about her son's pocket money?

(b) How would you describe her attitude to the idea of her son having a bank account?

    (i) Accepts it because it will help him to cope with the consumer society;

    (ii) horrified because it will cause rifts in their relationship;

    (iii) not concerned either way by the idea?

# Your home

(c) How would you describe her view of her son's money sense?
(i) He's completely unreasonable and has no money sense;
(ii) he saves on occasions;
(iii) he still lacks maturity when it comes to saving?

6 Write a letter of 100–130 words to your pen-friend who is going to visit you for the first time in the summer. Concentrate on asking her/him about her/his daily routine and likes/dislikes as regards food and activities. Make some suggestions about what you might do. Say how much you're looking forward to the visit.

## CHECK-LIST

**Essential language tasks**

(a) describe your house/flat/caravan etc.
(b) say where it is (e.g. near to town/village)
(c) talk about the rooms/garden etc.
(d) find out the same details as above about someone else's house
(e) ask where toilet/bathroom is in a home you are visiting
(f) describe your own bedroom (if you have one to yourself)
(g) say how you help around the house
(h) offer to help
(i) say you need washing materials e.g. soap, toothpaste
(j) say you would like food/drink/shower/bath when arriving in French home after long journey
(k) thank someone for hospitality during or at end of visit
(l) talk about your daily routine e.g. time of waking/eating/going to bed
(m) say what you do at weekends, e.g. part-time job
(n) talk about pocket money.

**Useful language tasks**

(a) ask for permission/explanation regarding what to do when staying in a French home e.g. washing dirty clothes; using the telephone; using electrical sockets
(b) explaining politely that things are missing/not working e.g. not enough coat-hangers; light bulb missing; no toilet paper
(c) showing a French visitor (who speaks little /no English) around your home and explaining the things she/he needs to know
(d) talking about your ideal home (if you had the money to afford it)
(e) talking about the differences you notice in daily routine at home and in the French family with whom you are staying.

# YOUR SURROUNDINGS AND THE WEATHER

### A  ENQUÊTE SUR L'HABITAT

Emplacement de votre domicile – agglomération/banlieue/petite ville/ville importante/village
Caractère – industriel/agricole
Région:            Nombre d'habitants:
Paysages voisins – urbain/campagne/mer/lac/forêt/montagne
Décor – plutôt beau/plutôt laid/intéressant/charmant/calme
Agréments/Équipements – anciens quartiers/villages pittoresques/monuments/musées/parcs/cinéma/théâtre/camping municipal/stade/grands magasins
Possibilités touristiques locales et régionales:
Aspects positifs:        Aspects négatifs:
Est-ce que vous vous plaisez ou vous vous ennuyez ici?
Pourquoi?

**Activity**
The above is a list of prompts for an interviewer carrying out an opinion poll on people's surroundings. Can you work out the questions in French and decide what you would answer in French about the place where you live.

### B  EXTRAIT D'UNE LETTRE:

'... j'habite dans une grande ville dans le sud-est de la France. Elle est entourée de montagnes. Ce n'est pas loin de la Suisse et de l'Italie. Il y a quelques industries. La rivière qui traverse la ville s'appelle l'Isère. Il y a un très beau musée de peinture dans le centre ville et de beaux parcs. La visite du château de Vizelle, qui se trouve à environ 17 km de Grenoble est vraiment intéressante. La ville possède un grand stade et aussi un 'anneau de vitesse' où ont eu lieu les épreuves olympiques de patinage en 1968. Le village olympique est situé dans la banlieue de Grenoble. De la ville même il est possible de prendre un téléphérique au pied de la colline de la Bastille. Du sommet on a un panorama magnifique sur la ville ... Ici, il fait très froid en hiver, mais l'air est sec. Nous avons beaucoup de neige. Heureusement les chasse-neige dégagent les routes rapidement. En été il fait chaud et de plus les montagnes abritent la ville du vent. Mais nous avons la pluie en février et les giboulées en mars ...'

## Your surroundings and the weather

**Activity**

Your neighbours show you the letter above which has come to their son who has only just started French. Could you explain to them what it is about and also write something in French which gives similar type of information about where you live?

## SKILLS PRACTICE

**SIGNS AND NOTICES**

1. Could you explain each of the following to a non-French speaker who was walking with you through a French town? In each case the location of the sign is given in brackets.
   - (a) POUSSEZ! (on a door)
   - (b) PEINTURE FRAICHE (on a door)
   - (c) RUE PIÉTONNE (on a street sign)
   - (d) PAR ARRETÉ PREFECTORAL LES ANIMAUX NE SONT PAS ADMIS DANS LE MAGASIN (on a shop door)
   - (e) CONFORMEZ-VOUS AU REGLEMENT DE LA PRÉFECTURE DE POLICE – NE FUMEZ PAS – JETEZ VOTRE CIGARETTE ICI – MERCI (in the foyer to a building)
   - (f) NE JETEZ RIEN A TERRE (on a street sign)
   - (g) CHANTIER INTERDIT AU PUBLIC (by a building site)
   - (h) DEFENSE D'AFFICHER (on a wall)
   - (i) EMPRUNTEZ LE PASSAGE SOUTERRAIN (by a busy road junction)
   - (j) SYNDICAT D'INITIATIVE (on a street sign)
   - (k) EXPOSITION HENRY MOORE (on a poster)
   - (l) DEFENSE DE MARCHER SUR LES PELOUSES (in a park)
   - (m) NEIGE? GEL? PLUIE? – RALENTIR! (a road sign)

2. You come across the following information in a free hand-out given to you by the tourist information office in the town hall of the place where you're camping.

   **POMPIERS:** Tel. 38–97–40–22
   **GENDARMERIE:** Tél. 38–97–40–22
   **ÉTAT DES ROUTES:** Inter Service Routes 16–1–48–58–33–33
   **OFFICE DE TOURISME:** 1er mai au 30 septembre tous les jours sauf dimanche après-midi et lundi. Tél. 38–00–97–60
   **CENTRE DE LOISIRS:** Tél. 38–97–92–03 (uniquement en juillet)
   **SOCIÉTÉ DE PECHE:** Tél. 38–97–34–83

   - (a) Which phone number might be handy from a motoring point of view and why?
   - (b) When would there be not much point in contacting the local tourist information office?
   - (c) Which two numbers might be vital in an emergency?
   - (d) What item of information is given about the leisure centre apart from the phone number?
   - (e) Of what use might the very last entry in the list be to you?

3

*TEMPS POUR VOS VOYAGES*

- Première colonne: temps à 14 heures (heure de Paris), le 27 juillet.
  (**S**: soleil; **N**: nuageux; **C**: couvert; **P**: pluie; **A**: averse; **O**: orage; **B**: brouillard; *****: neige).
- Deuxième colonne: température à 8 heures (heure de Paris), le 27 juillet.
- Troisième colonne: température à 14 heures (heure de Paris), le 27 juillet.

Étant donné l'important décalage horaire entre Paris et certaines stations étrangères (celles d'Extrême-Orient, en particulier), les températures qui y sont relevées à 8 heures (heure de Paris) peuvent être parfois supérieures à celles relevées à 14 heures (heure de Paris).

### FRANCE

| | | | |
|---|---|---|---|
| Ajaccio | N | 21 | 27 |
| Biarritz | C | 17 | 22 |
| Bordeaux | S | 14 | 25 |
| Brest | P | 15 | 16 |
| Cherbourg | S | 14 | 21 |
| Clermont-F | S | 16 | 26 |
| Dijon | S | 17 | 25 |
| Dinard | C | 18 | 22 |
| Embrun | S | 15 | 26 |
| Grenoble | S | 16 | 28 |
| La Rochelle | S | 19 | 23 |
| Lille | C | 16 | 23 |
| Limoges | S | 13 | 23 |
| Lorient | C | 16 | 19 |
| Lyon | S | 18 | 26 |
| Marseille | S | 21 | 29 |
| Nancy | C | 14 | 24 |
| Nantes | P | 18 | 20 |
| Nice | S | 21 | 27 |
| Paris | N | 19 | 25 |
| Pau | N | 16 | 23 |
| Perpignan | S | 22 | 29 |
| Rennes | C | 17 | 23 |
| Rouen | N | 16 | 24 |
| St-Étienne | S | 15 | 25 |
| Strasbourg | N | 18 | 25 |
| Toulouse | C | 17 | 25 |
| Tours | C | 17 | 22 |

### EUROPE

#### ILES BRITANNIQUES

| | | | |
|---|---|---|---|
| Brighton | N | 14 | 20 |
| Edimbourg | P | 15 | 19 |
| Londres | C | 13 | 21 |
| Cork | P | 14 | 15 |
| Dublin | P | 14 | 18 |

#### ALLEMAGNE – AUTRICHE

| | | | |
|---|---|---|---|
| Berlin | C | 16 | 23 |
| Bonn | N | 16 | 21 |
| Hambourg | N | 17 | 22 |
| Munich | C | 16 | 24 |
| Vienne | S | 18 | 24 |

#### BELGIQUE – PAYS-BAS

| | | | |
|---|---|---|---|
| Bruxelles | N | 17 | 23 |
| Amsterdam | N | 16 | 20 |

#### ESPAGNE – PORTUGAL

| | | | |
|---|---|---|---|
| Barcelone | S | 18 | 26 |
| Las Palmas | S | 20 | 24 |
| Madrid | S | 15 | 28 |
| Marbella | S | 18 | 25 |
| Palma Maj | S | 17 | 28 |
| Séville | S | 18 | 32 |
| Lisbonne | B | 16 | 26 |
| Madère | N | 19 | 22 |
| Porto | S | 12 | 23 |

#### ITALIE

| | | | |
|---|---|---|---|
| Florence | S | 20 | 27 |
| Milan | S | 19 | 27 |
| Naples | B | 20 | 32 |
| Olbia | S | 21 | 24 |
| Palermo | S | 26 | 32 |
| Reggio Cal | S | 24 | 28 |
| Rimini | N | 19 | 25 |
| Rome | S | 20 | 29 |

#### GRÈCE – TURQUIE

| | | | |
|---|---|---|---|
| Athènes | S | 29 | 32 |
| Corfou | S | 20 | 30 |
| Patras | S | 23 | 30 |
| Rhodes | S | 26 | 33 |
| Salonique | S | 23 | 29 |
| Ankara | S | 19 | 29 |
| Istanbul | M | 23 | 27 |

#### PAYS NORDIQUES

| | | | |
|---|---|---|---|
| Copenhague | C | 17 | 19 |
| Helsinki | S | 17 | 24 |
| Oslo | B | 15 | 16 |
| Stockholm | S | 15 | 22 |

#### SUISSE

| | | | |
|---|---|---|---|
| Bâle | N | 17 | 26 |
| Berne | S | 15 | 24 |
| Genève | S | 16 | 26 |

#### U.R.S.S.

| | | | |
|---|---|---|---|
| Leningrad | C | 23 | 26 |
| Moscou | C | 20 | 25 |
| Odessa | S | 21 | 24 |

#### YOUGOSLAVIE

| | | | |
|---|---|---|---|
| Belgrade | S | 16 | 26 |
| Dubrovnik | S | 22 | 27 |

## Your surroundings and the weather    43

When you're on holiday in France in July you buy a French newspaper and you're interested to see the reports on weather around the world because you have quite a few relatives, friends and neighbours who are on holiday at the same time as you in different countries.

(a)   Why are there two figures given for temperatures, in the second and third columns?
(b)   What was the weather report for that day for ... Dinard in France ... Rhodes in Greece ... Dublin in Ireland ... Bâle in Switzerland ... Lisbon in Portugal ...?
(c)   What do these three symbols stand for according to the key at the top? O–A–*

4   **Régions lyonnaise et stéphanoise.** – Après des résidus d'orages nocturnes, le ciel sera nuageux puis deviendra très nuageux. Et des foyers orageux éclateront en cours d'après-midi. Vent de sud-sud-ouest faible à modéré températures minimales 13 à 15 degrés, maximales 23 à 25 degrés.

**PREVISIONS DE DEMAIN**
Le ciel sera très nuageux à couvert. Et après des orages localement forts dès la matinée le temps deviendra pluvieux. Vent faible.

You also read the forecast for the area in which you are staying. Someone asks you to explain what you've read.
(a)   In today's forecast (on the left) what does it have to say about the morning and the afternoon?
(b)   What does it have to say about wind and temperature?
(c)   In tomorrow's forecast (on the right) what does it have to say about the sky? What is said about the weather after the storms?

5   In the tourist information office at Gérardmer you pick up the following information leaflet about the town.

### CE QUE L'ON DOIT SAVOIR DE GÉRARDMER

Commune couvrant 5.413 ha, dont 3.721 de forêts de résineux (plus de 5 millions de sapins et d'épicéas).
Jumelée avec Le Locle (Suisse) et Waremme (Belgique)
Population: 10.000 habitants, dont 7.700 en agglomération. 2.176 immeubles.
Altitude moyenne de la ville: 666 mètres.
Marchés: les jeudis et samedis (matin).
Nombreux et vastes parkings gratuits.

### LE LAC

Altitude 660 m – Surface 115,5 ha – Longueur maximum 2 200 m – Largeur maximum 750 m – profondeur maximum (entre Kattendycke et Croix Meyon) 38,40 m – Longitude 6° 93' E – Latitude 48° 4' N – Volume 19.510.000 m$^3$ – Origine glaciaire.

### LES INDUSTRIES

Textile (toile, jacquard, confection) – Bois (scierie, charpente, menuiserie, construction de chalets) – Profilés métalliques – Granit – Sablières – et le Tourisme.

### PRODUITS LOCAUX

de petite agriculture: Fromage «Le Gérômé», fabrication fermière – Truites de pisciculture, eau des ruisseaux de montagne – Pains d'anis – Miel de sapins – Spécialité de Fumé vosgien (lard et viandes).

Show how much of it you've understood by trying to fill in the following table:

Natural setting for the town: _____

Twin towns in other countries: _____

Population (total and number living in the urban area): _____

Height above sea-level: _____

Market days: _____

Arrangements for parking: _____

Length, width and depth of lake: _____

Origin of lake: _____

Examples of main industries: _____

Examples of local products: _____

**Extension**

Using all the clues which are there about what the town and the surroundings are like, imagine that you are writing a letter to a French pen-friend who lives in another part of France. Tell her/him how you are getting on and what kinds of things you have done or are planning to do during the course of your stay.

**6   APRÈS LA TRAVERSÉE**

CONDUISEZ A GAUCHE. C'est beaucoup plus facile que vous ne le croyez.

RESPECTEZ LES LIMITATIONS. En général, 30 miles en ville (48 km/h), 60 miles sur route (96 km/h), 70 miles sur autoroute (112 km/h), 50 miles avec une caravane (80 km/h).

SACHEZ STATIONNER. En ville, ne stationnez pas sur des lignes en zig-zag, ni le long de trottoirs peints d'une bande jaune. Une ligne jaune simple autorise le stationnement seulement en dehors des heures indiquées sur les panneaux proches.

SACHEZ CIRCULER. Les autoroutes sont indiquées sur des panneaux à fond bleu. Leurs numéros sont précédés de la lettre M. Les numéros des grandes routes sont précédés d'un A, ceux des routes secondaires d'un B.

SACHEZ FAIRE LE PLEIN. Sur routes principales et autoroutes, vous trouverez généralement des stations ouvertes 24 h sur 24. Si votre voiture roule à l'ordinaire, servez-vous à la pompe** (indice d'octane 91). Si vous roulez au super, il vous faut du **** (indice d'octane 97). Dans tous les cas, vous mesurerez en gallons, 1 gallon vaut 4,5 litres.

FAITES VOS ACHATS AUX BONNES HEURES. Vous êtes venus pour ça, alors allez-y à coup sûr. La plupart des magasins ouvrent à 9 h et ferment à 17 h 30. Dans certaines régions, ils peuvent fermer 1 h pour le déjeuner. Dans les grandes villes, les magasins sont ouverts jusqu'à 20 h une fois par semaine. A Londres, c'est le mercredi dans Knightsbridge, le jeudi dans le West End.

ALLEZ AUX PUBS. Les horaires d'ouverture changent selon les régions et les jours. En semaine, la règle générale, c'est 11 h–22 h 30 (23 h à Londres). Le vendredi et le samedi, beaucoup restent ouverts jusqu'à 23 h. Dans certaines régions, les pubs sont ouverts le dimanche, mais à horaires restreints. Il faut avoir dix-huit ans révolus pour y acheter ou consommer une boisson alcoolisée. A partir de quatorze ans, on peut y acheter et consommer des boissons non alcoolisées. A tout âge, on peut avoir accès aux restaurants possédant une licence.

ECRIVEZ; TELEPHONEZ. Les bureaux de poste sont ouverts généralement du lundi au vendredi de 9 h à 17 h 30, le samedi de 9 h à 12 h 30 ou 13 h.

CHANGEZ VOTRE ARGENT. Les banques sont ouvertes du lundi au vendredi, de 9 h 30 à 15 h 30. Dans certaines régions elles ferment à l'heure du déjeuner, mais sont alors ouvertes plus tard le soir. A Londres, quelques bureaux de change restent ouverts 24 h sur 24.

METTEZ-VOUS AU COURANT. La tension électrique en usage est de 240 V.

This information sheet is one given to French visitors to prepare them

## Your surroundings and the weather

for their visit to Great Britain. Check carefully through all the details and underline anything which you think is either out of date or inaccurate for the part of Great Britain in which you live.

**Extension**
Without copying directly from this handout, use some of its phrases, together with words and phrases of your own, to write a letter to the parents of your French pen-friend who are planning a mini weekend break on the South coast of England. Tell them the most important things they need to know as first-time visitors to this country.

7 **Les environs**

Partant de Manchester vers le nord-ouest, vous découvrirez les villes textiles du Lancashire, célèbres pour leurs filatures de coton à l'époque victorienne. Fières de leur héritage, elles ont gardé une grande partie des machines anciennes dans des musées. Dans la direction opposée se trouve le 'Peak National Park', un des plus grands parcs d'Angleterre. Le paysage accidenté si typique des collines du Derbyshire vous captivera tout autant que le décor souterrain autour de Castleton où se cachent d'immenses grottes naturelles et des mines construites par la main de l'homme. Plusieurs d'entre elles sont illuminées et valent une visite.

Au-delà des landes de la Forêt Macclesfield, vous entrerez dans le Cheshire où la douceur pastorale du paysage ne manquera pas de vous séduire. Ces collines ondoyantes s'étendent jusqu'au Wirral et aux stations balnéaires qui bordent la Mer d'Irlande. C'est dans cette région que se niche un véritable joyau de l'architecture élisabéthaine, la ville ancienne de Chester dont certains quartiers remontent même à l'époque romaine.

Quel que soit l'endroit où vous souhaitez vous rendre: dans les stations balnéaires animées de Blackpool et Southport, dans les montagnes Pennines au nord, ou dans le 'High Peak' au sud, vous y accéderez facilement grâce au très bon réseau de trains rapides, de routes et de cars. (N'oubliez pas la règle en campagne: Soyez prudents et propres!)

The above is a document produced in French by your local Town Hall to attract French visitors.
(a) Would you describe the main emphasis as being about
  (i) transport facilities
  (ii) facilities in towns, e.g. shopping precincts
  (iii) scenery and historical interest
  (iv) history.
(b) This is a very 'flowery', formal style of language. Could you write down a few sentences, using some of the same information as here, but in the sort of style you would use when recording a 'cassette letter' to your pen-friend in which you were talking about the town and its surroundings? Example: Ben .. alors .. au nord-ouest tu trouves les villes de textile qui étaient très célèbres et très importantes au 19ème siècle. M'enfin . . . maintenant les anciennes usines sont devenues des musées . .
(c) Why not ask your local or regional tourist bureau what information they have on your town or region in French. Suitably adpated, it could be useful for you in preparing things to say and write about this particular GCSE topic.

# French

## CHECK-LIST

**Essential language tasks**

(a)   talk about your town/village (e.g. where it is; urban, rural, seaside; what it's like; what the attractions/amenities are – shops, hotels, pubs, markets, festivals, special events)

(b)   give an opinion about where you live or about another area of Great Britain

(c)   talk about the weather at present and pass a comment on it

(d)   talk about the weather in general in the different seasons in the area where you live; ask about the differences in the part of France or the French-speaking country you are visiting

(e)   understand simple weather forecasts.

**Useful language tasks**

(a)   give a fuller description of your area e.g. local industry

(b)   talk about the possibilities for sight-seeing for foreign visitors to your area or to other areas in Great Britain

(c)   say which parts of Great Britain and which parts of French-speaking countries you have visited; comment on the visits

(d)   say how long you've lived where you are now

(e)   talk in more detail about the pluses and minuses of where you live now

(f)   say what your ideal place to live in would be or how you would improve the facilities in your town/village

(g)   talk about the differences in way of life when living in town/village/seaside

(h)   understand more complicated weather forecasts

(i)   say which season of the year you prefer and why.

# TRAVEL AND TRANSPORT

### A   DIALOGUE

1   *On va se rencontrer à . . .*
    SALLY   *Salut Jean-Luc. C'est Sally à l'appareil.*
    JEAN-LUC   *Tiens. Bonjour Sally. Ça va?*
    SALLY   *Bien merci. C'est simplement pour confirmer mon arrivée demain soir. J'arrive à l'aéroport de Nancy à 21 heures.*
    JEAN-LUC   *C'est parfait. Je viens te chercher en voiture.*
    SALLY   *C'est vraiment gentil. A demain donc. Au revoir!*

### Activity

1. Imagine the letter that was written prior to this confirmation by telephone. Write down what Sally might have said about her journey (i.e. times of arrival and departure) as well as details of how Jean-Luc might recognize her; if it's possible for him to meet her.
2. Work through your own version of the telephone conversation with a partner. Prepare beforehand (without showing your partner) six different sets of circumstances (i.e. date/time/venue: airport, railway station, bus station, boat station/how to recognize you), changed each of the six times you go through it. Your partner should listen carefully each time and jot down in English what you said in French. When you've finished, check your version of what you said against her/his version and see if you would have been met at the right place at the right time.

### B   DIALOGUE

1   *On cherche le chemin.*
    TOURISTE   *Pardon, Monsieur, où est le syndicat d'initiative, s'il vous plaît?*
    PASSANT   *Je suis désolé, mademoiselle, mais je ne suis pas d'ici. Mais je crois qu'il y a un plan de la ville sur la place principale au bout de cette avenue.*
    TOURISTE   *Merci bien, monsieur.*

    *Pardon, madame. On cherche le syndicat d'initiative. C'est près d'ici?*
    DAME   *C'est à dix minutes à pied. Vous prenez la première rue à droite puis vous allez tout droit jusqu'au pont. Traversez le pont et prenez la deuxième rue à gauche. C'est à 200 m. sur votre droite.*
    TOURISTE   *Merci beaucoup.*
    DAME   *Il n'y a pas de quoi.*

# French

### Activity
Using the above dialogue as a source of phrases and ideas, do some practice conversations with a partner on the town plan below. You're standing at the junction of the Boulevard de l'Hautil and the Boulevard de l'Oise, looking down towards the bus station. Write down for yourself the names of the places marked 1,4,7,8 and 9 on the map. Then without looking at the map, ask your partner the way to each of the places. Your partner gives you directions in French according to the map. You listen and write down in English the directions you are given each time. Check through each of the sets of directions you were given when you get to the end of the practice exercise.

1. Hôtel de Ville et centre culturel André Malraux
2. Préfecture
3. Parvis de la Préfecture
4. Piscine patinoire
5. E.D.F.
6. Essec
7. Gare S.N.C.F.
8. Gare d'autobus arrêt Prefecture
9. Centre commercial «Les 3 Fontaines»

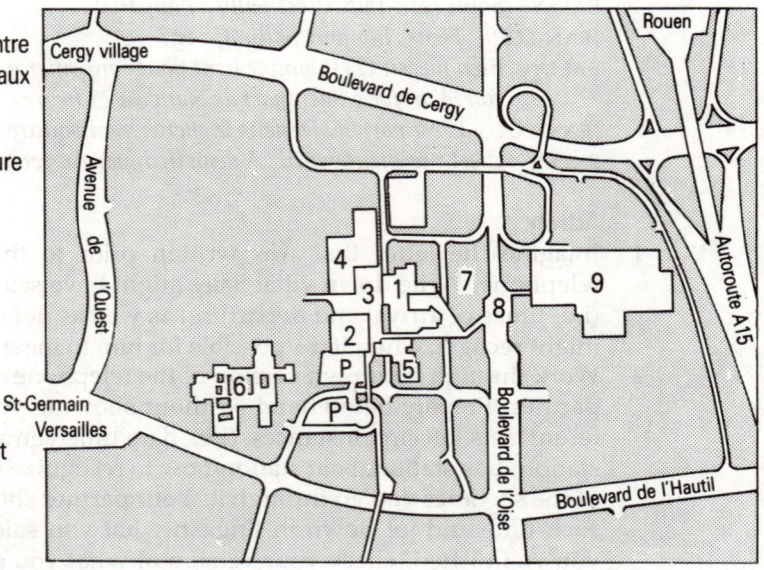

### C  DIALOGUE

*On ne connaît pas la ville . . .*

TOURISTE  Pardon, monsieur – on ne connaît pas la ville. On cherche le centre de loisirs. Est-ce qu'on peut y aller en autobus?

PASSANT  Oui, mademoiselle. Il y a un arrêt d'autobus à deux minutes d'ici, de l'autre côté de la rue.

TOURISTE  Merci, monsieur. Il faut prendre quelle ligne?

PASSANT  Vous devriez prendre le 78 ou le 65.

TOURISTE  Merci bien, monsieur.

### Activity
Would you know how to say in French: 'we're looking for the bus station/coach station/railway station . . . is it possible to go by taxi/underground/on foot? . . . is there a bus stop/underground station/taxi rank near here?'

# Travel and transport 49

**D  DIALOGUES**

*On prend des billets.*

1  *A la gare S.N.C.F.*
   VOYAGEUR   Un aller–retour pour Le Havre, s'il vous plaît, deuxième classe. Est-ce qu'il est possible de faire une réservation à l'avance?
   EMPLOYÉE   Bien sûr, monsieur. Fumeur ou non-fumeur?
   VOYAGEUR   Non-fumeur, s'il vous plaît.
   EMPLOYÉE   Alors, voiture 12, place 42, à côté de la fenêtre.
   VOYAGEUR   Merci bien. Ça part à 13.50, n'est-ce pas? C'est bien quai 8, voie A?
   EMPLOYÉE   Oui, monsieur. Je vous donne un horaire. N'oubliez pas de composter votre billet.

**Activity**

Could you change this dialogue and ask for a single ticket? How would you ask how frequent the trains are? How would you ask how long the journey takes and whether you have to change?

2  *Dans le métro.*
   VOYAGEUSE   Un ticket, s'il vous plaît.
   EMPLOYÉ     Première ou deuxième classe?
   VOYAGEUSE   Deuxième. C'est combien?
   EMPLOYÉ     4 francs 10.
   VOYAGEUR    Un carnet, s'il vous plaît.
   EMPLOYÉ     Oui, monsieur. Trente francs.
   TOURISTE    Un billet de tourisme, s'il vous plaît.
   EMPLOYÉ     Oui, madame. 2, 4 ou 7 jours?
   TOURISTE    Pour 4 jours, s'il vous plaît.
   EMPLOYÉ     Voilà madame. 42 francs.

**Activity**

How would you ask for two first class tickets? Three books of tickets? A 7-day tourist ticket?

**E  BRIBES DE CONVERSATION: RENSEIGNEMENTS DIVERS**

'... le train part dans combien de temps? ... là ce sont les trains de banlieue – les grandes lignes sont de l'autre côté ... de quel quai part le train pour Boulogne? ... où est-ce qu'on peut laisser les bagages? ... la salle d'attente est en face ... où est-ce que je dois descendre? ... vous avez la correspondance pour Boulogne à Amiens ...'.

**Activity**

Can you make sense of these bits of overheard questions at the railway station? Try to imagine what else was said in the parts of the conversations which are missing.

## F DIALOGUE

*En voiture*
TOURISTE   Pardon, madame. C'est occupé ici?
VOYAGEUSE   Non, non. C'est libre, mademoiselle.
TOURISTE   C'est bien le train pour Strasbourg?
VOYAGEUSE   Je l'espère bien!
TOURISTE   C'est quelle direction pour la voiture-buffet s'il vous plaît?
. . . Ah, bon. C'est par là. Merci.

### Activity
How would you check in French whether this was the train for Pouligny? How would you find out where the restaurant car was?

## G DIALOGUE

*A la station-service.*
CLIENT   Pour 200 francs de super, s'il vous plaît. Vous acceptez bien la carte VISA?
POMPISTE   Bien sûr, monsieur. Vous payez à la caisse à l'intérieur.
CLIENT 1   Est-ce que vous pouvez laver le pare-brise, s'il vous plaît?
POMPISTE   D'accord. Pas de problème.
CLIENTE 2   Faites le plein, s'il vous plaît.
POMPISTE   Oui, madame. Ordinaire ou super?
CLIENTE 2   Ah non, monsieur. Du gas-oil!
POMPISTE   Tiens – c'est un moteur vraiment silencieux. Je n'aurais pas su . . .
CLIENTE 2   Oui, c'est vrai. Voulez-vous bien vérifier la pression des pneus et aussi les niveaux d'huile et d'eau?

### Activity
How would you ask for 150 francs worth of two star and an oil level check? How would you ask for a full tank of four star and for the headlamps to be cleaned. How would you ask for 100 francs worth of diesel and a check on the water level in the battery? How would you find out if they sold road maps?

## H DIALOGUE

*En panne*
AUTOMOBILISTE   C'est bien le garage Jacquard?
GARAGISTE   Oui, monsieur. C'est pour quoi?
AUTOMOBILISTE   Je suis tombé en panne à 5 km d'Isigny sur la RN 13.
GARAGISTE   C'est quelle marque, monsieur?
AUTOMOBILISTE   Une Montego, anglaise, blanche, immatriculée A529 ODB.
GARAGISTE   D'accord, monsieur. On va envoyer un mécanicien tout de suite pour vous dépanner sur place. Si c'est grave, on va vous remorquer à l'atelier.

# Travel and transport 51

AUTOMOBILISTE  *Un renseignment, s'il vous plaît – est-ce que vous acceptez la carte American Express?*
GARAGISTE  *Oui, monsieur. On accepte toutes les cartes de crédit majeures.*

**Activity**

Could you give the details (colour, make, registration) of the vehicle you might travel in in France? Could you explain that you thought it was the battery? Could you ask whether they are going to repair on the spot or tow you in? Could you ask what the rate of payment is per hour or per kilometre for the tow? Could you ask if they accept ACCESS? Could you ask how long you will have to wait?

I  **QUELQUE VOCABULAIRE SPÉCIALISÉ POUR LES VOYAGES EN BATEAU ET EN AVION**

*. . . je voudrais confirmer ma réservation pour le vol numéro BA224 à Manchester International . . . Combien coûte le vol aller simple à Belfast? . . . Ça coûte combien la traversée Cherbourg-Portsmouth? . . . Où est-ce que je dois me présenter à l'enregistrement? . . . je dois aller à quelle porte? . . . c'est bien le ferry pour Ramsgate?*

**Activity**

How would you say: How much is a return flight to Newcastle? How long does the crossing to Folkestone last? Where do I check in for Birmingham? Which gate do I go to for flight SR181 for London? Is this the right flight for Dover?

J  **L'INATTENDU**

Sometimes things happen unexpectedly or people say things which you were not expecting. In each of the following situations consider carefully what action you would take and what you would say, if anything, in French.

1 *Au guichet*
  VOYAGEUR  *. . . Merci bien. Le prochain train part dans combien de minutes?*
  EMPLOYÉ  *Il y a un train à peu pres tous les quarts d'heure mais vous feriez mieux de consulter les horaires qui sont affichés à votre droite.*
  VOYAGEUR  *Il y a une voiture restaurant ou grill-express?*
  EMPLOYÉ  *Aucune idée, monsieur, mais vous n'avez qu'à regarder l'horaire.*

2 You have a reserved seat (and the printed reservation to prove it) but when you get to the correct carriage you find someone is already in it.

3 You get on a bus and have the following conversation with the driver:
  VOUS  *Pardon madame. Où est-ce qu'il faut descendre pour le centre commercial?*
  CONDUCTEUR  *Vous auriez dû prendre la ligne 16. Si vous prenez ce bus-ci vous aurez un quart d'heure de marche.*

4 You're with your family and arrive in the car at Boulogne to get the ferry home. Because you are delayed by roadworks, you get to the quay just as your sailing is leaving. Your mother says you have no

money left to pay for a night in a hotel. There's only one more sailing that night. You've got a younger brother and sister aged 2 and 4. The ferry official says there is no chance of getting on the last sailing because it's already fully booked. Try and work out the dialogue between you (the only one to speak any French) and the ferry official.

5   Imagine a different scenario at the hoverport. Your father discovers to his horror that he's left the flight tickets in the hotel bedroom at your last overnight stop. You know the name and address of the hotel but you cannot find the bill with the telephone number on it. How would you explain the problem in French to the officials and what action could you think of?

6   Going out to France on the coach/hovercraft service you're dismayed to find that one of your party's suitcases is not on the luggage conveyor belt when you arrive at Calais. The coach is waiting to take the hovercraft passengers on to Paris. Again, what would you do and say?

7   *A la douane*

DOUANIER   *Voulez-vous bien venir par ici, monsieur? C'est pour un contrôle de sécurité. Ouvrez votre valise, s'il vous plaît. Est-ce que vous avez fait votre valise vous-même? Personne ne vous a aidé? Vous l'avez gardée avec vous tout le temps depuis votre départ?*

How would you react?

8   *Contrôle de vitesse sur la route par la police routière.*

MOTARD   *Alors, monsieur – vous vous croyez au Paris–Dakar? Vous faisiez du 130 – on vous a contrôlé au radar. La limite est à 110 à l'heure. Vos papiers, s'il vous plaît!*

Could you explain that your father doesn't speak French and make some kind of polite excuse?

**ENQUÊTE SUR LES TRANSPORTS INDIVIDUELS ET LES TRANSPORTS EN COMMUN**

Est-ce que vous avez un permis de conduire pour moto ou voiture?
   Est-ce que vous aimeriez apprendre à conduire? Pourquoi?/Pourquoi pas?
   Est-ce que vous avez déjà ou est-ce que vous avez l'intention d'acheter un vélo, un vélomoteur, une moto ou une voiture? Pourquoi?
   Si vous voyagez en voiture, est-ce que vous préférez emprunter les autoroutes, les routes nationales ou les routes départementales? Pourquoi?
   Qu'est-ce que vous pensez des aires de service sur les autoroutes?
   Qu'est-ce vous pensez des transports en commun dans votre ville ou votre région?
   Que pensez-vous de la gare principale (de chemins de fer) de la gare routière et de l'aéroport qui desservent votre ville ou votre région?
   Si vous voyagez à l'étranger, est-ce que vous préférez prendre l'avion, le bateau ou faire de l'autostop, l'aéroglisseur. Qu'est-ce qui vous plaît le mieux – voyager en voiture ou en train, ou faire de l'autostop ou du vélo? Pourquoi?

Imagine the dialogue which would go on if you were asked to take part in the opinion poll above by an interviewer on a French street. Could you explain you were an English visitor but then go on and

# Travel and transport 53

have a go at giving your views in French. What could you say about each of the questions?

## SKILLS PRACTICE

**SIGNS AND NOTICES** 1 This is a topic area where you are bound to come across a large number of signs and notices during the course of a visit. How many of the following would you be able to understand or work out with some intelligent guesswork? In each case the location of the sign is given for you.

### ON THE ROAD

(a) CHAUSSÉE DÉFORMÉE SUR 2 KM (road sign)
(b) DÉVIATION – ROUTE BARRÉE A 3 KM (road sign)
(c) CONVOI EXCEPTIONNEL (on back of a lorry)
(d) REIMS PAR RN 4 (road sign)
(e) REIMS PAR AUTOROUTE (road sign)
(f) FEUX DE CIRCULATION A 800 M (road sign)
(g) TRAVAUX ENTRE ST QUENTIN ET L'ÉCHANGEUR 8 (at the entry road to the motorway)
(h) TRAVAUX A RAON L'ÉTAPE – ITINÉRAIRE RECOMMANDÉ A ST DIÉ SUR RAMBERVILLIERS (road sign)
(i) PARE-BRISE – 1 KM A GAUCHE – POSE RAPIDE (advertisement hoarding by roadside)
(j) AU FEU A GAUCHE – MIDAS CENTRE D'ÉCHAPPEMENT – POSE EN 30 MINUTES SANS RENDEZ-VOUS – CHANGEZ DE POT EN 30 MINUTES! (advertisement hoarding by roadside)
(k) STATIONNEMENT INTERDIT LE SAMEDI ET LE VENDREDI A PARTIR DE 20 HEURES (road sign at a market place)
(l) ATTENTION! CE CARBURANT EST DESTINÉ AUX VÉHICULES ÉQUIPÉS POUR FONCTIONNER AVEC DU CARBURANT SANS PLOMB (sign at petrol pump)
(m) JO=JOURS OUVRABLES Q=QUOTIDIEN (footnote on bus timetable)

### RAILWAY JOURNEYS

(a) PROCHAINS DÉPARTS (station sign above list of train times)
(b) ARRIVÉES – GRANDES LIGNES (station sign)
(c) TRAINS DE BANLIEUE (station sign)
(d) ACCESS AUX QUAIS (station sign)
(e) ACCUEIL – INFORMATIONS – SALLE D'ATTENTE (station sign)
(f) NON FUMEURS (in train carriage)
(g) EAU NON POTABLE (on washbasin in train toilet)
(h) TRAIN SUPPRIMÉ EN RAISON D'ACCIDENT (special note at entrance to platform at station)

## French

**MÉTRO JOURNEYS**

(a) CORRESPONDANCE (sign on platform)
(b) LIMITE DE VALIDITÉ DES BILLETS (sign as you are about to leave the tube station)

2  You see the following advert in a free news sheet in the town where you are camping.

VELO: POUR LES LOUER
Gare S.N.C.F. 02000 LAON – Tel. 23.23.23.25
TARIFS 1986

| Assurance comprise | ½ journée | Journée | Week-end | Semaine forfait |
|---|---|---|---|---|
| par personne | A1 14F | B1 23F | C1 35F | D1 85F |
| à partir de 4 personnes | A2 12F | B2 20F | C2 29F | D2 70F |
| Tandem | 29F | 40F | 65F | 160F |

CAUTION PAR VELO: 50F

(a) What is the facility which is advertised here?
(b) What is the rate per person per day if two people are involved?
(c) Is insurance extra?
(d) Is there anything else to pay?
(e) Where do you go in the town to arrange this service?

**Extension**

Imagine the conversation which would take place if you were booking this service along with a friend who was camping with you. Write down what you and the employee might say if you were booking for a weekend.

3  You read this footnote to a bus timetable, referring to a service which only runs on certain days of the week.

SERVICE SPECIAL MARCHÉ DE MONTARGIS – mercredi et samedi – départ 8.30
(place A. Chesneau – face au monument) retour mercredi et samedi à 11.55 (gare routière)

(a) What are the days and times of the journeys, outward and return?
(b) Where are the picking up and dropping off points?

**4** The following is part of a timetable and information sheet provided by French Railways.

**Symboles**

| | | | |
|---|---|---|---|
| A | Arrivée | ✕ | Voiture restaurant |
| D | Départ | ⊗ | Grill-express |
| TEE | Trans Europ Express | ▣ | Restauration à la place |
| ⟞ | Couchettes | 🍸 | Bar |
| 🛏 | Voitures-lits | ☕ | Vente ambulante |

**Remarque**

Certains trains circulant rarement ne sont pas repris dans cette fiche.

**Services offerts dans les gares**

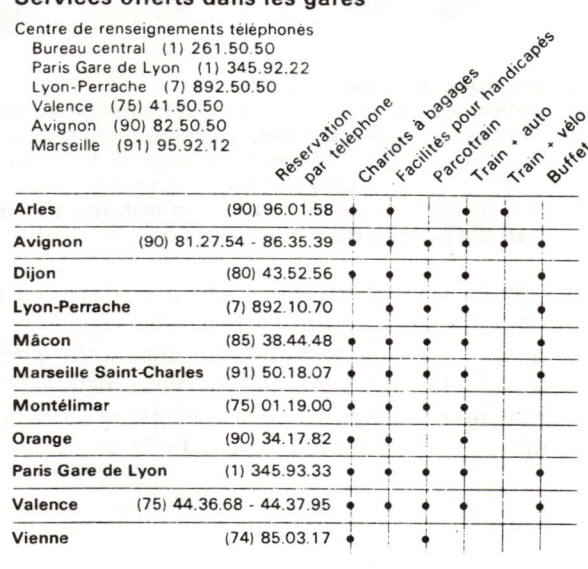

Centre de renseignements téléphonés
Bureau central (1) 261.50.50
Paris Gare de Lyon (1) 345.92.22
Lyon-Perrache (7) 892.50.50
Valence (75) 41.50.50
Avignon (90) 82.50.50
Marseille (91) 95.92.12

| | | Réservation par téléphone | Chariots à bagages | Facilités pour handicapés | Parcotrain | Train + auto | Train + vélo | Buffet |
|---|---|---|---|---|---|---|---|---|
| **Arles** | (90) 96.01.58 | • | • | | • | • | | |
| **Avignon** | (90) 81.27.54 - 86.35.39 | • | • | • | • | • | • | |
| **Dijon** | (80) 43.52.56 | • | • | • | • | | • | |
| **Lyon-Perrache** | (7) 892.10.70 | | • | • | • | | • | |
| **Mâcon** | (85) 38.44.48 | • | • | • | • | | • | |
| **Marseille Saint-Charles** | (91) 50.18.07 | • | • | • | • | | • | |
| **Montélimar** | (75) 01.19.00 | • | • | • | • | | | |
| **Orange** | (90) 34.17.82 | • | • | | • | | | |
| **Paris Gare de Lyon** | (1) 345.93.33 | • | • | • | • | | • | |
| **Valence** | (75) 44.36.68 - 44.37.95 | • | • | • | • | | • | |
| **Vienne** | (74) 85.03.17 | • | | • | | | | |

(*a*) Would you be able to explain the meaning of the symbols at the top of the sheet?

(*b*) What is the purpose of the list of stations?

(*c*) Why are two different telephone numbers given for each station?

5. At a motorway toll booth you are handed a leaflet from which the following is an extract.

**Le saviez-vous ?** L'autoroute est une voie sûre.
Pour votre sécurité, n'abusez pas de ses facilités.

● Respectez les vitesses autorisées !
**130 km/h** par temps sec. **110 km/h** par temps pluvieux.

● Gardez vos **distances**
Le véhicule qui vous précède peut freiner brusquement.
Si vous roulez à **60 km/h**, laissez un espace de 4 voitures
à **100 km/h**, un espace de 6 voitures
à **130 km/h**, un espace de 8 voitures
Quand la chaussée est mouillée, **n'oubliez pas d'augmenter ces distances de 50 %.**

(a) Does the leaflet start off by stressing the danger or the safety of motorways?
(b) Why are two different maximum speed limits stated?
(c) In asking you to keep your distance from the vehicle in front, how does it suggest that you measure the safe gap?
(d) When should the gap be increased by 50 per cent?

# Travel and transport

6   When you arrive at a car park you notice the ticket machine. This is what it looks like.

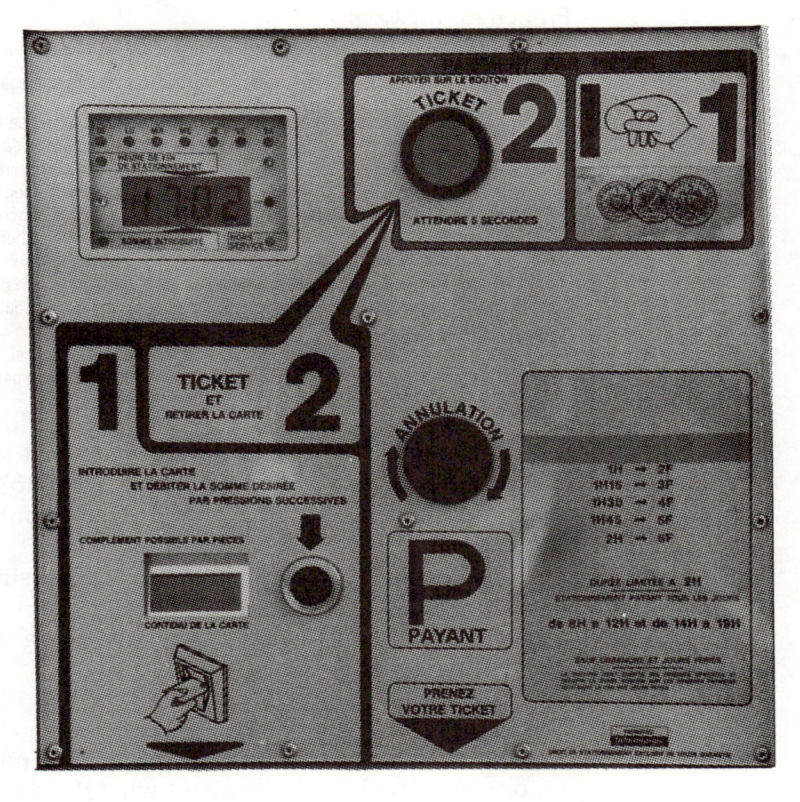

(a)   If it's 6.00 p.m. on a Sunday, do you still need to pay?

(b)   Write down exactly each step you would take to get your ticket from the machine, when paying with coins.

(c)   If it said at the bottom of the ticket PLACER CE TICKET DERRIERE VOTRE PARE-BRISE LISIBLE DE L'EXTÉRIEUR, what would you do with the ticket?

**Extension**

You put your money in and the coin jams. There is no other machine. You see a traffic warden just outside the car park. What do you say to her/him?

7 The thought of a breakdown on a motorway is always a bit worrying. You are given the following information leaflet about procedures on French motorways.

### En cas de panne: assistance et dépannage

Vous pouvez vous arrêter en cas de nécessité sur la bande d'arrêt d'urgence, en bordure des voies de circulation. Pensez à allumer vos feux de détresse ou à présignaler votre véhicule au moyen d'un triangle rouge réglementaire. Descendez toujours du côté droit de votre véhicule, afin de ne pas vous faire happer.

Un réseau permanent (et gratuit) de bornes d'appels téléphoniques d'urgence est à votre disposition; si vous tombez en panne allez jusqu'à la borne la plus proche qui est toujours distante de moins d'un km. Vous serez mis en communication avec la gendarmerie qui préviendra immédiatement le dépanneur de permanence, lequel se rendra rapidement auprès de vous pour vous remorquer jusqu'au garagiste de votre choix ou à son atelier.

Les tarifs de dépannage sont affichés sur les bornes d'appel. Sur simple demande, une notice sur les conditions de dépannage vous sera remise par les dépanneurs.

(a) What advice does it give about what to do when you have broken down *before* you go off to phone for help?

(b) What information are you given about the emergency telephone system on the motorways?

(c) Who will actually answer your distress call in the first instance?

(d) What is your safeguard against being 'ripped off' when you are charged for the tow?

**Extension**

Imagine you had to adapt this for French motorists using British motorways. Think carefully about what the differences might be and try to rewrite the information sheet in French with any adaptations.

8 The beginning of July is notorious for its traffic jams. You find you are in the Paris area during the first weekend in July, about to continue on the second leg of your journey down to the South of France on your camping holiday. You notice the diagram pictured opposite which accompanies an article in the newspaper.

(a) Over the two days covered by the diagram, which are the two worst periods during which to set off on your journey, i.e. between *which* times on each day?

(b) What is the significance of the columns with the diagonal stripes and the columns which are not shaded in any way?

# Travel and transport

**Colonnes sombres :** moment le plus défavorable pour prendre la route. **Colonnes claires :** heures de départ idéales pour éviter les bouchons. **Tranches horaires hachurées :** risques d'encombrements.

## La tendance en région parisienne

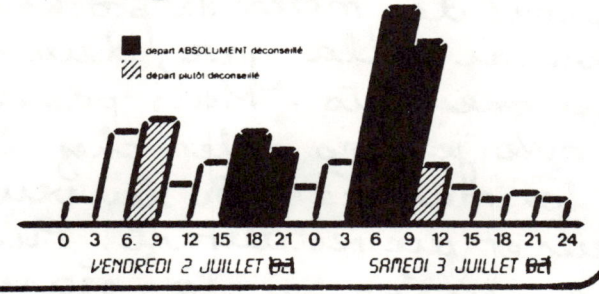

■ départ ABSOLUMENT déconseillé
▨ départ plutôt déconseillé

0  3  6  9  12  15  18  21   0  3  6  9  12  15  18  21  24
VENDREDI 2 JUILLET          SAMEDI 3 JUILLET

9   You read the following newspaper report of how the first day of the holiday exodus went.

### Encombrement normal sur les routes de France

A quelques exceptions près, ce premier jour de grands départs en vacances s'est plutôt bien déroulé sur les routes de France.

En fin de matinée, on annonçait un ralentissement sur trente kilomètres en arrivant sur l'autoroute A10, ainsi qu'un bouchon de six kilomètres sur la A63 à la sortie de cette ville. Les plus grands problèmes se sont posés dans un goulot d'étranglement dans la vallée du Rhône entre Vienne at Valence, où le trafic s'arrêta sur trente kilomètres sur l'autoroute A7 et sur treize kilomètres sur la N7. La circulation était bloquée sur dix-huit kilomètres de part et d'autre de Montpellier, sur l'autoroute A9 en allant vers le Sud-Ouest.

En fin d'après-midi, la situation en province se résorbait lentement, alors que les sorties de Paris devenaient difficiles.

(*a*)   Would you describe the tone of the article as sensational or low-key?
(*b*)   Which was the area with the largest jams?
(*c*)   How was the situation described by late afternoon in Paris and outside Paris in the regions?

**French**

10  You are in Paris and your French friend Daniel, who lives in Rouen, has invited you to visit him in Rouen for a couple of days. He sends this short note below:

> Salut,
>
> J'espère que tu n'as pas oublié notre rendez-vous de mercredi prochain. Je t'attendrai à la gare, devant le bureau de renseignements. Mais pas avant midi, parce que je dois aller chez le dentiste dans la matinée. Si tu veux, je t'invite à déjeuner au restaurant. Puis, nous irons au cinéma, à la séance de 14 heures. Il y a un bon film avec Michael Caine. Ensuite, nous irons à la piscine avec des copains à moi. Surtout, n'oublie pas d'apporter ton maillot de bain.
> A mercredi!
>
> Daniel.

(a) Where exactly will he meet you? (Give 2 details)
  i _____
  ii _____

(b) What activities has he planned for the afternoon? (Give 2 details)
  i _____
  ii _____

(c) What reminder does he give you?
  _____

## Travel and transport

(*d*) Look at the train time-table below and find what time there is a suitable train leaving Paris.

| Numéro du train | | 7005 | 7009 | 3115 | 7017 | 3139 | 7081 | 7019 | 309 | 7021 | 7023 | 3141 | 3195 | 7025 | 7027 | 3145 | 7087 |
|---|---|---|---|---|---|---|---|---|---|---|---|---|---|---|---|---|---|
| Notes à consulter | | 1 | 2 | 3 | 4 | 5 | 6 | 7 | 8 | 9 | 10 | 11 | 12 | 13 | 7 | 14 | 15 |
| | | | | + | | | | | | | | | | | | | |
| Paris Saint-Lazare | D | 06.08 | 07.04 | 07.49 | 08.39 | 09.15 | | 10.45 | 10.55 | 11.15 | 11.45 | 12.35 | | 12.45 | 13.45 | 13.45 | |
| Pontoise | D | 06.44 | 07.32 | 08.17 | 09.22 | | | 11.22 | | 12.00 | 12.22 | | | 13.22 | 14.22 | | |
| Chars | A | 07.05 | 07.54 | | 09.44 | | | 11.44 | | 12.22 | 12.44 | | | 13.44 | 14.44 | | |
| Gisors | A | 07.27 | 08.16 | 08.46 | 10.06 | | | 12.05 | | 12.44 | 13.06 | | | 14.06 | 15.06 | | |
| Gournay-Ferrières | A | | | | 09.04 | | | | | | | | | | | | |
| Forges-les-Eaux | A | | | | 09.21 | | | | | | | | | | | | |
| Serqueux | A | | | | 09.25 | | | | | | | | | | | | |
| Neufchatel-en-Bray | A | | | | 09.39 | | | | | | | | | | | | |
| Rouen | A | | | | | 10.26 | | 12.06 | | | | 13.44 | | | | 15.07 | |
| Rouen | D | | | | | | 10.36 | 12.17 | | | | | 13.53 | | | | 15.14 |
| Dieppe | A | | | | | 10.03 | 11.41 | 13.00 | | | | | 14.34 | | | | 16.18 |
| Dieppe Maritime | A | | | | | | | 13.10 | | | | | | | | | |

Tous les trains comportent des places assises en 1<sup>re</sup> et 2<sup>e</sup> cl. sauf indication contraire dans les notes + changement de train à Pontoise.

*Source: York Reading Extended Question 3*

**11** You see the following article in a local newspaper while you are in France.

### Zéro de conduite

Farid et Benasser ont vingt-six ans à eux deux, et ils se sont crus autorisés à «emprunter» une voiture à Petit-Quevilly pour une courte balade qui s'est mal terminée pour les galopins qui ont joué quelques instants au stock-car dans une rue de cette ville de la banlieue de Rouen.

Une fois dans le véhicule dont ils avaient brisé la vitre et pris le deuxième jeu de clés laissé négligemment sur la tableau de bord par son propriétaire, Farid, 14 ans, et Benasser, 12 ans, ont dû faire face à un problème délicat: ils n'avaient pas individuellement la taille requise pour occuper la place du conducteur et en assumer les fonctions.

Ils ont alors composé... Farid s'est assis à la place du chauffeur et Benasser s'est mis sur ses genoux, le premier s'occupant des pédales et passant les vitesses, le second se réservant le soin de piloter «à vue» l'automobile.

La «folle équipée» du véhicule s'est terminée assez rapidement, la voiture conduite par les duettistes allant heurter deux autres en stationnement sur le bord de la route à quelques mètres de là. Comble de malchance, les apprentis voleurs tentant une dernière manœuvre de repli pour se désencastrer, renversaient un malheureux passant qui devait être hospitalisé, la jambe brisée.

Farid et Benasser ont été emmenés au commissariat où ils ont dû s'expliquer sur leur «mauvaise conduite».

(*a*) What is the most startling thing about this incident?
(*b*) How did the two boys get into the car?
(*c*) Exactly what damage and injury were caused?

# 62  French

12  This is not the sort of question you would meet in the examination, but to round off your hard work on this section have a try at the following puzzle which is set in an airport!

### ÉNIGME
#### PAR BERLOCK HOLMES
Contresens

Bertrand se demande s'il ne va pas manquer l'avion qui part dans trois minutes. Courant à vive allure dans les couloirs de l'aéroport, il emprunte un passage interdit et aperçoit un tapis roulant qui conduit à l'embarcadère. Stupeur! Bertrand se trouve à contresens. Il va devoir courir, et vite! Le tapis, long de 400 mètres, se déroule à la vitesse constante de 6 km/h.

A QUELLE VITESSE BERTRAND DOIT-IL ALLER POUR PARCOURIR LA TOTALITÉ DU TAPIS A CONTRESENS EN DEUX MINUTES?

## CHECK-LIST

**Essential language tasks**
(a) say how you get to school (e.g. on foot; by bus; how long?)
(b) ask a passer-by politely where a place is
(c) understand/ask for explanation of the route given in reply
(d) ask how long it will take to get there
(e) ask if a facility is available nearby (e.g. bank, supermarket)
(f) ask about different means of transport available (e.g. bus, tube, train)
(g) ask which bus, train etc. to get to a particular destination
(h) buy tickets, or book of tickets, saying which class/single/return
(i) ask about cost for adult/child
(j) find out times of departure and arrival/length of journey
(k) ask about frequency of services
(l) check whether you have correct station, bus stop, platform, bus, train
(m) find out where platform, bus stop, waiting room, enquiry office, buffet, toilets are
(n) ask about changing buses/trains
(o) ask where you have to get off
(p) find out whether a seat is free for you to sit on
(q) buy petrol/diesel (asking for correct grade and quantity in litres; or asking for, say, 200 francs worth; or asking the attendant to fill the tank)
(r) ask for checks on oil, water, battery and tyres
(s) ask for windscreen to be cleaned
(t) ask for toilets, shop facilities at the petrol station (e.g. for sweets, crisps), nearest restaurant/hotel
(u) ask for a map and for advice on the route.

# Travel and transport 63

**Useful language tasks**

(a) talk in more detail about a complex journey e.g. from the UK to France

(b) talk about public transport service in your area and give an opinion on it

(c) discuss the advantages and disadvantages of different types of transport, public and private

(d) say whether you prefer motorways or ordinary roads and why

(e) explain reductions in public transport available to foreign visitors to your area

(f) talk about the railway stations, ports, airports available in your part of the country and pass an opinion on them

(g) talk about your personal means of transport (e.g. bike, moped, car – whether you are learning to drive a moped or car – whether you have ever hitch-hiked)

(h) give directions to strangers who ask you the way, or say you are not from around there

(i) give information to a foreign visitor about the best way and means of transport to get to somewhere in the UK.

(j) ask whether you need to reserve a seat in advance

(k) ask whether there is any supplement to pay on the ticket

(l) ask about price reductions

(m) ask for and request explanation about timetables and plans of bus/tube/rail routes

(n) ask someone else to enquire for you about cost of flight/crossing on a sea/air/hovercraft journey

(o) check in and say where you would like to sit (e.g. non smoking; by the window)

(p) check you have the correct 'gate' for the flight or the correct ferry

(q) respond to security checks (e.g. say what's in your case and whether you packed it yourself)

(r) deal with the unexpected e.g. lost luggage, lost tickets, delayed or cancelled flight/ferry/train

(s) request more detailed information about road routes, different classes of roads, where to park, motorway service facilities

(t) understand advice about traffic regulations from officials and others

(u) explain similar traffic information and regulations relating to the UK to a foreign visitor

(v) report you have broken down (where; make of car and colour; registration number; how long will you have to wait?; what will it cost?

(w) ask for a receipt after the breakdown

(x) enquire about hiring a bike or a car and give the relevant details to the hirer (e.g. cost; length of time required; age of persons concerned).

# HOLIDAYS

### A  AU SYNDICAT D'INITIATIVE

TOURISTE  *Bonjour, monsieur. Nous venons d'arriver à Clermont-Ferrand – nous sommes des touristes anglais. On cherche d'abord un plan de la ville. Vous avez aussi quelques renseignements sur les distractions?*

EMPLOYÉ  *Voilà, madame. Vous trouverez tout dans cette brochure – le programme des distractions, cinéma, théâtre etc. , et aussi une liste des restaurants.*

TOURISTE  *Merci, monsieur. Qu'est-ce qu'on peut voir dans la ville elle-même?*

EMPLOYÉ  *Alors, ici vous avez des dépliants sur les différents musées – par exemple le musée Lecocq. C'est ouvert normalement toute la journée, depuis 9 heures du matin. Mais il est fermé aujourd'hui puisque c'est mardi.*

TOURISTE  *Ça ne nous dit pas grand'chose. Il y a d'autres choses à voir?*

EMPLOYÉ  *Il est intéressant de visiter les quartiers anciens de la ville.*

TOURISTE  *Qu'est-ce qu'il y a qui est vraiment du pays?*

EMPLOYÉ  *Ah peut-être les crémeries de Clermont-Ferrand?*

TOURISTE  *Mais oui. Ça se trouve où?*

EMPLOYÉ  *Juste en face, madame – et c'est ouvert aujourd'hui.*

TOURISTE  *Merci bien, monsieur.*

EMPLOYÉ  *A votre service. Bon séjour!*

**Activity**

Using the dialogue above as a stimulus, try to write a simple letter to a tourist information office in a town where you are thinking of spending part of your holiday. State the number in your party and their ages, as well as when you are planning to go and how long you intend to stay. Ask for information on the different possibilities for accommodation in the area (e.g. medium price hotels, campsites, gîtes) as well as a list of restaurants. Ask also for brochures and pamphlets giving details of tourist possibilities. Give an idea of the sort of things you like doing so that they are able to select appropriate documents for you.

### B  A LA CAISSE DU MUSÉE

CAISSIÈRE  *Vous êtes combien?*

TOURISTE  *Deux adultes et trois enfants.*

# Holidays

CAISSIÈRE  *Les enfants ont quel âge?*
TOURISTE  *13, 11 et 9.*
CAISSIÈRE  *Alors, deux adultes à 5 francs et trois enfants à 2.50. Ça fait 17.50 en tout.*
TOURISTE  *Merci bien, madame. Est-ce qu'on peut prendre des photos?*
CAISSIÈRE  *Oui, mais il faut payer un forfait de 3 francs.*
TOURISTE  *Alors, c'est moi le photographe . . . voilà 3 francs. On n'a pas beaucoup de temps aujourd'hui. Si on veut revenir un autre jour, vous êtes ouvert tous les jours?*
CAISSIÈRE  *Tous les jours sauf le mardi. On est ouvert le dimanche et les jours fériés. L'entrée est gratuite ces jours-là.*
TOURISTE  *Tiens . . . on ne savait pas ça!*

**Activity**

Could you ask these further questions? Are there guided visits? Where can I leave my bag? May we take flash photographs? Are there any guidebooks? What time do you close?

**Extension**

When on holiday in France you come across an exhibition which really interests you. Unfortunately it's toward the end of your last day, but you're still very anxious to have a quick look around if only for ten minutes. What would you say in French if this is what the person at the entrance desk said to you?

CAISSIÈRE  *. . . Je suis désolée, mademoiselle . . . on ferme dans un quart d'heure . . . je ne peux pas vous laisser entrer. Vous devriez revenir demain . . .*

## ENQUÊTE SUR LES VACANCES

The French National Tourist Office are doing a survey among British holidaymakers in the streets of Paris. They're trying to collect information which will help them to promote certain types of holiday packages throughout France. What would you want to say in French in response to the various questions?

Comment est-ce que vous passez vos vacances normalement? (*a*) Sans partir en vacances (c'est-à-dire vous restez chez vous)? (*b*) En vacances en Grande-Bretagne? (*c*) En vacances à l'étranger?
Si vous partez en vacances, est-ce que vous allez (*a*) Au bord de la mer (ou au bord d'un lac)? (*b*) À la campagne? (*c*) Faire un séjour dans une grande ville?
Est-ce que vous faites un séjour chez des amis ou chez des parents?
(*a*) Vous partez seul(e)? (*b*) Avec des parents? (*c*) Avec des amis? Vous partez pour (*a*) 8 jours? (*b*) 15 jours? (*c*) plus?
Donnez quelques détails sur la dernière fois que vous êtes parti(e) en vacances
(*a*) Quand? (*b*) Où? (*c*) Avec qui?
  Pendant combien de temps?
  Quel temps a-t-il fait?
  Qu'est-ce que vous avez fait/vu?

# French

Vos impressions générales?
Qu'est-ce qui vous a plu/déplu?
Est-ce que vous avez des projets pour un séjour éventuel? Quels sont les facteurs importants pour vous quand vous sélectionnez un voyage organisé? (a) Prix? (b) Le lieu de séjour? (c) L'ambiance? (d) Le temps? (e) Des sites naturels/historiques?

## SKILLS PRACTICE

**SIGNS AND NOTICES**

1   While you're holidaying you are likely to have to read a lot of signs and notices. What would your explanation of the following be to someone who was with you who did not understand any French?

(a)   ANNULABLE SELON SAISON, MÉTÉO ET ÉCONOMIE D'ÉNERGIE – SE RENSEIGNER (on a board at the landing stage for boat trips)
(b)   DÉPARTS SUPPLÉMENTAIRES – SE RENSEIGNER (on a board advertising departure times for coach trips)
(c)   SYNDICAT D'INITIATIVE – A VOTRE DISPOSITION POUR TOUS RENSEIGNEMENTS (outside a public building)
(d)   VISITE DE VILLE: Visites proposées du 1er juillet au 15 septembre. Prix groupe à la demande. (notice outside town hall)
(e)   CIRCUITS RÉGIONAUX: Circuits proposés de juillet à septembre. Entrée payante dans les monuments. Départs: Place du Capitole devant l'horloge de la mairie. (notice outside travel agency)
(f)   DINER – 20h30 – TENUE "HABILLÉE" DE RIGUEUR – ENFANTS DE –12 ANS DÉCONSEILLÉS (on a sign advertising evening river cruises with a meal)

2   The following are the section headings from a guide to 'Adresses Utiles' in the town of Avignon. How many of them do you understand?

Divers .. Services Publics .. Services d'Urgences .. Ambulances .. Agences de Voyages .. Banques .. Change .. Bibliothèques .. Cabaret/Discothèques .. Campings .. Cinémas .. Clubs .. Cultes (Catholique + Autres) .. Culture et Loisirs .. Enseignement .. Garages .. Hébergements .. Journaux Locaux .. Location Cycles .. Location Voitures .. Musées et Monuments .. Parkings .. Radio Locale .. Sports et Détente .. Stations de Taxi .. Hôtels centre-ville .. Hôtels environs immédiats .. Restaurants moins de 50f .. Restaurants de 50 à 80f .. Restaurants 100f et au-delà

3   Whilst staying in Arles you come across the following document on historic buildings and museums.
(a)   Why are two sets of prices given?
(b)   What is a **carte globale** likely to be?

# Holidays

## MONUMENTS ET MUSÉES

**ARLES**

|  | Plein tarif | Tarif réduit |
|---|---|---|
| MONUMENTS (Arènes, Théâtre, Les Alyscamps) | 4,30 F | 3,25 F |
| CLOITRE SAINT TROPHIME | 5,00 F | 4,00 F |
| MUSEES (Païen, Chrétien, Réattu) | 3,25 F | 2,10 F |
| MUSEON ARLATEN | 3,00 F | 1,50 F |
| **CARTE GLOBALE** En période d'exposition | 18,00 F | 13,00 F |
| Hors exposition | 16,00 F | 11,00 F |

**MONUMENTS HISTORIQUES**

| | | |
|---|---|---|
| Abbaye de Montmajour, Fouilles de Glanum Château du Roi René | 8,00 F | 4,00 F |
| MOULIN DE DAUDET (FONTVIEILLE) | 4,00 F | 2,00 F |
| CHATEAU DE BARBENTANE | 12,00 F | 7,00 F |
| LES BAUX DE PROVENCE | 6,00 F | 3,00 F |

**HORAIRES DES MONUMENTS D'ARLES**

HEURES OUVERTURE  
MATIN:  9 h 30 de janvier à mars  
        8 h 30 autres mois  
SOIR:  14 h 00 toute l'année

HEURES FERMETURE  
MATIN: 12 h 00 de janvier à mai  
        12 h 30 les autres mois  
SOIR:  16 h 30 janvier, février, décembre  
        17 h 30 mars, novembre  
        18 h 00 avril et du 15-09 au 15-10  
        19 h 00 de mai au 15 septembre

\* Entrée gratuite pour les groupes de scolaires de l'enseignement primaire et secondaire sur présentation d'une attestation à l'en-tête de l'Ecole (hors vacances scolaires).

(c)  Complete this table giving the opening hours for the historic buildings in Arles for *August*.

A. M.   Open:            Closed:  
P.M.    Open:            Closed:

**4** While on holiday you are weighing up the relative value of a couple of trips advertised by a coach and boat firm, which you are thinking of making during the weekend of 13/14 September of your visit. Complete the table below as a way of making a comparison and helping you to make up your mind. You're staying in *Orléans*.

*Croisière
sur la Seine*
Samedi 28 Juin
Samedi 13 Septembre

Départ BLOIS/VENDOME 5 h 30, ORLÉANS 6 h 30. BOULOGNE, embarquement à 8 h 30 Quai du Point du Jour pour la Croisière. petit déjeuner, déjeuner, boisson comprise, animation et commentaire sur le bateau. Arrivée vers 17 h 45 à l'Écluse du Bois du Roy à FONTAINEBLEAU. Retour en direct par PITHIVIERS.
**Prix d'Orléans: 420 F.**
**Blois/Vendôme: 450 F.**
Comprenant: le transport, le déjeuner, croisière.

**NOUVEAU**
*Croisière
sur le Canal de Briare*
Dimanche 1$^{er}$ Juin
Dimanche 14 Septembre

Départ de notre région, VENDOME 7 h, BLOIS 7 h 30, ORLÉANS 8 h 30. GIEN: visite du musée de la Chasse. 11 h 45: embarquement pour la croisière, déjeuner sur le Canal de BRIARE. Il traverse des paysages verdoyants et vallonnés. Vous assisterez au passage d'écluses pittoresques. 15 h: débarquement. BRIARE: visite du musée des vieilles voitures. Temps libre, puis retour en soirée.
**Prix de Blois/Vendôme: 300 F.**
**Prix d'Orleans: 280 F.**
Comprenant: voyage, déjeuner, croisière, visites.

|   | | *Cruise on Seine* | *Cruise on Canal* |
|---|---|---|---|
| 1 | Day of departure | | |
| 2 | Time of departure | | |
| 3 | Meals and drinks included | | |
| 4 | Visits to museums (which/what type?) | | |
| 5 | Other attractions? (e.g. scenery, points of interest?) | | |
| 6 | Price | | |

## Holidays

5  The items below are from a guide to places of interest just off the A9 motorway which runs from Orange right through to the Spanish border.

        1                        2                      3

**1.** Ouvrage comportant de puissants dispositifs militaires, le palais épiscopal de Narbonne qui commandait à la fois la ville et le port, aurait servi de modèle d'après Viollet-le-Duc, pour le palais des Papes d'Avignon.
. Il possède trois tours carrées: tours de la Madeleine et St-Martial (13ᵉ siècle) – et le donjon Gilles Aycelin (14⁴ siècle).
. La cathédrale St-Just, limitée en 1354 à un chœur gothique, aux voûtes parmi les plus hautes d'Europe.

**2.** Érigée sous le règne d'Auguste au 1ᵉʳ siècle avant Jésus-Christ, la Maison carrée est un temple romain pourvu de sculptures. C'est aujourd'hui un musée des Antiques.
. Gladiateurs et bêtes fauves se livraient à des combats sans merci dans les arènes de Nîmes, à présent devenues un lieu de prédilection pour les courses de taureaux provençales.

**3.** Port d'embarquement pour les croisades élu par Saint Louis, la cité d'Aigues-Mortes est à présent ensablée.

(*a*)  According to item 1, what is the connection between the Bishop's Palace at Narbonne and the Popes' Palace at Avignon? How many towers does the Bishop's Palace have and how old are they?

(*b*)  According to item 2, what was the original function of the Maison Carrée in Nîmes and what is its present function?

(*c*)  According to item 2, what was the original function of les Arènes and what use is the building put to at present?

(*d*)  According to item 3, why can Aigues-Mortes no longer fulfil the function it did at the time of the Crusades?

6  While on holiday in Reims you are interested in visiting the Charbonneaux Motorcar Museum. Below are two extracts from different publicity leaflets for this museum.

### 1
**MUSÉE DE L'AUTOMOBILE FRANÇAISE**

Collection privée CHARBONNEAUX – 160 véhicules en parfait état de 1895 à nos jours. Cet ensemble de voitures uniquement françaises est unique au monde.
Il comprend des véhicules historiques tel un taxi de la Marne, la Panhard du Roi d'Espagne, la Peugeot du Général GOURAUD, la Renault du Maréchal PETAIN, la Scarab du Général EISENHOWER…
34, avenue Georges Clémenceau – Tel: 26.82.83.84

• OUVERTURE TOUS LES JOURS
DE 10 H A 12 H ET DE 14 H A 19 H

ENTREE: 20 F
ÉTUDIANTS ET GROUPE DE 20 PERSONNES: 15 F

### 2

Une rarissime présentation de modèles réduits pour enfants et jouets anciens sont exposés, ainsi qu'un exceptionnel ensemble de plus de 100 affiches automobiles d'époque.

Une salle vidéo située à l'entrée du Centre présente en permanence des dispositives explicatives et commentées sur ses voitures, ainsi que des films retraçant l'épopée automobile. Des expositions temporaires seront organisées plusieurs fois par an.

Une boutique-librairie et un "bistrot" (sur podium), sont à la disposition des visiteurs.

Hervé Charbonneaux (expert en automobiles de collection) se tiendra souvent au Centre pour renseigner, conseiller, ou expertiser tous véhicules de collection.

(a) Use item 1 to complete the following table of basic information about the museum.
  (i) Price and special reductions:
  (ii) Number of vehicles and age span represented:
  (iii) Nationalities of vehicles:
  (iv) Opening hours:
(b) Use item 2 to gather the following additional information.
  (i) Audio-visual and other sources of information about the vehicles:
  (ii) Shop/facilities for visitors:
  (iii) Additional exhibits apart from full-size cars.

7 Read these extracts from a survey on holidays published in a French magazine. Explain briefly the questions asked and the most popular reply in each case. Answer by completing the sentences below in English. (The first one has been done for you as an example.)

Avez-vous l'intention de partir en vacances l'été prochain, c'est-à-dire de passer au moins 4 jours consécutifs hors de votre domicile entre le 1er juin et le 30 septembre?

| ENSEMBLE DES INTERVIEWÉS | 1 161 = 100% |
|---|---|
| • Oui, sûrement | 45% |
| • Oui, peut-être | 10% |
| • Non, ne pensent pas | 13% |
| • Non, sûrement pas | 32% |
| • Ne savent pas | — |

A When asked: **Are you going on holiday next summer?** the most popular reply was: **yes, definitely**.

De quelle façon vous logerez-vous?

| ENSEMBLE DES INTERVIEWÉS PENSANT PARTIR EN VACANCES EN FRANCE | 488 = 100% |
|---|---|
| – Pensent être logés: | |
| • à l'hôtel | 12% |
| • en location meublée | 15% |
| • dans un gîte rural, une maison familiale, dans un V.V.F. | 8% |
| • en camping-caravaning | 26% |
| • chez des parents ou des amis | 32% |
| • dans votre résidence secondaire | 10% |
| – Ne savent pas | 4% |

B When asked: _____ the most popular reply was: _____

# Holidays

Où avez-vous l'intention de partir principalement en vacances l'été prochain? Si à l'étranger, partirez-vous avec un groupe organisé ou en voyage individuel?

| ENSEMBLE DES INTERVIEWÉS PENSANT PARTIR EN VACANCES | 634 = 100% |
|---|---|

– Pensent partir:
- ... en France .......................... 77%
- ... à l'étranger ....................... 20%
- dont: • avec un groupe organisé ............ 3%
- • en voyage individuel ............... 17%
- • ne savent pas ...................... —
– Ne connaissent pas encore leur destination ....... 3%

Et au cours de ces vacances effectuerez-vous un circuit ou resterez-vous le plus souvent au même endroit? Si même endroit, est-ce que ce sera, à la mer, à la campagne, à la montagne ou en ville?

| ENSEMBLE DES INTERVIEWÉS PENSANT PARTIR EN VACANCES EN FRANCE | 488 = 100% |
|---|---|

– Pendant leurs vacances en France, pensent:
- ... effecteur un circuit .......... 31%
- ... rester au même endroit ........ 66%
- dont: • à la mer ........................ 32%
- • à la campagne .................. 11%
- • à la montagne .................. 14%
- • en ville ....................... 1%
- • ne savent pas .................. 8%
– Ne savent pas encore comment s'organiseront leurs vacances ........................... 3%

**C** When asked: **i** _____

and **ii** _____

the most popular replies were:
**i** _____
and **ii** _____

**D** When asked: **i** _____

and **ii** _____

the most popular replies were:
**i** _____
and **ii** _____

> JE VAIS EN FRANCE, JE SUIS ALLERGIQUE AUX LANGUES ETRANGÈRES

**E** Now look at this cartoon. Which extract (A, B, C or D) do you think it best illustrates?

Answer: _____

*Source: York Reading Extended Question 5*

# French

8  Don't forget that in the examination you may have to talk/write not only about what you've done or are planning to do on holiday, but that you might also be asked about festivals you celebrate at home at certain times of the year. As a practice for this, write down some short accounts in French (or say them on to cassette tape) about how you celebrate, or have celebrated your birthday, Christmas, Eid, Divali etc. As well as talking about the length of school holidays in a letter, be prepared also to respond to enquiries in a letter about the Bank Holidays in Great Britain and to say roughly how many weeks holiday people have in a working year.

## CHECK-LIST

Any item from Section C which helps you to pass an opinion on a holiday or holiday activity.

**Essential language tasks**

(a)  say where you go for your holidays, when you take them and for how long
(b)  say whom you go with and what you do on holiday
(c)  talk about a holiday you've been on, whether you enjoyed yourself, what the weather was like
(d)  talk about your plans for your next holidays
(e)  say if you've been to a French-speaking country, where you went and what you did
(f)  explain in a tourist information office how long you're staying in the area and ask for information about the town/region (e.g. details of where to stay, where to eat, what to visit)
(g)  ask about coach trips/boat excursions etc. and book tickets
(h)  give a reaction to suggestions made about trips/visits/excursions which are available
(i)  write a short letter to a local tourist office asking in advance for the kinds of details listed here.

**Useful language tasks**

(a)  talk about the way you celebrate important events and festivals at home
(b)  talk about any holiday jobs you may have had
(c)  talk about presents you might give/receive (or have given/have received) on particular occasions
(d)  compare the length of public holidays in France and the UK.
(e)  talk about the kind of visits/trips/excursions/activities which you enjoy when on holiday
(f)  talk about your own town's/area's tourist possibilities for foreign visitors coming to stay there
(g)  understand a short historical account in a brochure or as part of a spoken commentary on a guided tour (e.g. details of a famous building or the site of a famous battle).

# ACCOMMODATION

### A  ON FAIT DES RÉSERVATIONS

1  '... Je voudrais réserver une chambre à grand lit et (à côté) une chambre à deux lits du 15 au 20 août, pour mon mari et moi et nos deux enfants. On aimerait des chambres calmes, avec une salle de bains complète (w.c., lavabo, baignoire ou douche) dans chaque cas. J'attends votre réponse et je vous envoie mes salutations distinguées ...'

2  '... Nous serons cinq – trois jeunes filles et deux garçons. Nous avons l'intention de passer 5 nuits à l'auberge. Nous espérons arriver le soir du 11 juillet et partir le matin du 16. On voudrait prendre le petit déjeuner seulement. Est-ce qu'il est possible de louer des sacs de couchage? ...'

3  '... Je vous écris pour réserver un emplacement pour une caravane du 20 au 24 juillet. Nous serons trois, deux adultes et un garçon de 8 ans ..'

**Activity**

The extracts above are from letters written several months prior to trips to France as people made their accommodation arrangements. Using the clues which are there and adding in extra details yourself, try to reconstruct the conversations which went on when each of the three parties arrived at the hotel, youth hostel or campsite.

**Extension**

What would you say in French if you were in the party going to the hotel and were told by the receptionist, 'Je suis désolé, mais il y a deux petits problèmes ... nous n'avons qu'une seule chambre avec salle de bains complète. Et il a été impossible de vous mettre à côté. Votre chambre est au premier étage et celle des enfants au deuxième.'

How would you react if you were in the parties going to the youth hostel or campsite if you were told, 'Je ne trouve pas votre nom ici ... non je n'ai pas de réservation à ce nom-là ..'

### B  DEVANT LE GÎTE

AGENT   Bonjour madame, monsieur. Je m'appelle Reynaud. Je suis là pour vous accueillir de la part de M. et Mme Canault, les propriétaires. Alors vous voyez bien que c'est une ancienne ferme restaurée avec des pelouses devant et derrière. Alors on va passer à l'intérieur? Voici la clef pour la porte d'entrée et voici celle pour la porte de derrière. Voulez-vous bien me suivre? C'est à un étage. Alors tout est au rez-de-chaussée.

TOURISTE  *Pouvez-vous nous montrer comment faire marcher le chauffage?*
AGENT  *Ah oui, naturellement. En principe c'est automatique pour l'eau chaude . . . voici la minuterie. Voici l'interrupteur pour mettre le chauffage en marche si vous en avez besoin.*
TOURISTE  *Merci, ce n'est pas trop compliqué, heureusement.*
AGENT  *Vous avez apporté le linge de maison . . . c'est-à-dire draps, serviettes . . .*
TOURISTE  *Bien sûr.*
AGENT  *Je crois que vous trouverez tout l'équipement et tous les meubles en bon état. Voulez-vous bien signer ici, s'il vous plaît?*
TOURISTE  *Voilà . . . on a tout payé à l'avance par virement bancaire de notre banque en Angleterre. Voici une copie de la facture.*
AGENT  *Merci – tout est en règle. Je vous verrai dans deux semaines au moment de votre départ. Je vous souhaite un excellent séjour.*

**Activity**

If you were the visitor in the dialogue above, what additional questions would you want to ask in French about the rented property itself, the immediate surroundings and the area within 20 km or so?

C  Below are bits and pieces of many conversations where people are asking for information at the beginning of their stay. Read each one and decide whether it would most likely have been asked at (*a*) a hotel (*b*) a campsite (*c*) a youth hostel (*d*) in rented property. Some could be in more than one but in the majority of cases there should be a clue which makes it clear which type of accommodation is involved.

(i) '. . . *à quelle heure est-ce qu'on doit libérer les chambres demain matin? . . . notre train ne part qu'à 11 heures . .*'
(ii) '. . . *est-ce qu'on peut allumer un barbecue? . . .*'
(iii) '. . . *est-ce que la porte d'entrée est fermée après minuit? . . . il y a un portier peut-être? . . .*'
(iv) '. . . *où est le magasin d'alimentation le plus proche? . . .*'
(v) '. . . *est-ce qu'on peut louer des draps? . . .*'
(vi) '. . . *est-ce qu'il faut ranger les chambres ou faire la vaisselle? . . .*'
(vii) '. . . *est-ce qu'on peut laisser les bagages à la réception? . . . le taxi vient nous chercher à 11.45 . . .*'
(viii) '. . . *est-ce que l'eau dans le bloc sanitaire est potable? . . .*'
(ix) '. . . *est-ce qu'on peut fumer dans les dortoirs? . . .*'
(x) '. . . *est-ce que le terrain est éclairé la nuit? . . .*'
(xi) '. . . *est-ce qu'on peut cueillir des fruits dans le jardin? . . .*'
(xii) '. . . *où est-ce qu'on peut acheter une bouteille de gaz? . . .*'
(xiii) '. . . *qu'est-ce qu'on peut faire le soir? . . . il y a une salle de jeux peut-être? . . .*'
(xiv) '. . . *quels sont les sites naturels et historiques les plus intéressants de la région? . . .*'

D  **Some more extracts** – in fact a long catalogue of complaints about the things that do sometimes go wrong in hotels . . . although not usually all at once! Imagine that each of the problems happened to you when

# Accommodation

staying in a French hotel. Work out what you would say to the receptionist in order to bring the problem to her/his attention as politely but firmly as possible. Can you also think of what you would suggest should be *done* about each problem?

'. . . le lavabo est bouché . . . il n'y a pas d'eau chaude . . . la douche ne marche pas . . . il n'y a pas de bonde dans la baignoire . . . il y a trop de bruit parce que la chambre donne sur la rue . . . je ne peux pas dormir à cause du bruit qui vient de la plomberie . . . l'armoire est trop petite . . . le lit est trop petit . . . le téléviseur . . . le téléphone . . . la radio . . . le chauffage . . . l'ascenseur . . . ne marche pas . . . il n'y a pas d'ampoule dans la salle de bains . . . il n'y a pas de cintres dans l'armoire . . . il n'y a pas de serviette/de papier hygiénique/de savon . . . la chambre n'est pas propre . . . on n'a pas encore apporté nos valises à notre chambre . . .'

### Extension

Below is part of a letter of complaint to a Tourist Office. Can you imagine the conversation which went on as this gentleman left his hotel?

'. . . et je voudrais en plus vous signaler que l'Hôtel des Noyers de votre ville ne correspond pas à la brochure que vous m'avez envoyée. La chambre était peu confortable et la nourriture mal préparée. Je ne suis pas satisfait du tout de mon séjour . . .'

## E   DES PROBLÈMES À SIGNALER APRÈS UN SÉJOUR DANS UN GÎTE

PROPRIÉTAIRE   Madame, Monsieur. C'est terminé, maintenant, malheureusement. Mais le séjour s'est bien passé?

TOURISTE   Ah, oui, à part deux petits problèmes. D'abord on a remarqué une petite fuite d'eau sur un des radiateurs. Il a fallu téléphoner au plombier pour nous dépanner. On a essayé de vous contacter mais vous n'étiez pas là. Voici sa facture.

PROPRIÉTAIRE   Ah, bon. Je suis désolé. Et l'autre problème?

TOURISTE   C'est que notre petit garçon a cassé un vase qui était sur le buffet. On est vraiment désolé . . . on va vous rembourser naturellement.

PROPRIÉTAIRE   Ah non . . . ce n'était pas un objet de grande valeur. Ça arrive de temps en temps avec les enfants . . . c'est normal.

TOURISTE   C'est vraiment gentil. On a passé de très bonnes vacances. On aimerait réserver les deux mêmes semaines l'année prochaine si elles ne sont pas déjà prises.

PROPRIÉTAIRE   Un instant. Il faut que je consulte mon agenda. Oui, ça va . . . aucun problème.

TOURISTE   A l'année prochaine alors!

PROPRIÉTAIRE   Oui, c'est ça, hein. Alors bonne route et bonne rentrée en Angleterre!

### Activity

Can you think of other problems which might have cropped up during a two-week stay in rented accommodation? How would you break the news very politely and gently to the owner? Here are some possibilities for starters: the central heating broke down ... the shower isn't working ... an electrical appliance (say which one) isn't working ... we've broken two plates ...

### F  LE DÉPART DE L'HÔTEL

TOURISTE  Je voudrais régler maintenant, s'il vous plaît. Je n'aurai pas beaucoup de temps demain matin.
RÉCEPTIONNISTE  Oui, madame. Vous êtes restée combien de nuits en tout?
TOURISTE  Six.
RÉCEPTIONNISTE  Alors, ça fait 360 francs. Vous n'avez pas mangé à l'hôtel le soir?
TOURISTE  Non, j'ai pris le petit déjeuner seulement.
RÉCEPTIONNISTE  D'accord. Six petits déjeuners à 12 francs, et vous avez pris chaque jour un jus d'orange ... ça fait un supplément de 24 francs. Voilà ... 456 francs en tout ... toutes taxes comprises.
TOURISTE  Merci bien. Mon séjour m'a plu énormément. J'aimerais revenir une autre fois ...
RÉCEPTIONNISTE  Merci bien. A la prochaine, alors!

**Activity**

Is the bill correct? How would you say you thought there was a mistake? How would you ask if you could pay by credit card?

### G  ENQUÊTE SUR L'HÉBERGEMENT

Combien de fois par an en moyenne faites-vous un séjour dans un hôtel/un terrain de camping/une auberge de jeunesse/un gîte?
Plusieurs fois/une fois/jamais?
Quelle formule d'hébergement avez-vous choisie pour votre séjour de vacances le plus récent?
Hôtel/Terrain de camping/Auberge de Jeunesse/Gîte?
Pourquoi avez-vous choisi cette formule?
Avez-vous réservé à l'avance?
Est-ce que vous êtes satisfait(e) de votre séjour?
Qu'est-ce qui vous a plu/déplu?
Est-ce que vous avez l'intention de retourner au même endroit?

**Activity**

If you were stopped in the street and asked to answer some questions in French for the opinion poll above, what could you manage to say in response to each question?

# Accommodation

## SKILLS PRACTICE

**SIGNS AND NOTICES**     1    Accommodation is a topic area which is bound to involve many signs and notices. How well could you explain the following in the various settings indicated?

### CAMPSITE

(*a*)      SALLE DE RÉUNION .. SALLE DE JEUX .. TERRAIN DE BOULES .. POUBELLES .. BLOC SANITAIRE .. BUREAU D'ACCUEIL (all on direction signs)
(*b*)      EAU NON POTABLE (above a wash basin)
(*c*)      PRISE DE COURANT POUR RASOIR (above an electrical socket in the wash rooms)

### YOUTH HOSTEL

(*a*)      DORTOIR DES FILLES .. DORTOIR DES GARCONS .. CANTINE .. SALLE DE SEJOUR .. INSTALLATIONS SANITAIRES (all on direction signs)
(*b*)      IL EST FORMELLEMENT INTERDIT DE FUMER DANS LA SALLE A MANGER (sign on wall of dining room)
(*c*)      GARDEZ L'AUBERGE PROPRE. UTILISEZ LES POUBELLES! (sign on notice board)
(*d*)      LE SOIR, MINIBUS POSSIBLE SUR DEMANDE (MINIMUM 6 PERSONNES (notice at reception)
(*e*)      HORAIRES DES REPAS (sign in canteen)
(*f*)      DANS LES CHAMBRES NE LAISSEZ PAS D'OBJETS DE VALEUR (notice at reception)

### HOTEL

(*a*)      SORTIE DE SECOURS (sign on a door)
(*b*)      EN CAS DE PANNE, N'ESSAYEZ PAS DE SORTIR. APPUYEZ SUR LE BOUTON D'ALARME! (sign in a lift)
(*c*)      CABINE HORS DE SERVICE (sign on a telephone booth)
(*d*)      POUR PROLONGER VOTRE SÉJOUR, ADRESSEZ-VOUS A LA RÉCEPTION AVANT 10H DU MATIN (sign at reception)
(*e*)      PRIERE DE FAIRE MA CHAMBRE .. PRIERE DE NE PAS DÉRANGER (double-sided sign to hang on the outside of your bedroom door)

2    When you write off for information about French campsites you receive the following information as part of a leaflet.

*LE CAMP*

Classé «4 étoiles», le terrain de Camping Caravaning se situe au centre de la Forêt de Montgeon, et l'on accède par des routes excellentes. Ses six hectares ombragés de bouleaux, peuvent recevoir 800 campeurs, qui trouveront des équipements modernes et confortables, salles de réunions et de jeux, etc...

Le Parc de loisirs de Montgeon leur offre, sur 250 hectares, un cadre forestier exceptionnel, dont 25 hectares équipés pour les loisirs, avec plaines de jeux, enclos

pour animaux, terrains de boules et pétanque, lac pour canotage, pelouses fleuries, etc…
La Ville, la plage et le port sont à quelques minutes, et d'un accès aisé.

(a) What information is there about the site itself under the following headings? Surface area, capacity, amenities, location, access, shade.

(b) How much information can you work out about the nearby Leisure Park?

(c) Which other nearby amenities/attractions are said to be within easy reach of the campsite?

3 The following is part of a brochure which is sent to you after writing to the French Youth Hostelling Federation.

---
**LES INDIVIDUELS**
---

Les A. J. ont été créées pour permettre aux jeunes de voyager économiquement, rencontrer d'autres jeunes … Très différentes les unes des autres, elles offrent toujours des chambres collectives ou petits dortoirs, installations sanitaires, salles à manger, séjour, souvent une cuisine 'individuelle'.

Une Auberge de Jeunesse est la maison de tous les jeunes. C'est pourquoi il te sera parfois demandé d'assurer quelque service. Ne considère pas cela comme une contrainte, mais comme une simple participation à la vie en commun.

Et nos amis les bêtes? Désolés, ils ne sont pas admis dans les A.J.!

---
**HORAIRES**
---

En général, de 7.30 à 10.00 h. et de 17.00 à 22.00 h. l'hiver et 23.00 h. l'été.
Horaires différents à PARIS 'Jules Ferry', 'd'Artagnan', CHOISY-LE-ROI, qui ferment à 1.00 ou 2.00 h. du matin.

---
**TARIFS**
---

| HÉBERGEMENT* (selon catégorie) | REPAS (boissons non comprises) |
|---|---|
| Catégorie 🏠 ............ 30,00 F | Petit déjeuner ............................. 9,50 F |
| | Déjeuner ou dîner ..................... 31,50 F |
| Catégorie 🏠 ............ 26,00 F | Plat unique (aux individuels ..... 20,50 F seulement et dans certaines A.J.) |
| Catégorie ⛺ ............ 18,00 F | Location draps/sacs couchage (de 1 à 7 nuits) ........................... 11,00 F |

(a) Which part of the first section (**LES INDIVIDUELS**) has something to say about *attitude*? What is it saying exactly?

(b) What does the first section have to say about animals?

(c) What is the change in the opening hours between winter and summer? What are the exceptions to the general opening hours given?

(d) What do the two sets of prices in the bottom right- and left-hand columns refer to?

(e) What does the leaflet have to say about drinks, sheets and sleeping bags?

## Accommodation

**Extension**

Try to write a dialogue which might take place at the reception of this hostel, between the warden and two visitors who have not had this leaflet beforehand. Imagine the questions they might ask about the hostel regulations and the process they would go through to book in for two nights, hiring sleeping bags.

4  You receive some brochures when you are planning a holiday stay in a French gîte. Here are some extracts.

**LES GÎTES RURAUX** sont des locations meublées (maison ou appartement) situées à la campagne, dans un village agréable ou dans le cadre d'une ferme. Les aménagements sont faits selon des normes précises et les propriétaires ont gagné la « charte des Gîtes de France ». RESERVATION: à la semaine du samedi 16 h au samedi 10 h), ou du week-end.

**Légendes des tarifs:**
- A = prix semaine, Juillet – Août
- B = prix semaine + petits congés
- C = prix semaine, hors saison
- D = prix week-end.

**SAINT-MARTIN-D'ABBAT**
(855 habitants). (G. 6).
N° A. 19, 3 épis, capacité maximum 6 personnes. **Animaux admis.** Gîte indépendant, situé sur un domaine boisé et parsemé d'étangs. Le gîte comprend: 1 salle de séjour avec cheminée, coin cuisine, 3 chambres équipées de salle de bains, terrain. Loisirs à proximité: pêche et chasse sur place, tennis et piscine: 5 km. Ville à proximité: Châteauneuf-sur-Loire: 5 km.

| A | B | C | D |
|---|---|---|---|
| 1.130 F | 905 F | 720 F | 410 F |

**LIGNY-LE-RIBAULT**
(960 habitants). (C. 8).
N° B. 3; 1 épi, capacité maximum 3 adultes. **Animaux admis.** Situé en pleine Sologne et dans le cadre d'une ferme typique, ce petit gîte donnera la possibilité de découvrir les charmes d'une région réputée. Le gîte comprend: 1 cuisine, 1 salle de séjour, 1 chambre, douche, jardin. Loisirs à proximité: pêche: 1 km; piscine: 14 km; équitation: 8 km. Villes à proximité: La Ferté-Saint-Aubin: 14 km; Orléans: 32 km.

| A | B | C | D |
|---|---|---|---|
| 575 F | 470 F | 365 F | – |

(*a*) From the top extract what can you find out about what exactly a gîte is, where they are situated, what the booking arrangements are (e.g. is mid-week to mid-week possible?) and which price code you will have to follow for a week's stay in August?

(*b*) Using the bottom extracts, complete the table below on the two properties, comparing the points listed.

|   | Property A19 | Property B3 |
|---|---|---|
| 1 Number of bedrooms |   |   |
| 2 Bathroom facilities |   |   |
| 3 Maximum capacity |   |   |
| 4 Leisure facilities |   |   |

5   Whilst staying in a gîte in Champagne you notice the following item in the Reims local paper.

**Bonjour les odeurs!**
La plupart des Rémois sortent dans l'après-midi leurs poubelles pour la collecte du lendemain matin. Cette pratique entraîne des odeurs et des salissures (sacs éventrés, renversés...).
Il serait souhaitable de ne sortir les déchets ménagers qu'à partir de 19 h 30. En outre, il est rappelé qu'il est inutile de sortir quoi que ce soit le mardi soir puisque la collecte n'est pas effectuée le mercredi mardi.
A votre service, ALLO PROPRETÉ : 26.40.22.33.

(a) What exactly are they requesting you to do about your dustbin and why?
(b) What does the article say about Tuesday evening?
(c) Can you spot the misprint in the last but one sentence? What word should have been printed instead of mardi? (in ... pas effectuée le mercredi mardi).

6   You read the following notice on the back of your hotel bedroom door.

**PRIX DE VENTE DE LA CHAMBRE N°**

|  | Avec TV couleur | Sans TV |
|---|---|---|
| **Chambre occupée par 1 personne** | : _____ | _____ |
| **Chambre occupée par 2 personnes** | : _____ | _____ |
| **Lit supplémentaire** | : _____ | |
| **Animal** | : _____ | |

**Petit déjeuner continental par personne :**
**Prix impulsion téléphonique :**

PRIX NET / NET PRICE / PRIX, TAXES ET SERVICE COMPRIS

**HORAIRES**

– Hôtel ouvert de 7 h à 23 h.
  Si vous pensez rentrer tardivement, conservez votre clef et demandez le N° du code qui vous permettra l'accès de la porte de l'hôtel au-delà de 23 h.
– Petit déjeuner servi de 7 h à 9 h 30 au restaurant et de 7 h 30 à 9 h 30 en chambre.
– Restaurant «LE GAULOIS» ouvert de 12 h à 22 h.
  Les menus et la carte sont servis de 12 h à 14 h 30 et de 19 h à 22 h.
  Entre ces plages horaires, une prestation simplifiée Vous sera proposée.

**PARKING**

**Parking gratuit non gardé.**
**Veuillez prendre toutes les précautions d'usage et ne rien laisser dans votre véhicule.**

**URGENCES**

De 23 h à 7 h, nous n'assurons pas de permanence de nuit, cependant, en cas de malaises ou d'incendie, appeler le N°:

★★   NN                                               ★★   NN

## Accommodation

(a) What are the instructions regarding returning to the hotel after 11.00 p.m.?
(b) What is available if you feel hungry at around 4.00 in the afternoon?
(c) Which of the following are 'extras', i.e. over and above the basic minimum price of the room: tax . . . service . . . breakfast?
(d) What two warnings are given about car parking?

## CHECK-LIST

**Essential language tasks**
(a) talk about campsites, youth hostels, hotels etc. you have used
(b) write a short letter enquiring about whether accommodation is available, what the price is and what facilities exist
(c) write a short letter making a booking
(d) understand a letter/brochure/guide book giving accommodation details
(e) ask in a hotel if rooms are available
(f) say whether or not you've reserved
(g) state what sort of a room you need
(h) ask about price per night
(i) say if it is too dear for you
(j) say you would like to see the room
(k) accept or reject the room offered
(l) ask if there are other hotels nearby
(m) book in
(n) enquire where the room is
(o) ask about keys (e.g. is there key to front door as well as to bedroom?)
(p) ask if there is a restaurant in or near the hotel
(q) ask where lift, lounge, t.v. room, telephone, car park are
(r) ask if any meals are included, especially breakfast, and where they are taken
(s) pay on departure and thank/congratulate
(t) ask in a youth hostel if there is room
(u) say how long you're staying and how many males/females in your party
(v) fill in the registration details
(w) ask about costs
(x) ask about facilities e.g. cooking, eating, bathing and toilet arrangements i.e. availability, times of availability, cost and location
(y) ask about amenities in the nearest town/village, e.g. shops, restaurants and leisure facilities
(z) pay on departure, confirming the number of nights you've stayed, meals you've taken etc.
(aa) ask at a campsite if there is room
(bb) say for how many nights, how many people, how many tents/caravans etc.

(*cc*) asking cost for adults/children/vehicle per night
(*dd*) ask where the pitch is
(*ee*) ask about amenities (e.g. showers, hot water, electricity points, restaurant, take away meals, shops, games room etc.) i.e. if available and where?
(*ff*) say what your needs are in the camp shop (e.g. tin opener, batteries, gas)
(*gg*) pay at end of stay and thank for service
(*hh*) when arriving at a gîte, identify yourself and ask to be shown around
(*ii*) enquire about the keys
(*jj*) enquire about heating and hot water.

**Useful language tasks**
(*a*) talk about the advantages/disadvantages of different types of accommodation (e.g. camping versus hotel)
(*b*) make complaints about problems in any of the types of accommodation (e.g. no plug in wash bowl; light bulb not working; no toilet paper; dirty towels; room too hot/too cold; no coathangers; not enough blankets; gas/water leaks; too much noise; wish to change room
(*c*) in a hotel, enquire about half-board and full board rates
(*d*) in a youth hostel, ask about any rules and regulations e.g. attitude towards alcohol; where to leave valuables; chores which have to be done
(*e*) ask about hiring a sleeping bag or sheets
(*f*) at a campsite, ask about rules and regulations e.g. attitude towards barbecues, whether camp gates are locked at night
(*g*) at a gîte, ask about procedure for booking next year
(*h*) explain any problems which have occurred during the course of your stay e.g. something you've broken, some appliance that has broken down.

# TOPIC SEVEN

# EATING AND DRINKING

### A  AU CAFÉ

FRANÇOIS  *Alors, Stephen, qu'est-ce que tu prends?*
STEPHEN  *Pour moi, un coca, s'il te plaît.*
SYLVIE  *Et pour moi aussi.*
JACQUELINE  *Moi, je prends plutôt un soda orange.*
FRANÇOIS  *Mademoiselle . . . deux cocas et deux sodas orange, s'il vous plaît. Qu'est-ce que vous avez à manger? Des sandwiches ou d'autres choses?*
SERVEUSE  *Des sandwiches – jambon, pâté, camembert – des croque-monsieur et des hot-dogs.*
FRANÇOIS  *Qu'est-ce qu'on prend alors?*
STEPHEN  *Rien pour moi, merci. Je n'ai pas faim.*
FRANÇOIS  *Tu es sûr? Sylvie? Jacqueline?*
SYLVIE  *Un sandwich au camembert . . .*
JACQUELINE  *Moi, je voudrais bien un croque-monsieur.*
FRANÇOIS  *Et pour moi, un hot-dog, s'il vous plaît.*
SERVEUSE  *Tout de suite.*
STEPHEN  *Qu'est-ce qu'il y a à faire dans un café français? Ce n'est pas tout à fait la même chose qu'un 'pub'.*
FRANÇOIS  *Bien, très souvent, on trouve des jeux électroniques, un babyfoot, un juke-box ou un jeu de flippers.*

**Activity**

Re-write the sort of dialogue which might have taken place between these four people if they were in the café whose price list appears on page 87. What questions would you need to ask the waiter/waitress to find out if the café had the entertainment facilities mentioned by François above?

### B  AU RESTAURANT

GARÇON  *Vous êtes combien, madame?*
DAME  *Nous sommes quatre.*
GARÇON  *Vous avez fait une réservation?*
DAME  *Non. Vous avez de la place?*
GARÇON  *Ah, oui . . . je crois bien. Il n'y a pas beaucoup de monde ce soir. Voilà une table libre au fond. C'est à côté de la fenêtre. Cela ne vous pose aucun inconvénient?*
DAME  *Au contraire . . .*

MONSIEUR  On prend un apéritif?
DAME  Merci, pas pour moi. Et les enfants?
ENFANTS  Non, merci.

GARÇON  Vous avez choisi?
DAME  Alors, quatre menus à 60, s'il vous plaît. Pour commencer, deux œufs mayonnaise et deux salades de tomates. Pour suivre, deux steaks saignants, une escalope et un poulet. Et moi, je prends pas de frites . . . je les digère très mal.
GARÇON  On peut très facilement vous servir du riz, madame.
DAME  Très bien.
GARÇON  Et comme boisson?
DAME  Une carafe de rouge et deux limonades, s'il vous plaît.

MONSIEUR  Le café n'est pas compris dans le menu à prix fixe, n'est-ce pas?
GARÇON  Non monsieur.
MONSIEUR  Apportez-nous quatre cafés, s'il vous plaît.

DAME  L'addition, s'il vous plaît.
GARÇON  Alors, quatres menus à 60 . . . ça fait 240 . . . plus les boissons . . . 32 francs . . . et les cafés 16 francs . . . 288 francs en tout.
DAME  Le service est compris?
GARÇON  Oui, c'est compris, madame.
DAME  Je suppose que les toilettes sont au sous-sol.
GARÇON  Oui, madame.
MONSIEUR  Est-ce qu'on peut téléphoner d'ici?
GARÇON  C'est aussi en bas, monsieur, au fond du couloir.
DAME  Merci bien, monsieur. On a vraiment bien mangé ce soir.

**Activity**

Using this dialogue as a basis, make a list of all the key phrases in French you feel you would need to use if you were helping parents or friends in a French-speaking country to get a meal in a restaurant. List them in order, from the moment you enter the restaurant until the time you pay and leave. What phrases are missing from the dialogue here which you might need to say? Some examples: 'Are the drinks included? What do you recommend? Can you explain what this is? What's the dish of the day? Can you pay by credit card?'

**C   DES PROBLÈMES . . . ET DES RÉCLAMATIONS**

Have a look at the following list of phrases overheard in restaurants when people have had some kind of problem or wanted to complain about something. Decide for each one whether you would be most likely to say it

(a)   as you arrive
(b)   whilst you are waiting for the waiter to take your order
(c)   when ordering
(d)   when the food arrives

## Eating and drinking

(e) once you've started to eat the food
(f) at the end of the meal. Ask yourself in each case why you feel it might be a, b, c, d, e or f. Some comments could occur at more than one time, so there isn't always a right or wrong answer.

(i) '. . . je crois que vous avez fait une erreur . . . le café est compris dans le menu à prix fixe . . .'
(ii) '. . . qu'est-ce que c'est . . . la salade niçoise?'
(iii) '. . . on peut avoir de la moutarde, s'il vous plaît?'
(iv) '. . . alors, vous n'avez plus de truite . . .'
(v) '. . . pourriez-vous me chercher un autre verre? Celui-ci n'est pas propre . . .'
(vi) '. . . on peut commander maintenant?'
(vii) '. . . cette assiette est froide . . .'
(viii) '. . . il nous manque des cuillères . . .'
(ix) '. . . mon mari a horreur des courants d'air . . . on ne veut pas être trop près de la fenêtre . . .'
(x) '. . . pouvez-vous nettoyer la table après les clients qui viennent de partir, s'il vous plaît?'
(xi) '. . . ça ne sera pas trop long, j'espère. On n'a pas beaucoup de temps . . .'

### D  ON DÎNE CHEZ DES AMIS

MME HOLEC  Bonsoir Hélène, bonsoir Olivier. Salut, Simone. Ce jeune homme doit être ton correspondant anglais.
NICKY  C'est ça, madame. Enchanté . . .
MME HOLEC  Alors, entrez . . . je vous en prie. Tout le monde connaît Alain, je crois, à part Nicky. Nicky, je te présente Alain, mon mari.
NICKY  Enchanté, monsieur.
ALAIN  Et moi aussi, Nicky. On a beaucoup parlé de toi . . . Tenez, je vous prends vos manteaux et puis on va s'installer dans le salon.
MME MÉNAGE  Un tout petit cadeau, Edith, pour te dire merci . . .
MME HOLEC  Mais tu n'aurais pas dû, vraiment. Regarde, Alain . . .
ALAIN  C'est gentil, hein . . . mais il ne fallait pas.
MME HOLEC  Alors . . . qu'est-ce qu'on vous offre comme apéritif? J'ai du porto, du whisky, du martini et du vin doux . . . et pour les enfants des jus de fruits et du coca . . .

MME HOLEC  A table, tout le monde!
MME MÉNAGE  Mmm, ça sent bon.
MME HOLEC  C'est Alain qui a tout préparé . . .
ALAIN  Ah . . . vous savez . . . c'est un repas très simple . . . mais j'espère que ça va vous plaire quand même . . . Bon appétit!

ALAIN  Tiens . . . encore quelques haricots, Nicky.
NICKY  Non, merci, monsieur. J'en ai déjà repris une fois.
ALAIN  Tu es sûr? Je ne peux pas t'en resservir quelques-uns?
NICKY  Non, merci. C'était délicieux . . . mais j'ai vraiment bien mangé déjà.
ALAIN  Olivier . . . je peux t'en redonner?

OLIVIER  *Ah, oui, bien volontiers, Alain.*

**Activity**

Make a comparison of this dialogue and the one set in the restaurant on page 83. In each situation certain phrases are required to do certain things, e.g. to attract attention, to ask for explanation, to order, to ask for something extra, to accept an offer and to refuse, to compliment, to thank. Try to make a list of all these phrases and put them into one of the following three categories: (*a*) phrases you could only use at a restaurant (*b*) phrases you could only use when eating with a French family at home and (*c*) phrases you could use both in a restaurant and at a meal in someone's home.

**Extension**

If you were Nicky in the dialogue, what would you say to Mme Holec at the end of the evening before you left with the Ménage family?

**Enquête**

Est-ce que vous avez mangé récemment dans un restaurant/self-service/établissement fast-food?
Vous avez mangé seul(e) ou avec des amis?
Qu'est-ce que vous avez mangé?
Gamme de prix: plutôt cher/prix modérés/pas cher?
Qu'est-ce qui vous a plu/déplu?

Est-ce que vous recevez des amis pour manger souvent/rarement/jamais?
Qu'est-ce que vous offrez typiquement à manger?
Est-ce que vous aidez à préparer le repas?
Est-ce que vous pouvez penser à un plat qui a été très réussi/moins réussi?

Quand vous êtes chez vous, à quels moments de la journée mangez-vous, normalement?
Quel est pour vous le repas principal de la journée?
Pourquoi?
Quel est votre repas favori quotidien? Et quand vous fêtez quelque chose de spécial?
Quel est votre repas le moins préféré?
Si vous êtes au collège, est-ce que vous mangez à midi dans la cantine? Quelle est votre opinion sur les repas du point de vue de variété/quantité des portions/prix/équilibre nutritionnel?

**Activity**

What sort of responses could you make in French to the questions being asked in the opinion poll above?

# Eating and drinking 87

## SKILLS PRACTICE

**SIGNS AND NOTICES**

1 What would you make of these signs and notices which are all connected with food and drink?
   (a)   TÉLÉPHONE AU SOUS-SOL (sign in a café)
   (b)   COIN NON-FUMEURS (sign in a restaurant)
   (c)   SPÉCIAL ÉTÉ – 20F LE MENU 'DE LUXE' – * UN CHEESEBURGER 'DE LUXE' * UNE PETITE PORTION DE FRITES * UNE BOISSON 25 CL. (sign on window of fast food restaurant)
   (d)   NE JAMAIS RECONGELER UN PRODUIT DÉCONGELÉ (note on back of frozen food packet)
   (e)   * GRILL A TOUTE HEURE * SALON DE THÉ * GLACE PATISSERIE * OUVERT DE 11 H A 22 H MEME LE DIMANCHE (roadside advert)
   (f)   VOUS POUVEZ TROUVER A VOTRE DISPOSITION DES PRODUITS ALIMENTAIRES 'A EMPORTER', TELS QU'ÉPICERIE, CHARCUTERIE, PAIN, BOISSONS ... DANS LA PLUPART DES STATIONS-SERVICE ET RESTAURANTS (note in a leaflet about French motorways)

2 You come across the following drinks list in a French café

| | 1/4 | 1/2 | 1/1 |
|---|---|---|---|
| **EAUX MINERALES** | | | |
| Evian, Badoit | 8,00 | 10,00 | 14,00 |
| **BIERES, JUS DE FRUITS, SODAS** | | | |
| Bières françaises | (25 cl) | | 10,00 |
| Autres bières | (33 cl) | | 17,00 |
| Jus de tomate, raisin, orange, pamplemousse | (20 cl) | | 8,00 |
| Coca-cola, Schweppes, Orangina, sodas divers | (20 cl) | | 10,00 |
| **FRUITS FRAIS PRESSÉS** | ( 6 cl) | | 18,00 |

   (a)   Why are there three separate prices given for mineral water?
   (b)   What is the difference in origin between the two types of beer?
   (c)   How much would a freshly squeezed orange drink be?
   (d)   What would the order be, in French, for the following? 2×quarter litre Evian mineral water – a grapefruit juice – a fizzy orange

**Extension**
Write a dialogue between the four people who eventually give this order, from the point when they are deciding what to have (include questions to each other about their choice, changes of mind etc.), to the giving of the order to the waiter and finally to the stage of asking for the bill, enquiring whether service is included, and paying.

**3** You see this sign outside a restaurant.

> Le petit creux à toute heure
> PAM
> restauration rapide
> fast food
> 45 RUE DE PARIS tel: 51.04.80
> burger . croque monsieur
> pizza . frite . sandwich
> boissons
> Milk Shake
> coupe glacée . chantilly
> NOS PIZZAS FAMILIALES
> à emporter
> OUVERT SANS INTERRUPTION

(a) What does it tell you about opening hours?
(b) Which four hot foods are available?
(c) Are there any desserts available? If so, what?
(d) What is available for take away?

## Eating and drinking

4   You see this advert for a 41.20 F set meal in a restaurant.

> **UN CHOIX DE GRILLADES AU FEU DE BOIS ET DE SPÉCIALITÉS AUX MEILLEURS PRIX**
>
> **QUELQUES EXEMPLES:**
> La côte de porc grillée garnie (pommes frites et salade)
> et
> la tarte aux pommes maison ................ **41,20 F**
>
> Service 15% non compris.

(a)   What exactly do you get for your 41.20 F? Is a tip included?

5   The following are extracts from a leaflet which is given to customers at a motorway service area restaurant.

**Les réchauffe-plats**
Pour vous permettre de prendre votre temps pendant vos repas et pour que votre plat chaud reste chaud, MAREST a mis à votre disposition des fours à micro-ondes. (Attention, n'y introduisez pas d'objets métalliques).

**Les cafés**
Demandez à notre caissière votre jeton-café. Vous pourrez en échange finir votre repas en dégustant tranquillement un café bien chaud.

(a)   What facility is the left-hand item telling you about? What warning does it give?
(b)   The right-hand item is obviously something to do with coffee. What does it advise you to do in order to avoid your coffee going cold by the time you are ready for it at the end of the meal?

6   You are given the following questionnaire to fill in as you leave the self-service restaurant in a hypermarket at Calais, where you are catching the ferry back home.

> Monsieur, Madame,
>
> Vous pouvez nous aider à mieux vous satisfaire en répondant à ces quelques questions.
>
> 1. – Qu'appréciez-vous chez FLUNCH?
>
> 2. – Avez-vous des critiques à formuler? Lesquelles?
>
> 3. – Avez-vous des suggestions à faire? Lesquelles?
>
> 4. – En moyenne, à quelle fréquence venez-vous chez FLUNCH?
>
> . tous les jours ☐
> . 3 à 4 fois / semaine ☐
> . 2 à 3 fois / semaine ☐
> . tous les 15 jours ☐
> . tous les mois ☐
> . occasionnellement ☐

(a)   What are the four things they want you to tell them?

**Extension**

Think of possible replies and fill the form in.

7  You find the following information about breakfast in your hotel in a leaflet in your room.

> Si vous désirez prendre le petit déjeuner dans votre chambre, veuillez suspendre votre commande dès ce soir à la poignée extérieure de votre porte. Merci. Il est également servi au restaurant. La plupart des NOVOTEL proposent maintenant une formule de petit déjeuner buffet (voir cavalier dans votre chambre). Nous vous souhaitons une bonne nuit.
>
> **petit déjeuner Continental**
>
> Jus de fruit, petit pain et croissant, beurre, confiture, boisson chaude au choix.
>
> Café noir ☐
> Café au lait ☐
> Thé au lait ☐
> Thé citron ☐
> Chocolat ☐

(a)  What are the instructions about ordering breakfast?
(b)  Where is breakfast served?
(c)  What does the continental breakfast consist of exactly and what is the choice of hot drinks?

8  You read the following information about catering on French high-speed trains.

**1 – LE BAR**

Dans chaque rame, le bar est ouvert pendant toute la durée du trajet. Ce bar offre aux voyageurs des deux classes:
- des coffrets repas,
- des plat simples chauds et froids,
- des sandwichs,
- des boissons chaudes et froides.

**2 – LA RESTAURATION A LA PLACE EN 1re CLASSE**

Dans les voitures 1re classe réservées à la restauration, un service à la place est assuré dans tous les TGV circulant aux heures habituelles des repas.
Ce service, proche de la restauration traditionnelle, offre:
- le petit déjeuner,
- à midi, un menu avec possibilité de choix entre le plat du jour et une grillade,
- le soir, une formule allégée autour d'un plat.

Les menus sont souvent renouvelés à l'intention des voyageurs se déplaçant fréquemment.
Réservez votre place à l'avance dans ces voitures.

**3 – LA VENTE AMBULANTE**

Une vente ambulante est assurée dans certains TGV. Elle offre des sandwichs, des pâtisseries et des boissons, ainsi que, aux heures de petit déjeuner, des boissons chaudes et des croissants.

(a)  What are the opening hours of the bar/buffet?
(b)  Can you get a full hot meal in the bar/buffet?
(c)  If you're a first class passenger, at what times of the day can you get a full meal served at your seat?
(d)  Will there always be a food/drinks trolley service on every train?

## Eating and drinking

(e) What range of food and drinks is available from the trolley service?

9. It's important to understand correctly the instructions for keeping food which you have bought. Here are two extracts from labels.

**1**

**Conservation:**
24 heures dans un réfrigérateur.
3 jours dans le compartiment à glace d'un réfrigérateur.
Plusieurs mois dans le compartiment *** à –18° d'un congélateur, dans la limite du délai optimal de consommation.

**2**

**rians**

**LAIT FRAIS PASTEURISÉ DEMI-ÉCRÉMÉ**
La remontée de crème sur le lait frais pasteurisé est normale.
Agiter avant utilisation.
Conserver à +6°C max.
Laiteries H. Triballat 18220 Rians

18194 JLP

(a) Explain very carefully to the person in your party who is looking after food and supplies how each product has to be kept. No 1 is a frozen product and number 2 milk.

10. While on your camping holiday you notice the following recipe in a local newspaper.

**Pommes de terre barbecue**

**Préparation:** 10 mn.

**Cuisson:** 45 à 60 mn.

**Pour 4 personnes:** 8 pommes de terre de bonne taille – 200 grs de crème fraîche (ou de fromage blanc battu) – ciboulette – persil – estragon – sel et poivre.

Laver et brosser les pommes de terre. Envelopper chacune dans un carré de papier alu. Les poser sur le gril chaud. Retourner 4 fois pendant la cuisson sans percer le papier. A partir de 45 mn, piquer les pommes de terre avec une brochette pour vérifier la cuisson.

Elle doit pénétrer facilement. Pendant ce temps, ajouter à la crème ou au fromage blanc, les fines herbes hâchées. Saler et poivrer. Servir brûlant sans développer les papillottes. Chaque convive fend sa pomme de terre en 2, la recouvre de sauce et la mange avec une petite cuiller.

(a) Write down for the persons who are going to be involved in making this dish very precise directions. Use the following headings: (a) Preparing the potatoes (b) Cooking them (c) Testing whether ready (d) Making the sauce (e) How to serve (f) How to eat.

# French

**11** For supper one evening you have decided to have sole and noisette potatoes, as they are both available frozen in the campsite shop. Here are the directions from the back of the packets.

**Conseils de cuisson:**
Nous vous conseillons de cuisiner ces filets de limande panés sans décongélation préalable.

**Suggestion culinaire:**
Après avoir suivi les conseils de cuisson, faites frire les filets dans une poêle avec du beurre pendant 2 ou 3 minutes. Au moment de servir, ajoutez du jus de citron et un peu de persil haché.

**Modes d'emploi**
**1 – Dans une poêle:** faites chauffer un mélange d'huile et de beurre (ou de margarine). Lorsque le mélange est chaud, mettez-y les pommes noisettes encore surgelées. Laissez brunir à feu doux durant 5 minutes en agitant la poêle de temps à autre.

(a) Do the sole fillets have to be defrosted?
(b) What are the directions for cooking the sole fillets? What is it suggested you add when serving?
(c) Do the noisette potatoes have to be defrosted? What are the exact steps suggested for cooking them?

## CHECK-LIST

**Essential language tasks**
(a) talk about your likes/dislikes/preferences in food and drink
(b) talk about your meal times and eating habits at home
(c) in a public eating place, attract the waiter's attention
(d) order a drink/snack/meal
(e) ask for a menu at a set price
(f) ask for a table for a certain number
(g) ask whether they have certain foods and drinks
(h) ask about cost of food/drink
(i) ask for something on the menu or drinks list to be described/explained for you
(j) say what you think about the drink/food
(k) refuse or accept suggestions
(l) ask about any service charge
(m) ask if the following are available/where they are – toilets; telephone; pinball machine; computer game; juke box
(n) when eating in a French home, say you're hungry/thirsty
(o) ask where and when the family normally eats
(p) ask for things to be passed to you at table
(q) ask politely for a little more/a lot
(r) accept offers of food politely/refuse politely
(s) say how much you've enjoyed the meal i.e. pay compliments
(t) drink toasts in French.

**Useful language tasks**
(a) explain to a French person what a particular British dish is like
(b) understand simple recipes

# Eating and drinking

(c) say certain foods/drinks don't agree with you
(d) ask for a table in a particular place in a restaurant e.g. on the terrace, near the window
(e) ask for a change of table and give the reason
(f) ask if you can have something slightly different from the set menu
(g) complain about something missing e.g. glass, knife, serviette
(h) complain about the food/service e.g. too cold, too slow, dirty cloth
(i) talk about a special meal you once had in someone's house or in a restaurant
(j) say how you help/cook in the kitchen at home
(k) talk about differences in eating/drinking habits in homes/public eating places in France and the UK.

# SHOPPING

### A  TROUVER LE BON MAGASIN

TOURISTE   Pardon, monsieur. On cherche une boulangerie. Est-ce qu'il y en a une près d'ici?

PASSANT   Ah, oui, jeune homme. Prenez la première rue à droite et vous en trouverez une en face du bureau de poste.

TOURISTE   Merci bien, monsieur. C'est ouvert maintenant, vous croyez?

PASSANT   On ferme normalement entre une heure et deux heures trente. Vous avez encore du temps si vous vous dépêchez.

### B  TROUVER LE BON RAYON DANS UN GRAND MAGASIN

TOURISTE   Où est le rayon vêtements femmes, s'il vous plaît? C'est ici au rez-de-chaussée?

EMPLOYÉE   Ah non, c'est au quatrième étage. Vous pouvez prendre l'escalier roulant ou l'ascenseur.

TOURISTE   Merci bien, madame. Il me faut aussi du papier à lettres.

EMPLOYÉE   La papeterie est au sous-sol, madame.

### C  DANS UN MAGASIN D'ALIMENTATION

CLIENT   Bonjour . . . il y a quelqu'un?

COMMERÇANT   J'arrive tout de suite monsieur. Qu'est-ce qu'il y a pour votre service?

CLIENT   Je voudrais du pâté pour quatre personnes, s'il vous plaît. C'est pour un pique-nique.

COMMERÇANT   Alors à peu près 200 grammes. Et avec ça, monsieur?

CLIENT   Il me faut aussi quatre tranches de jambon et une boîte de camembert.

COMMERÇANT   Voilà. C'est tout?

CLIENT   Oui, c'est tout, merci.

### D  DANS UN MAGASIN DE VÊTEMENTS

TOURISTE   Est-ce que je peux essayer cette veste, s'il vous plaît?

EMPLOYÉ   Oui, bien sûr, monsieur. Les cabines d'essayage sont sur votre droite.

TOURISTE   C'est un peu trop petit. Vous n'avez pas d'autres à me montrer qui sont plus grandes?

# Shopping

EMPLOYÉ   *Je suis désolé, monsieur. Il n'y en a plus. C'est un article qui s'est vendu comme des petits pains. Il y aura une nouvelle livraison la semaine prochaine.*

TOURISTE   *Tant pis . . . je ne reste ici que pour quelques jours. Qu'est-ce que vous avez comme tee-shirts.*

EMPLOYÉ   *On a un grand choix. Vous pensez à une couleur en particulier?*

TOURISTE   *Bleu clair. Voyons . . . je prends celui-ci.*

EMPLOYÉ   *Très bien. Voulez-vous bien passer à la caisse?*

## E   UNE SITUATION PLUS COMPLIQUÉE

TOURISTE   *Bonjour, madame. Je suis là en vacances . . . je suis britannique. C'est l'anniversaire de mon père dans quelques jours et je voudrais lui offrir un disque français.*

EMPLOYÉE   *Quels sont ses goûts?*

TOURISTE   *Il aime la musique militaire. Qu'est-ce que vous avez comme disques de ce type que vous pouvez conseiller?*

EMPLOYÉE   *Nous avons celui-ci à 70 francs.*

TOURISTE   *Vous n'avez rien de moins cher?*

EMPLOYÉE   *Si . . . celui-ci à 55 francs mais celui-là est meilleur.*

TOURISTE   *Bon, alors je prends celui-là.*

EMPLOYÉE   *Vous avez bien choisi. Puisque c'est pour offrir à votre père, je vais vous l'envelopper. Vous savez qu'on ne peut ni reprendre ni n'échanger les disques. Vous ne pouvez pas vous faire rembourser.*

TOURISTE   *Oui, ça c'est clair. C'est comme chez nous en Angleterre. J'aimerais aussi acheter une carte d'anniversaire pour lui. Ce sera un petit peu spécial pour lui de recevoir une carte en français. Vous n'avez pas de cartes . . .?*

EMPLOYÉE   *Ah, non.*

TOURISTE   *Où pourrai-je en trouver?*

EMPLOYÉE   *Vous avez une librairie-papeterie à 500 mètres d'ici en sortant du magasin. Vous allez à gauche.*

## F   A LA CAISSE

CLIENTE   *Je suis désolée . . . je n'ai plus de petite monnaie. Je n'ai qu'un billet de 100 francs.*

CAISSIER   *Ça va comme ça, madame.*

CLIENTE   *Pouvez-vous me donner des pièces de cinq francs? J'en ai besoin pour la machine au parking payant.*

DEUXIÈME CLIENT   *Est-ce que je peux régler par Eurochèque, s'il vous plaît?*

CAISSIER   *Oui, monsieur. Vous avez une pièce d'identité?*

DEUXIÈME CLIENT   *Voici mon passeport.*

CAISSIER   *C'est parfait. Voulez-vous bien signer ici?*

## G   UNE RÉCLAMATION

CLIENT   *Je viens d'acheter ce pot de yaourt. Quand on l'a ouvert, on s'est aperçu tout de suite qu'il avait tourné.*

MARCHAND  *Ah, oui monsieur. Ça c'est évident. Vous avez gardé votre ticket?*
CLIENT  *Oui, monsieur. Le voici.*
MARCHAND  *Voulez-vous l'échanger ou vous faire rembourser?*
CLIENT  *Je voudrais l'échanger contre un autre, s'il vous plaît.*

### ACTIVITY

You're probably very familiar with shopping situations since they feature very heavily in many courses. Go through these dialogues and see if you can identify any key phrases which you need to say or understand which are missing. Here is one obvious one that no one actually says in the short collection of dialogues above – 'how much is it?' Another one might be how to say 'it's my turn' in French.

### ENQUÊTE

Qui fait les achats normalement dans votre famille? Où est-ce qu'on fait la plus grande partie des achats? Dans un centre commercial? Aux grands magasins ou au supermarché? Dans des petites boutiques locales?

Qu'est-ce qui influence le plus votre choix? Les prix? La qualité des produits? Le choix des produits? Le service? Les heures d'ouverture? La proximité? (c'est-à-dire pas trop loin de chez vous)

Pouvez-vous donner quelques détails sur la dernière occasion où vous avez passé une matinée ou un après-midi à faire des achats? Quand? Où? Avec qui? Quels magasins? Qu'est-ce que vous avez acheté?

Où feriez-vous vos achats si vous n'étiez pas obligé de considérer les prix?

### Activity

What could you find to say if asked to take part in this survey in French?

---

## SKILLS PRACTICE

**SIGNS AND NOTICES**  1  How well could you explain the following signs in shops?
(a)   NE PAS TOUCHER AUX FRUITS (in a green grocer's)
(b)   ENTRÉE LIBRE (sign at entrance to shop)
(c)   CAISSE – SOLDES – PROMOTION (three separate signs in a big store)
(d)   PRIERE DE TENIR LA MAIN COURANTE (sign on an escalator)
(e)   AVEZ-VOUS PRIS VOTRE CHARIOT? (sign above door in supermarket)
(f)   GARDEZ VOTRE TICKET. UN CONTROLE PEUT ETRE EFFECTUÉ A LA SORTIE (sign at check-out in supermarket)
(g)   FERMEZ LA PORTE S'IL VOUS PLAIT (sign on door)
(h)   OUVERT SANS INTERRUPTION DU LUNDI AU VENDREDI DE 8.30 A 18.30 (sign on shop door)

# Shopping

2 At another supermarket you come across this large notice in the car park.

**CONSIGNE GRATUITE**

AVANT VOTRE MARCHÉ
introduisez 10 f.
poussez, puis tirez

APRÈS VOTRE MARCHÉ
enclenchez
récupérez vos 10 f.

(*a*) What is the notice telling you? What exactly do you have to do before and after shopping?

3 You see this advert for special offers in a local shop.

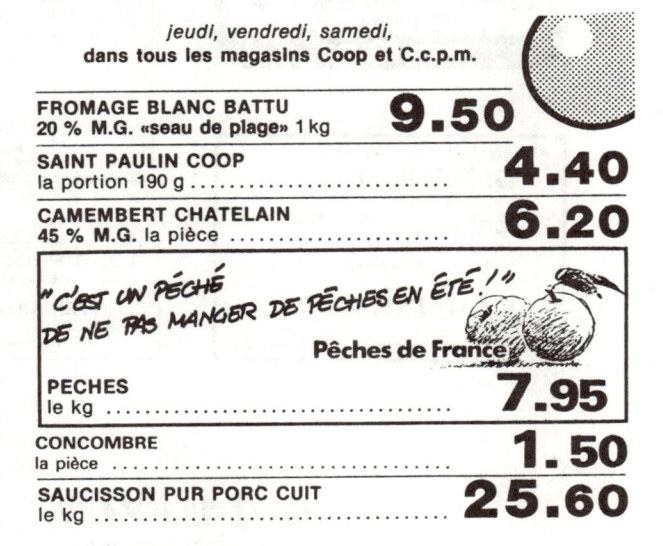

*jeudi, vendredi, samedi,*
**dans tous les magasins Coop et C.c.p.m.**

| | |
|---|---|
| **FROMAGE BLANC BATTU** 20 % M.G. «seau de plage» 1 kg | **9.50** |
| **SAINT PAULIN COOP** la portion 190 g | **4.40** |
| **CAMEMBERT CHATELAIN** 45 % M.G. la pièce | **6.20** |

"C'EST UN PÉCHÉ DE NE PAS MANGER DE PÊCHES EN ÉTÉ!"
Pêches de France

| | |
|---|---|
| **PECHES** le kg | **7.95** |
| **CONCOMBRE** la pièce | **1.50** |
| **SAUCISSON PUR PORC CUIT** le kg | **25.60** |

(*a*)   You go into the shop on a day when you are planning a picnic. How would you say the following things? – There are four of us; we're going to picnic. We'd like some cooked sausage and cheese for four people, half a cucumber, half a dozen peaches – we've already got bread and butter in the caravan.

**Extension**

Imagine and write/act out with a partner the full conversation with the shopkeeper, including the 'small talk'. Are you on holiday, are you staying in a hotel in the village? Don't forget the usual shopping phrases: is that all, that comes to, and so on.

4   You read the following page of advertisements for local shops in a free newspaper.

**AU PANIER GOURMAND**

Maison Loustau
1, rue de l'Hôtel-de-Ville
95300 PONTOISE – 038.54.27

• Sélection Fauchon •

Alimentation générale :
2, rue d'Herblay — ST-OUEN-L'AUMONE

**Transports Démas**

VOYAGES TOURISTIQUES
EXCURSIONS

Bureaux : 7 Av. René Gasnier
49000 ANGERS        Tél. 48.38.13

**C.P.A.**   Concessionnaire   Z.I. OSNY
CERGY-PONTOISE AUTOMOBILES   030.12.12

VEHICULES NEUFS ET D'OCCASION
LOCATION Tourisme et Utilitaires
TARIF DEGRESSIF à compter du 2ᵉ jour

**PEUGEOT**

**Pénélope**
Prêt à porter féminin   (tailles du 38 au 50)
11, rue de l'Oisellerie – 49000 ANGERS
Tél. 87.02.66

**SUPER**
L'HYPER MARCHÉ DU CENTRE VILLE
Sans Problème de Parking

AUVENTS DE CARAVANES
**G. PAIN**
Sellier - Voilier
36, chemin des Chesnaies ANGERS
Tél. 43.71.76
ATELIER : R.N. 23, Maison-Neuve
CORZÉ après Maisons de l'Avenir

**CAMPING**   RÉPARATION
TRANSFORMATION
RÉIMPERMÉABILISATION
ET TOUTES CONFECTIONS INDUSTRIELLES

**ANJOU FÊTES**
S. DECAUX
40, rue Saint-Laud - ANGERS - Tél. 87.76.49
Farces - Attrapes - Gadgets - Cotillons - Artifices

TOUS PRODUITS LAITIERS
ET ŒUFS EN GROS
**Bernard LANGÉ**
45, rue de Poitiers        49 SAUMUR
TÉLÉPHONE : 51.24.32

**RALLYE**
L'Hyper Solidaire
Route des Sables. 49300 CHOLET (face au centre hospitalier) Tél. 62.33.41
Essence. Centre Auto. Parking gratuit 1200 places. Cafétéria Ondine. 42 commerces

# Shopping

(a) Which business would you go to if your Dormobile roof developed a serious leak during the course of your stay?

(b) If you wanted to combine a shopping trip with a fill-up of petrol which establishment might be a good bet?

(c) If you didn't fancy a trip to a very large store out of town, which business would be the best for doing the weekend shopping?

(d) If you were thinking of taking some French delicacy home with you, which might be a good shop to investigate?

(e) How exclusive does the ladies' clothes shop which is advertised appear to be from what you read about it?

5 You see a big newspaper advert giving the latest offers in a supermarket.

**CONFITURES "BONNE MAMAN"**
Fraise : les 2 pots de 370 g (prix kg : 16,89 F)  **12 F 50**
Abricot : les 2 pots de 370 g (prix kg : 14,72 F)  **10 F 90**

**SERVIETTES DE TABLE LOTUS**
à jeter, décors au choix
34 x 34 cm
le sachet de 20  **4 F 90**

**SACS POUBELLE HANDY BAG**
40 sacs de 30 litres  **23 F 90**
10 sacs de 100 litres  **16 F 90**

**COCA-COLA**
la bouteille de 1 litre
(verre consigné)  **3 F 40**

**CAFE MOULU "TRADITION" STENTOR**
les 4 paquets de 250 g  **49 F 90**

**BRUT DE POMME**
le pack de 8 x 25 cl (dont 2 bouteilles gratuites)
(prix au litre : 7,10 F)  **14 F 20**

**LIQUIDE VAISSELLE PAIC CITRON**
le flacon de 1500 ml
(prix au litre : 10,60 F)  **15 F 90**

(a) What information are you given about the serviettes?
(b) What is the attraction of the beer pack?
(c) Is the coffee instant granules, instant powder, beans for grinding or ready ground? How exactly is it packed and in what quantities?
(d) What exactly are the bags for which are advertised here?
(e) What is in the container marked PAIC?
(f) What is the price of strawberry jam?
(g) Apart from price and volume, what information is given about the Coca-Cola bottle?

## CHECK-LIST

**Essential language tasks**
(a) ask whether/where certain shops, supermarkets, shopping centres are available
(b) ask for a specific section/department in a shop or shopping area
(c) ask whether certain goods are available
(d) say what you want i.e. the item, quantity, size, colour, whom for (saying it's a present if you want it gift wrapped)
(e) ask about price
(f) ask to see a particular item
(g) ask to try on a particular item
(h) refuse or accept suggestions
(i) comment on whether an item is too dear/too small/too big etc.
(j) ask for something cheaper/smaller/larger/of different colour etc.
(k) ask about opening and closing hours
(l) say you need nothing else
(m) ask for a bag
(n) ask for the cash point.

**Useful language tasks**
(a) talk about the advantages/disadvantages of using different types of shops
(b) talk about your own shopping preferences
(c) talk about a recent shopping expedition
(d) talk about what you would buy if money were no object
(e) ask whether other shops might stock the item you are looking for
(f) query the change if you think a mistake has been made
(g) return items which are unsatisfactory – e.g. food/drink which has gone off; wrong size when tried on after leaving the shop – and ask for your money back or alternative goods.

# SERVICES

### A  AU BUREAU DE POSTE...

TOURISTE  *Bonjour madame. Je voudrais envoyer cette lettre à l'étranger, s'il vous plaît. C'est combien une lettre pour l'Angleterre?*
EMPLOYÉE  *2 francs 50.*
TOURISTE  *Merci, et une carte postale?*
EMPLOYÉE  *1 franc 90.*
TOURISTE  *Alors donnez-moi trois timbres à 2,50 et six à 1,90 s'il vous plaît.*
EMPLOYÉE  *Voilà, madame. Ça fait 18,90 en tout.*
TOURISTE  *Où est la boîte aux lettres la plus proche s'il vous plaît?*
EMPLOYÉE  *Devant le bureau de poste, à gauche de la sortie.*

**Activity**

Could you also say, 'I would like to send a parcel to Great Britain.'? How would you ask for ten 1.50 stamps and six 2.20 stamps? If you asked for five 2 franc stamps and were told, *Je n'ai plus de timbres à 2 francs* what might be your reply to the counter clerk in French? What would you need to say in French to find out the following information from the counter clerk: 1 the location of the nearest phone box; 2 how long the letter will take to reach England; 3 the opening and closing times of the post office?

### B  IDENTIFIEZ LE GUICHET!

Study carefully the following four conversations from the post office, then try to identify at which 'window' the conversation is most likely to have taken place from these possibilities:

Annuaires Téléphoniques – Télégraphe – Poste Restante – Envoi tous mandats – Paiement tous mandats – Timbres à tous les guichets – Timbres de Collection – Téléphone – Retraits C.C.P./Change

1  CLIENT  *Où est le guichet de la poste restante, s'il vous plaît?*
   EMPLOYÉ  *C'est le troisième guichet, au fond, monsieur.*
   CLIENT  *Merci, monsieur.*

   *Bonjour madame. Est-ce que vous avez des lettres adressées à Coleman, s'il vous plaît?*
   EMPLOYÉE  *Ça s'écrit comment?*
   CLIENT  *C-O-L-E-M-A-N.*

EMPLOYÉE   Attendez un petit moment. Je vais regarder.

Voilà une lettre pour vous. Vous avez une pièce d'identité?
CLIENT   Oui, voici mon passeport. A quelle heure arrive le prochain courrier?
EMPLOYÉE   Cet après-midi, à 15 heures.

2   CLIENTE   Est-ce que je peux téléphoner d'ici en Angleterre?
EMPLOYÉ   Oui, bien sûr. Vous avez le numéro déjà?
CLIENTE   Oui, mais je ne sais pas si j'ai le bon code.
EMPLOYÉ   Vous pouvez très facilement le vérifier en consultant les annuaires à côté des cabines.
CLIENTE   Pouvez-vous m'expliquer comment téléphoner en Angleterre?
EMPLOYÉ   Vous composez le 19 et vous attendez la tonalité, c'est-à-dire la sonnerie spéciale pour appeler l'étranger. Puis vous faites le 44; suivi du code de la ville ou de la région . . . et bien sûr vous terminez par le numéro de votre correspondant. Voulez-vous bien utiliser la cabine 7, s'il vous plaît?
CLIENTE   Merci bien, monsieur. Votre aide m'a été très utile.

3   EMPLOYÉE   C'est à vous maintenant, madame.
CLIENTE   Ah bon. C'est bien ici que je peux toucher cet Eurochèque?
EMPLOYÉE   Oui, madame. Vous avez une pièce d'identité – passeport, carte d'identité . . .?
CLIENTE   J'ai mon passeport. Combien vaut la livre sterling en ce moment?
EMPLOYÉE   Elle est à 9.80, madame. Il faut signer là et là. Il n'y a pas de commission.
CLIENTE   Vous avez des billets de 100 francs?
EMPLOYÉE   Bien sûr, madame. Voici votre argent et aussi votre reçu. Bon séjour!

4   CLIENT   Je voudrais envoyer un télégramme, s'il vous plaît.
EMPLOYÉE   Il faut remplir une formule, monsieur.
CLIENT   Laquelle, s'il vous plaît?
EMPLOYÉE   Celle en bas, à gauche.

CLIENT   Voilà . . . c'est rempli. 19 mots.
EMPLOYÉE   Voilà . . . ça fait 52 francs en tout.

## C   AU TÉLÉPHONE

1   MÈRE DE FAMILLE   Alors, Timothy – tu voudrais téléphoner à tes parents peut-être ce soir?
TIMOTHY   Ah, oui – volontiers, madame. Est-ce que je peux appeler en p.c.v.?
MÈRE DE FAMILLE   Tu n'as pas besoin d'appeler en p.c.v., Timothy. Il est bien probable que Xavier va nous téléphoner de chez toi, quand il sera en Angleterre.

## Services

2    DEMANDEUR    *Allô . . . je voudrais parler à Mme Gorgeon, s'il vous plaît.*
     VOUS    *Je suis désolé . . . il n'y a personne de ce nom ici.*
     DEMANDEUR    *Tiens? C'est bien le 36-08-47?*
     VOUS    *Ah, non. C'est le 36-07-47. Je crois que vous vous êtes trompé de numéro.*
     DEMANDEUR    *C'est bien ça. Je suis désolé de vous déranger.*

3    DEMANDEUR    *Je voudrais parler à Jeanne, s'il vous plaît.*
     VOUS    *Ah bon. C'est sa correspondante anglaise à l'appareil. Attendez un instant. Je vais l'appeler. Ne quittez pas!*

        *Je suis désolée . . . je croyais qu'elle était dans sa chambre. Elle a dû sortir pour faire une petite course. Il n'y a personne d'autre à la maison.*
     DEMANDEUR    *Ça ne fait rien. Je peux très facilement laisser un message avec vous. C'est Marcel qui parle.*
     VOUS    *Oui, avec plaisir. Mais voulez-vous bien parler assez lentement, puisque je suis anglaise . . .?*
     MARCEL    *Ah bon. Dites-lui, s'il vous plaît, de me retrouver devant le cinéma à 21 heures jeudi soir.*
     VOUS    *Alors . . . devant le cinéma . . . à 9 heures du soir . . . jeudi prochain?*
     MARCEL    *C'est exact. Merci bien. Au revoir . . .*

### Activity
Make a list of 'telephone phrases' which you need (*a*) to say yourself and (*b*) to understand, when handling and making telephone calls during the course of a visit to a French-speaking country. Can you think of any important phrases which are not used in any of the three situations above? If you were the English girl in conversation 3, what exactly would you say to Jeanne, in French, when she came back from her errand?

### D    CHEZ LE TEINTURIER

     TOURISTE    *Bonjour madame. Nous sommes anglais . . . nous faisons du camping tout près du village. Malheureusement j'ai renversé une tasse de café hier soir, quand nous étions en train de manger. Vous voyez la tache sur cette chemise . . .*
     EMPLOYÉE    *Voyons . . . il n'est pas toujours possible d'enlever une tache comme ça. Mais je pense que ça ira. On ne peut qu'essayer, en tout cas. Pouvez-vous repasser dans trois jours?*
     TOURISTE    *Mais nous ne sommes là que pour deux jours encore.*
     EMPLOYÉE    *On n'a pas de machines ici, vous savez. C'est pour ça qu'il faut trois jours normalement. Mais puisque vous partez dans deux jours . . . on fera un effort spécial.*
     TOURISTE    *Ça c'est vraiment gentil. J'en suis vraiment reconnaissant. Ça va coûter combien, vous croyez?*
     EMPLOYÉE    *Dans les 25 francs. Je ne peux pas vous dire le prix exact . . . ça*

> dépend du travail qu'il faut . . . Vous vous appelez comment, monsieur?
>
> TOURISTE   Johnston . . . J–O–H–N–S–T–O–N.
> EMPLOYÉE   Et vous êtes bien au Camping des Pins?
> TOURISTE   Oui, c'est ça.
> EMPLOYÉE   Voici votre ticket.
> TOURISTE   Merci bien. A jeudi alors . . .

### Activity
How would this conversation have gone had you been staying in the Hôtel des Alpes . . . knocked over a glass of wine . . . stained a skirt . . . were there for a week . . . asked if you should come back tomorrow? The dialogue above ends happily because the man at the dry-cleaners makes a special effort to hurry things up. What sort of phrases would you be able to use in French if you genuinely felt you were being let down and wanted to express your disappointment and anger at the situation?

### E   A LA LAVERIE

> TOURISTE   Bonjour, monsieur. Nous sommes des touristes anglais. Pourriez-vous nous expliquer comment ça marche?
> EMPLOYÉ   Bien sûr, monsieur. Alors . . . pour une machine de 5 kilos, ça coûte 13 francs. Vous achetez un jeton pour faire marcher la machine. Vous mettez votre linge là-dedans . . . bien refermez la porte . . . mettez la lessive et sélectionnez le programme. Introduisez votre jeton et poussez la glissière. Et voilà . . . Pour les couleurs ça dure normalement 35 minutes. Après, vous pouvez passer aux séchoirs. Deux francs les dix minutes.

### Activity
Having worked through the dialogue above, set in the launderette, would you be able to find out the following information in French? Whether the machines work with coins or tokens . . . do you put the money-token in first? . . . when do you put the powder in? . . . how long does the wash take? how much do the dryers cost and how long do you get?

### F   AU MAGASIN D'APPAREILS-PHOTO

> TOURISTE   Pardon, madame. J'ai un problème avec mon appareil. Je crois que la pellicule est coincée . . . Je suis là en vacances et j'en ai vraiment besoin. Est-ce que vous pouvez me dire ce qui ne va pas?
> EMPLOYÉE   Tenez, monsieur. Je vais l'ouvrir dans la chambre noire.
>
> Malheureusement il y a un petit défaut dans le mécanisme. Je peux le réparer en deux jours. Ça ira?
> TOURISTE   Oui, bien sûr . . . je vous suis très reconnaissant, madame. Vous pourriez peut-être me donner une idée du prix de la réparation?

EMPLOYÉE  *Ça, c'est un peu difficile, monsieur. Ça dépend des pièces de rechange. La main-d'œuvre sera dans les 30 francs.*

### Activity

How do you say these four key things in French: what's wrong? . . . can it be repaired? . . . when will it be ready? . . . I'm really grateful . . .

### G  ON FAIT UNE RÉCLAMATION

CLIENT  *Bonjour madame. J'ai acheté cette cassette pré-enregistrée il y a quelques jours et la qualité du son s'est vraiment dégradée. Je ne l'ai passée que deux ou trois fois.*

EMPLOYÉE  *Je suis désolée, monsieur, mais les disques et les cassettes ne sont ni repris ni échangés. C'est la règle de la maison.*

CLIENT  *Mais c'est inadmissible! Il doit y avoir une garantie . . .*

EMPLOYÉE  *Pas pour les cassettes, monsieur.*

CLIENT  *Je tiens à vous dire que je ne suis pas content du tout. C'est presque neuf . . .*

EMPLOYÉE  *Vous êtes sûr que le problème est dans la cassette et pas dans le lecteur . . .*

CLIENT  *Pas possible . . . mon walkman est en très bon état.*

### Activity

Work out an adaptation of the dialogue above, preferably with a partner. Agree on five shops in which you are going to set each of your dialogues. Spend some time preparing your respective roles. In each case you think of something you might have bought in France while on holiday. Jot down some complaint which you feel you are able to explain in French. Your partner should prepare some things to say which are going to 'block' your complaint, like the employee in the dialogue set in the record shop. Try to improvise a little dialogue set in the five different shops which you agreed on. Your partner should make a note of the complaint each time. When you've finished all five dialogues you should look at these notes and see whether you communicated your complaint successfully in French. By all means become indignant and blow your top. Are there things which you could threaten to do which are not said in the dialogue printed here?

### H  AU COMMISSARIAT

TOURISTE  *Quelle horreur! . . . On m'a volé mon chéquier, mes chèques de voyage et mes cartes de crédit . . .*

AGENT  *Qu'est-ce qui s'est passé exactement monsieur? On vous a agressé?*

TOURISTE  *Effectivement . . . Oui. Ça est arrivé il y a quelques moments devant le bureau de poste. J'étais en train de retirer de l'argent d'un distributeur de billets, quand un jeune homme m'a menacé avec un couteau.*

AGENT  *Comment était-il?*
TOURISTE  *Jeune . . . assez grand . . . costaud . . . des cheveux noirs frisés. Il était habillé en blue-jean . . . et il portait un tee-shirt blanc. Je n'aurais pas de difficulté à le reconnaître.*
AGENT  *Vous n'êtes pas blessé, alors?*
TOURISTE  *Non . . . je lui ai tout donné puisqu'il était armé d'un couteau . . .*
AGENT  *Alors je peux très bien comprendre que vous êtes en état de choc, monsieur. Mais je pense qu'il vaut mieux aller faire votre déclaration. Vous devez vous adresser à la réception au fond de ce couloir. Malheureusement il y a énormément de vols de ce type en été . . .*

**Activity**
Working from the dialogue above as a starting point, would you be able to say the following things yourself in French in a similar situation? I'd like to report a theft – my passport and my wallet have been stolen. It happened ten minutes ago in front of the bank – a man mugged me. He was small with straight brown hair, wearing black trousers and a green sweater. I've got minor injuries and would like to see a doctor when I've finished making the statement.

**Extension**
What might the policeman's written report of the incident look like when he had taken down all the details from the man who had been threatened with the knife? Can you think of any questions which he might have asked which are not there in the printed dialogue?

## SKILLS PRACTICE

**SIGNS AND NOTICES**  1  How well would you cope with these examples of typical signs and notices connected with this topic?
(a)  DERNIÈRE LEVÉE 18.00 (on a post box)
(b)  PARIS – PROVINCE – ÉTRANGER (three separate labels to slots on post boxes)
(c)  TARIF RÉDUIT – TARIF NORMAL (two separate labels to slots on post boxes)
(d)  CABINE HORS D'ÉTAT? FAITES LE 13, C'EST GRATUIT! (notice in telephone booth)
(e)  'LAVOMATIQUE' NE PEUT ETRE TENU POUR RESPONSABLE DE LINGE PERDU, DÉCHIRÉ, BRULÉ, VOLÉ, ETC. (sign in launderette)
2  You read this information in a guide to local services.

Ouverture des guichets: 9 h à 12h – 14h 30 à 17h 30 – le samedi de 9h à 12h.
Départ de la distribution: 9h 15 et 10h 15, le courrier arrivant entre 7h 35 et 7 h 50.
Téléphone: 38 97 41 52 et 38 97 33 36.

**Services** 107

(*a*)   What are the opening hours of this local post office? If you were expecting some mail to be sent to your holiday address, what would be the earliest you could expect the postman to deliver?

3   You read these two notices which are on display in the post office, all about postage rates.

| LETTRES ET PAQUETS AFFRANCHIS ET TARIF DES LETTRES ORDINAIRES | | Jusqu'à ... | 20 g |
|---|---|---|---|
| RÉGIME GÉNÉRAL (sauf tarifs spéciaux ci-dessous) | | | 3,40 F |
| Tarifs spéciaux | Canada | | 2,20 F |
| | Allemagne (Rép. Féd.) • Luxembourg | | 2,20 F |
| | Belgique • Danemark • Pays-Bas • Irlande | | 2,20 F |
| | Italie • Saint-Marin | | 2,20 F |
| | Autriche • Espagne • Gde-Bret. • Grèce • Liechtenstein • Portugal • Suisse | | 2,50 F |

| CARTES POSTALES | | Ordinaires ou illustrées | Illustrées avec 5 mots de vœux au maximum |
|---|---|---|---|
| RÉGIME GÉNÉRAL (sauf tarifs spéciaux ci-dessous) ET RÉGIME PARTICULIER | | 2,70 F | 2,00 F |
| Tarifs spéciaux | Allemagne (Rép. Féd.) • Autriche • Belgique • Canada • Danemark • Espagne • Grande-Bretagne • Grèce • Irlande • Italie • Liechtenstein • Luxembourg • Pays-Bas • Portugal • Saint-Marin • Suisse | 1,90 F | 1,90 F |

(*a*)   What is the rate given for a postcard of 20 words to the United Kingdom?

(*b*)   How much is a 15 gm letter to England?

4   Because of a hitch in your travel plans, you are delayed in Paris on your way to visit your French friend in the South. You know they have no telephone in their summer villa so the only way to get in touch with them quickly is to send a telegram.

(*a*)   How would you ask in French in the post office where the telegram forms are? How would you find out in French which counter to go to, after you'd completed it?

(*b*)   What would you write on the form to convey this message:

Hovercraft service on strike – missed last train to Avignon – will arrive at 11.00 a.m. Thursday

(c)   What are the exact instructions given on the telegram form below regarding how you should fill it in?

| Services spéciaux demandés : (voir au verso) | Inscrire en **CAPITALES** l'adresse complète (rue, n° bloc, bâtiment, escalier, etc...), le texte et la signature (une lettre par case ; **laisser une case blanche entre les mots**). |
|---|---|
| | Nom et adresse |

TEXTE et éventuellement signature très lisible

5   You come across the following information leaflet about the services offered by the French Post Office for foreign visitors.

### Vous désirez téléphoner ...

Utilisez, en vous munissant préalablement de pièces de monnaie (page 15), une des 198 000 cabines placées dans les lieux publics* ou adressez-vous au guichet téléphone d'un de nos 17 000 bureaux de poste*. Si vous appelez à partir de votre hôtel, d'un café ou d'un restaurant, votre facturation risque d'être supérieure à la taxe officielle (maximum 30%).

● **Tarifs réduits**
– du lundi au samedi
de 20 h à 10 h pour le Canada et les États-Unis.
de 21 h 30 à 8 h pour Israël.
de 23 h à 9 h 30 pour le Portugal.
– du lundi au vendredi de 21 h 30 à 8 h et le samedi à partir de 14 h pour les autres pays de la CEE, la Suisse, l'Autriche et la Yougoslavie.
– et pour ces mêmes pays les dimanches et jours fériés français toute la journée.

### ... télégraphier

Vous pouvez déposer votre texte au guichet d'un bureau de poste, ou le téléphoner depuis votre hôtel.

### ... recevoir votre courrier

● Votre adresse en France comporte un numéro de code à 5 chiffres : n'oubliez pas de le communiquer à vos correspondants.
● Le courrier adressé en 'poste restante', dans une ville ayant plusieurs bureaux, est, sauf précision, disponible au bureau principal. Le retrait d'une correspondance donne lieu à paiement d'une taxe.
● Pour toute opération de retrait de courrier ou d'argent au guichet, on vous demandera votre passeport ou une pièce d'identité, pensez-y !

### ... expédier vos envois

● **Les timbres-poste:** vous pouvez vous les procurer dans les bureaux de poste (où on vend également des aérogrammes), les bureaux de tabac ou les distributeurs automatiques jaunes disposés sur la façade de certains bureaux de poste.

### ... envoyer ou recevoir de l'argent

● Pour le paiement ou l'émission de mandats ou l'échange de 'postchèques', adressez-vous directement au bureau de poste de votre choix.
● Dans les principales villes, vous pouvez changer votre argent dans 170 bureaux de poste signalés par un autocollant 'CHANGE'.
● Si vous êtes porteur d'une carte visa ou d'une carte de garantie Eurochèque délivrée par votre banque, vous pouvez retirer de l'argent dans un des 780 bureaux de poste signalés par un autocollant $\frac{CB}{VISA}$ ou EC*.

(a)   What are the five main services being advertised here?

## Services

(b) What warning is given about telephoning from a hotel, café or restaurant?

(c) What are the days and times when you can phone Great Britain at cheap rates?

(d) What two things will you have to do in order to pick up your letters from a 'poste restante' box at a post office?

(e) What are the three possibilities given for buying stamps?

(f) What is the procedure suggested for (i) changing £ sterling into French francs at a post office and (ii) using your Visa card or Eurochèque card to change currency?

6   You read this notice in the window of a dry-cleaner's.

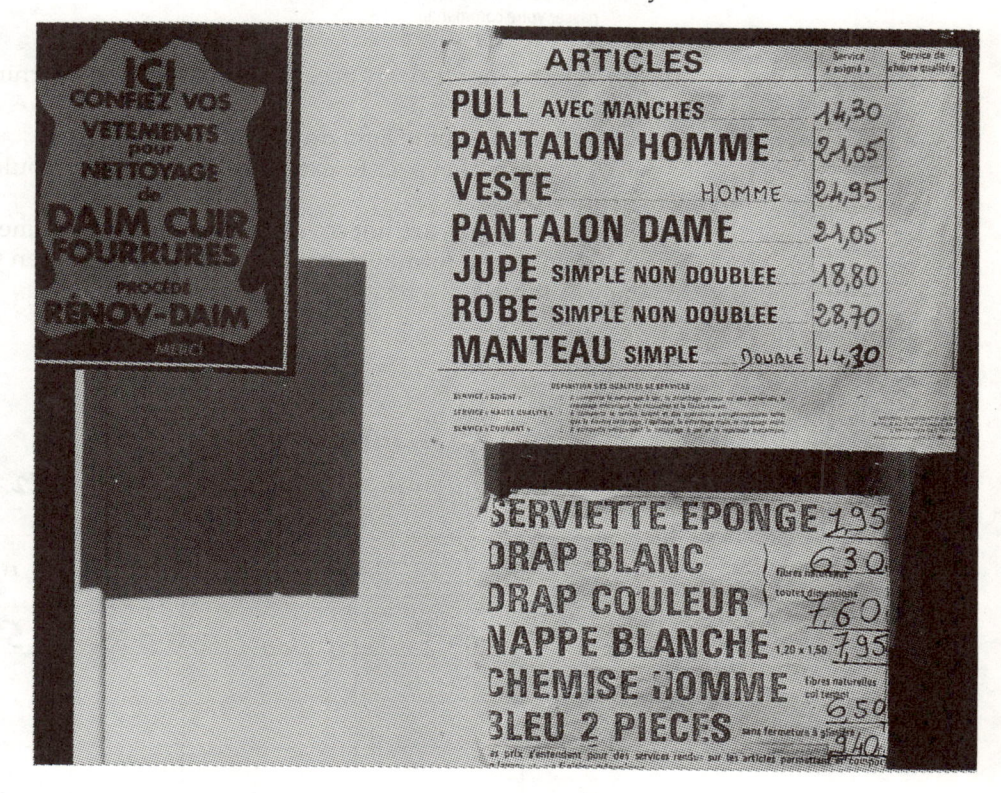

| ARTICLES | Service soigné | Service de haute qualité |
|---|---|---|
| PULL AVEC MANCHES | 14,30 | |
| PANTALON HOMME | 21,05 | |
| VESTE HOMME | 24,95 | |
| PANTALON DAME | 21,05 | |
| JUPE SIMPLE NON DOUBLEE | 18,80 | |
| ROBE SIMPLE NON DOUBLEE | 28,70 | |
| MANTEAU SIMPLE  DOUBLE | 44,30 | |

ICI CONFIEZ VOS VETEMENTS pour NETTOYAGE de DAIM CUIR FOURRURES procédé RÉNOV-DAIM MERCI

| | |
|---|---|
| SERVIETTE EPONGE | 1,95 |
| DRAP BLANC | 6,30 |
| DRAP COULEUR | 7,60 |
| NAPPE BLANCHE 1,20 x 1,50 | 7,95 |
| CHEMISE HOMME | 6,50 |
| BLEU 2 PIECES | 9,40 |

(a) You've had a bit of a spill in your caravan which has involved a pot of coffee, your mum's skirt, your dad's trousers and shirt and a towel. How much is it going to cost for each of these items?

# French

7   You see some bargains in a catalogue for a local discount warehouse in the town where you are staying but you're naturally a bit suspicious about the wisdom of buying something away from where you live. Here's what it says about returning goods.

> ET SI QUELQUE CHOSE N'ALLAIT PAS?
>
> • Profitez de notre garantie totale. Si un article ne vous convient pas, ou si vous avez changé d'avis, il vous suffit de nous le retourner dans les 15 jours. Joignez votre bordereau de livraison et suivez les instructions qui y sont portées. Il vous sera échangé ou remboursé sans discussion.
>
> • Attention! Les tissus vendus au mètre ne sont ni repris, ni échangés (sauf erreur de notre part): nous vous conseillons donc de demander des échantillons avant de passer votre commande.

(a) What does it say are acceptable reasons for returning goods to them?
(b) Is there any time limit on the return date?
(c) Would you expect to exchange the goods or could you have your money back?
(d) Which goods are not covered by the return scheme?

8   Below is a copy of a form which is filled in by banks when you change currency or travellers' cheques.

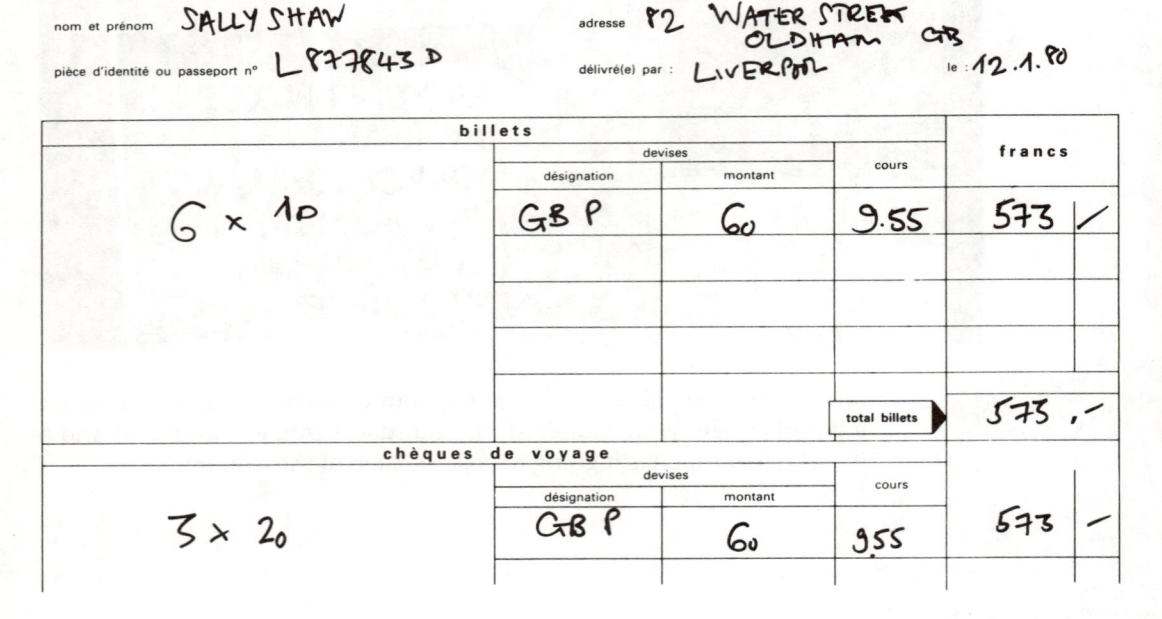

| date: 09.08.87 | agence: TOURS | | | |
|---|---|---|---|---|
| nom et prénom: SALLY SHAW | | adresse: 82 WATER STREET, OLDHAM GB | | |
| pièce d'identité ou passeport n°: L877843 D | | délivré(e) par: LIVERPOOL | | le: 12.1.80 |

**billets**

| | devises | | cours | francs |
|---|---|---|---|---|
| | désignation | montant | | |
| 6 × 10 | GB P | 60 | 9.55 | 573 ✓ |
| | | | | |
| | | | | |
| | | | total billets | 573,— |

**chèques de voyage**

| | devises | | cours | francs |
|---|---|---|---|---|
| | désignation | montant | | |
| 3 × 20 | GB P | 60 | 9.55 | 573 — |
| | | | | |

(a) How much in cash and how much in travellers' cheques was changed?
(b) Imagine – and write down – the dialogue which must have taken place on 9 August 1987 when Ms Shaw went into the bank in

## Services

Tours. Work out the scene from start to finish, from finding the correct queue for the exchange counter to explaining what she wanted, enquiring about the exchange rate, asking if there is any commission, giving the personal details at the top of the form, signing the travellers' cheques, being asked to move on to the cashier, getting the money from the cashier, thanking and saying goodbye.

## CHECK-LIST

**Essential language tasks**
- (a) find out where the nearest post office or bureau de tabac is
- (b) find out where the nearest letter box is
- (c) check if there is a special slot for letters going abroad
- (d) ask about postage rates for post cards and letters to particular countries
- (e) ask for stamps of a certain denomination
- (f) find out the opening hours of the post office
- (g) say you wish to make a telephone call and give the number
- (h) say you wish to change some £ sterling or some travellers' cheques
- (i) say you need to have something mended or cleaned.

**Useful language tasks**
- (a) ask about and retrieve letters from the *poste restante* service
- (b) find out where telephone calls can be made from
- (c) ask if and when you could contact someone by phone
- (d) ask for a reversed charge call
- (e) ask for coins to make a call from a coin box
- (f) answer the phone
- (g) ask who is speaking on the phone
- (h) tell someone s/he has got the wrong number
- (i) take a simple phone message
- (j) explain British post boxes (i.e. different colour/shape), first and second class post and British phone boxes to a foreign visitor
- (k) send a telegram
- (l) in a bank or change office, find the correct counter and confirm it's your turn
- (m) ask for bank notes of a certain value
- (n) confirm the rates of exchange and the commission
- (o) report that you have lost something/had something stolen
- (p) describe the circumstances in which the loss/theft took place
- (q) describe the item(s) concerned, e.g. value, age, colour, size
- (r) say how surprised, annoyed, disappointed etc. you are
- (s) give details about something which you need to have repaired because it has been damaged or has gone wrong
- (t) ask whether it can be repaired, how long it will take and how much it will cost
- (u) ask for assistance/advice

(v) ask to borrow something which might help you to repair it yourself
(w) ask for something to be cleaned or washed
(x) find out at dry cleaner's what it will cost and how long it will take
(y) ask for advice on how an automatic launderette works
(z) thank for service or express disappointment at the service.

# TOPIC TEN

# HEALTH AND WELFARE

### A  ON NE SE SENT PAS BIEN

NATHALIE  Tu n'as pas bonne mine ce soir, Monica. Qu'est-ce qui ne va pas?
MONICA  Je ne sais pas... j'ai mal dormi cette nuit et je ne me sens pas bien du tout. J'ai mal à la tête depuis ce matin.
NATHALIE  Je crois que le mieux serait de te coucher et de prendre deux aspirines. Tu n'es pas allergique à l'aspirine, non?
MONICA  Ah non.
NATHALIE  Alors, tu as besoin de quelque chose...?
MONICA  Non, merci. Je vais m'allonger maintenant.

**Activity**

If you were Monica and needed to explain what was wrong with you, would you be able to say the following things? I've had a headache for four hours; I've got a temperature; I feel sick (i.e. nauseous); I need to go to the toilet; may I lie down? I've got tooth-ache.

### B  CA VA MIEUX MAINTENANT?

SACHA  Salut, Virginie! Comment ça va?
VIRGINIE  Ça va beaucoup mieux maintenant... la semaine passée je ne me sentais pas bien du tout. J'avais de la fièvre et un mal de tête affreux.
SACHA  C'était la grippe, tu crois?
VIRGINIE  Je ne sais pas... le plus important c'est que je me suis remise maintenant... plus ou moins.

**Activity**

How would you say: my father wasn't well two or three weeks ago but he's completely recovered now.

### C  A LA PHARMACIE

PREMIER CLIENT  J'ai une angine affreuse depuis quelques jours. Vous avez quelque chose pour la soigner?
PHARMACIENNE  Je peux vous conseiller ces comprimés. Ils sont vraiment efficaces. Lisez soigneusement les indications... pas plus de huit par période de 24 heures.
PREMIER CLIENT  Est-ce qu'on doit les prendre avant les repas?

PHARMACIENNE  *Ça n'importe pas. Est-ce que vous prenez d'autres médicaments en ce moment?*
PREMIER CLIENT  *Je suis obligé de prendre des comprimés contre mon rhume de foins . . . mais ce n'est pas encore la saison.*
PHARMACIENNE  *Bon. Si vous n'allez pas mieux dans quelques jours, venez me revoir ou allez voir un médecin.*
PREMIER CLIENT  *Merci bien, madame.*
DEUXIÈME CLIENTE  *Un insecte vient de me piquer . . . ça me fait mal au bras.*
PREMIER CLIENT  *Vous me permettez de regarder? Ah . . . rien de grave. Ne vous en faites, pas madame. Vous trouverez cette crème ici très adoucissante contre les piqûres.*
TROISIÈME CLIENT  *Je viens de tomber dans la rue en essayant d'éviter un cycliste. Je me suis blessé la jambe.*
PHARMACIENNE  *Calmez-vous, monsieur. Je peux tout de suite vous mettre de l'antiseptique et un pansement pour protéger votre blessure. Vous n'aurez pas de difficulté à marcher, mais évitez de vous baigner aujourd'hui.*
QUATRIÈME CLIENTE  *Je suis enrhumée déjà depuis dix jours. J'ai le nez qui coule et je tousse continuellement.*
PHARMACIENNE  *Vous pourriez essayer ce sirop. Mais attention, ça fait endormir et vous ne devriez pas boire d'alcool avec. Si ça ne va pas mieux en quelques jours, il vaudrait mieux aller voir un médecin et demander une ordonnance.*

## Activity

Using the material in this dialogue and other words and phrases which you know, would you be able to communicate the following things in French if you weren't feeling well or had some kind of accident? Do you have any tablets for a cold? May I have some antiseptic and a plaster? How many times a day must I take the tablets? Do I take the tablets before or after meals? I'm already taking this medicine for my cough. Do I have to come back? Are the instructions on the bottle? Do you have a soothing cream for sun-burn? I've cut myself opening a tin. Am I allowed to bathe? Does the medicine make you feel drowsy?

### D  ON FIXE UN RENDEZ-VOUS

RÉCEPTIONNISTE  *Allô . . . cabinet du docteur Grandperret.*
M. GROSGURIN  *Bonjour, monsieur. Je téléphone de la part d'un jeune Anglais de 15 ans qui est chez nous en ce moment. On s'inquiète un petit peu parce qu'il ne se sent pas bien depuis plusieurs jours. Il a de la fièvre et il n'arrête pas de tousser.*
RÉCEPTIONNISTE  *Alors, monsieur. Quand voulez-vous venir avec lui?*
M. GROSGURIN  *Le plus tôt possible . . . cet après-midi?*
RÉCEPTIONNISTE  *Le docteur n'est pas là cet après-midi. Mais il consulte à partir de 6 heures du soir. Disons 18.35. Ça vous convient?*

## Health and welfare

M. GROSGURIN   *Peut-être un petit peu plus tard. M. le docteur est libre à 19 heures?*
RÉCEPTIONNISTE   *Oui . . . on peut vous caser à 19 heures. Le nom du jeune Anglais?*
M. GROSGURIN   *Jones – J–O–N–E–S. Il s'appelle Christopher de prénom.*
RÉCEPTIONNISTE   *Merci, monsieur. A ce soir.*

**Activity**

1   Make a list for yourself of the French phrases which you feel are the most important when trying to fix an appointment as in the dialogue above. Start by picking out ones from the dialogue, but add on any others which are not used here.

2   Imagine one of your parents is ill and you have to help by ringing up a doctor's surgery to find out what the consulting hours are. As a way of finding out how good you would be at this, try to find a partner who will work with you. She/he should look at the document on page 116 about consulting hours. You pretend you are ringing up and your partner has to communicate in French as much as she/he can of the information which is printed. You must not look at the information but you should try to write down in English what your partner explains in French to you. You should compare notes at the end to see how much information was accurately conveyed.

### E   UN ACCIDENT DANS LA RUE

MONSIEUR   *Aidez-moi . . . quelqu'un . . . mon bras . . .*
VOUS   *Qu'est-ce qui s'est passé, monsieur?*
MONSIEUR   *Un cycliste m'est rentré dedans . . . je crois qu'il est allé appeler une ambulance, mais je ne suis pas certain.*
VOUS   *Je vais chercher quelqu'un pour vous aider monsieur. Je ne suis pas d'ici – je suis anglais.*

*Madame, pouvez-vous m'aider, s'il vous plaît? C'est urgent.*
DAME   *Oui, jeune homme. Qu'est-ce qu'il y a?*
VOUS   *Je suis anglais. Je ne sais pas que faire exactement. Au coin de la rue il y a un monsieur qui s'est blessé le bras dans un accident.*
DAME   *Restez calme! On cherchera un téléphone pour appeler la police-secours.*

### F   UN ACCIDENT SUR L'AUTOROUTE

OPÉRATEUR   *Allô . . . police-secours.*
AUTOMOBILISTE   *Je vous appelle de la borne de secours numéro 18 sur l'autoroute A13 entre les échangeurs de Louviers Sud et Louviers Nord direction Paris. Je suis rentré en collision avec une autre voiture.*
OPÉRATEUR   *Il y a combien de blessés, monsieur?*
AUTOMOBILISTE   *J'étais seul dans la voiture. Moi, je ne suis que légèrement blessé. Les deux personnes dans l'autre voiture ne sont pas*

conscientes. Il faut les dégager d'urgence . . . ça pourrait prendre feu.

OPÉRATEUR  On enverra immédiatement une ambulance et les sapeurs-pompiers. En attendant, essayez de dégager la chaussée pour éviter d'autres collisions. Ne touchez pas aux blessés.

**Activity**

In a real emergency it would be wisest to find help and get someone else to pass on the details of what has happened to ambulance, police or fire brigade. If you were on your own, however, could you manage to explain these things in French? There's been an accident. Someone has hurt her leg. We need the police/ambulance/fire brigade. It's necessary to get the driver out of the car.

## SKILLS PRACTICE

1  What warning and what advice are being given in this roadside notice?

> Un simple bout de cigarette jeté de votre voiture peut détruire la forêt, utilisez votre cendrier de bord

2  You read this list of consulting times in the town guide to the place where you are staying.

**MÉDECINS** : Cabinet Médical: Tel. 38 97 43 94
*Pendant la fermeture et la nuit, suivre les indications du répondeur téléphonique.*

**HORAIRE DES CONSULTATIONS AU CABINET MÉDICAL**

|  | Docteur MOUIAL | Docteur ROGNON | Docteur GUILBAULT |
|---|---|---|---|
| Lundi | 13.30 à 15.30 | 18.00 à 20.00 | 8.00 à 10.00 |
| Mardi | Absent | 8.00 à 10.00 | 13.30 à 15.30 |
| Mercredi | 8.00 à 10.00 | Absent | 17.30 à 19.00 |
| Jeudi | 13.30 à 15.30 | 13.30 à 15.30 | 8.00 à 10.00 |
| Vendredi | 17.00 à 19.00 | 8.00 à 10.00 | Absent |
| Samedi | 8.00 à 10.00 | 13.30 à 15.30 | 13.30 à 15.30 |

What should you do if you need a doctor urgently at 8.00 p.m. on a Saturday night?

# Health and welfare

3   You see this sign at a bathing beach by a river.

**LIMITE DE PLAGE SURVEILLÉE**

▶ BAIGNADE SURVEILLÉE, ABSENCE DE DANGER PARTICULIER.

▶▶ BAIGNADE DANGEREUSE MAIS SURVEILLÉE.

▶ BAIGNADE INTERDITE

(*a*)   What boundary is it marking?

(*b*)   Unfortunately, all three triangular symbols look the same in black and white but in fact they are colour coded. What does the printed message tell you about the significance of each of the three symbols?

4   The following is an extract from an article on road safety in France.

### POUR LES JEUNES, 4 GRANDES PRIORITÉS...

La lutte contre l'alcoolisme au volant est de loin la mesure la plus citée. Pour plus des trois quarts des jeunes, l'efficacité passe par des sanctions plus sévères. Pour 1 jeune sur 2 c'est même la mesure la plus efficace.

Viennent ensuite le port obligatoire de la ceinture de sécurité et du casque pour les motards et la limitation de vitesse sur route et autoroute. Ces 4 mesures se détachent nettement. On notera qu'elles correspondent aux grandes campagnes menées par la Sécurité Routière.

(*a*)   According to the young people surveyed, what are the four measures which are most likely to result in a lowering of the accident statistics?

(*b*)   What, according to the article, is the connection between these four suggestions from young people and the current national road safety policies which are being pursued in France?

5   You read the following notice on the back of your hotel bedroom door.

fimotel

### CONSIGNE INCENDIE

**EN CAS D'INCENDIE DANS VOTRE CHAMBRE**
- Garder votre sang-froid;
- quittez votre chambre en refermant la porte et en laissant la clé dessus;
- prévenez immédiatement la personne de service, N°
- gagnez sans affolement le rez-de-chaussée par les escaliers;
- prévenez la réception. Veillez à l'appel des sapeurs-pompiers.

**EN CAS D'INCENDIE AILLEURS QUE DANS VOTRE CHAMBRE**
A l'audition du signal d'évacuation donné par les sonneries d'étage pendant une minute par intermittence ou sur appel du personnel:
- quittez votre chambre dans le calme après avoir fermé les fenêtres;
- refermez derrière vous la porte de votre chambre en laissant la clé dessus;
- gagnez la sortie de l'établissement par les escaliers;
- suivez les consignes de la direction;
- si les couloirs et escaliers sont envahis complètement par la fumée, restez chez vous. Une porte fermée, mouillée et bien calfeutrée, protège longtemps. Allez aux fenêtres et manifestez votre présence.

(*a*)   Why are there two sets of fire instructions under two different paragraph headings?
(*b*)   In the first set of instructions, what is the exact advice on leaving your room and where to report to?
(*c*)   What is the advice about how to leave your room in the second set of instructions? Where are you told to go this time and by what route?
(*d*)   In the second set of instructions, under what circumstances should you remain in your room?

**Extension**

Imagine you are a guest in a hotel when a fire breaks out. You are amongst several witnesses who are interviewed by local radio. Use some of the vocabulary in the notice above, plus your own ideas, to construct the interview in French.

## Health and welfare

6  You see the following article in a magazine which you are flicking through whilst staying in a holiday gîte in the South of France. You think your parents might be interested in it because you have your three-year-old brother with you.

**L'ÉTÉ: À LA MER**

**Le coup de soleil**

**Ce qu'il faut faire:**

Vous pouvez calmer la douleur avec des liquides adoucissants spécialisés que votre pharmacien vous conseillera. Vous pouvez aussi couper en deux une tomate bien mûre et étaler le jus sur son coup de soleil. Vous pouvez répéter cette application 1 heure après.

**Ce qu'il ne faut pas faire:**

Il ne faut pas le laisser au soleil les 2 ou 3 jours suivants sans avoir protégé par un vêtement toute la peau rougie, sinon il risque d'avoir une brûlure du 2$^e$ degré avec des cloques.

**Le coup de chaleur**

Votre enfant se plaint de mal à la tête, parfois il vomit, il a le visage congestionné.

**Ce qu'il faut faire:**

L'allonger immédiatement à l'ombre dans un endroit frais aéré. Surélevez-lui légèrement la tête.
  Rafraîchissez-lui le front, le crâne sans oublier la nuque avec des linges humides, frais.
  Faites-lui boire de l'eau fraîche.
  Si ça ne passe pas très vite: appelez un médecin ou emmenez-le à l'hôpital.

**Ce qu'il faut pour l'éviter:**

Il ne faut pas le couvrir trop.
Il ne faut pas le laisser jouer trop longtemps en plein soleil, surtout aux heures les plus chaudes de la journée.
Faites-le se reposer de temps en temps.
Donnez-lui à boire frais régulièrement.

(a)  What do the top two paragraphs give advice on?
(b)  What do the bottom two paragraphs give advice on?
(c)  What tip is given in the top left-hand paragraph which could be helpful if you are unable to find a chemist's?
(d)  What precaution is suggested in the top right-hand paragraph to avoid aggravating the child's condition?
(e)  What warning is given right at the end of the bottom left-hand paragraph?
(f)  What four tips are given in the bottom right-hand paragraph to help you avoid the child suffering this condition?

**7** The following two documents are taken from a newspaper and from a leaflet on motorway emergency services.

POUR DEMANDER DU SECOURS

POUSSEZ

RELACHEZ

ATTENDEZ LA RÉPONSE DE L'OPÉRATEUR

Donnez:
- lieu de l'appel
- lieu de l'accident, sens de circulation
- nombre de véhicules impliqués
- nombre éventuel de blessés
(leur état, nécessité de les dégager du véhicule, etc...)

Sur l'autoroute A 6

**Un pneu éclate; deux blessés**

Une voiture a été victime d'un accident, lundi soir, sur l'autoroute A6, dans la traversée du massif bellifontain, à hauteur d'Arbonne. Par suite de l'éclatement du pneu arrière droit, une Renault 4, se dirigeant vers la province, s'est renversée.

La conductrice, Mme Jacqueline Viguie, trente et un ans, de Paris, a été légèrement blessée mais son jeune passager, un enfant de dix ans, Thomas Jean-mougin (fils du propriétaire de la voiture), sérieusement blessé, a dû être transporté à l'hôpital de Fontainebleau.

(a) What are the three steps involved in working the emergency telephones on the hard shoulder of motorways?

(b) Four categories of information are listed which you are asked to give when reporting an accident or breakdown. Read the newspaper article carefully, then write down in English as much information in each category as you can relating to this incident. All the necessary information may not be contained in the article.

# Health and welfare

**Extension**

Imagine you are Mme Jacqueline Viguie in the article. Write down the dialogue which would go on between you and the operator as you used the emergency telephone to report the accident which you had just had in your Renault 4.

8 You read this report of an accident whilst you are on holiday in France.

Le chauffeur du car de pèlerins britanniques cherchait son ticket de péage...

### 3 morts, 27 blessé pour une seconde d'inattention

Trois morts, vingt-sept blessés dont neuf grièvement atteints: l'accident de l'autocar de pèlerins britanniques sur l'autoroute A 10 à hauteur de Tours a été particulièrement meurtrier. Quatre ans après la tragédie de Beaune, c'est toujours la même question angoissante de la sécurité des transports collectifs qui se pose. Cette fois, c'est certainement l'inattention du chauffeur qui est à l'origine du drame. Un drame qui aurait donc pu être évité?

A 3 heures du matin hier. L'autoroute A 10 est presque déserte. Un petit bus immatriculé dans le Kent, une région du sud de l'Angleterre, roule à une vitesse normale. A bord, quarante-quatre pèlerins qui vont à Lourdes. Dans deux kilomètres, c'est le péage. La route est excellente, il n'y a pas de brouillard: les passagers se sont pour la plupart endormis. Et puis soudain, le car fait des zigzags. Un bruit terrible: le véhicule s'effondre dans un fossé.

**Panique**

Trois passagers sont éjectés: on retrouvera leurs corps à quelques mètres du car. C'est la panique, hommes et femmes essaient de sortir du bus. Vingt-sept sont touchés aux jambes et aux bras et ont bien du mal à s'extraire de l'autocar couché sur le sol. Très vite les secours sont là. Les pompiers aident les premiers blessés, redressent le bus. Dix ambulances arrivent. Les rescapés seront hébergés à la base aérienne de Tours toute proche.

«Alors pourquoi un tel accident? Le bus roulait à 90 kilomètres à l'heure, la boîte noire l'a révélé. Le chauffeur très frappé par l'accident a quand même pu dire aux gendarmes: «J'ai voulu préparer mon ticket et l'argent pour le péage.» Un instant qui a suffi pour provoquer le drame....

(a) Why might this article be of particular interest to you as a British holiday maker?
(b) What *opinion*, rather than a fact, does the article put forward right at the end of the first paragraph?
(c) What appears to have been the cause of the accident?
(d) Complete the table below, gathering the facts as reported in the article.

---

Nationality of vehicle and driver:
Number of passengers:
Destination of passengers:
Time of accident:      Place of accident:
Road and weather conditions:      Speed:

First sign of a problem:
Other vehicles involved:
Nature/place of impact:
Number of fatalities:        Number of serious injuries:
Number of minor injuries:
Nature of injuries:
Emergency services – speed of arrival:
                  – order of arrival:
                  – number of units:
Survivors taken to:
Was the tachograph recovered?     yes/no

## Extension

You are one of the passengers who escapes with minor injuries. As one of the few people who speaks French you are interviewed by the local radio station. Write the interview between yourself and the reporter, using the article as a source of information and vocabulary but adding in your own ideas. Explain to the reporter all the background as well as the details of the accident itself.

## CHECK-LIST

**Essential language tasks**

(a)    say how you feel (as well as ask others) i.e. state of health, hungry, thirsty, tired, hot, cold
(b)    say you would like to rest/lie down/go to bed
(c)    say you've forgotten to bring towel, soap, toothpaste and ask for some
(d)    say what hurts/what is troubling you if you're not feeling well
(e)    shout for help
(f)    tell other people about possible dangers.

**Useful language tasks**

(a)    explain minor health problems, e.g. headache, sore throat, nausea, flu, cough, cold, nose bleed, temperature, sunburn
(b)    enquire at a chemist's what they have for such problems
(c)    explain how long you've had symptoms
(d)    ask for an appointment to be made with a dentist or doctor
(e)    find about surgery hours
(f)    ask for the nearest hospital
(g)    explain what medicine you are already taking, if any, how long you've been taking it and how often
(h)    say if you're insured and ask for any receipts you will need to claim medical expenses back
(i)    ask how long you will need to take any medicine and whether you will need to make another visit to the doctor/dentist

# Health and welfare

(k) ask if there are things you should not do e.g. sunbathe or bathe
(l) in the event of an accident, ask someone to telephone for the emergency services
(m) if involved in a road accident, ask for the other driver's name and address
(n) suggest that you fill in a *constat aimable*
(o) say it was not your fault
(p) describe an accident you saw or read about e.g. number of vehicles, how serious.

# LEISURE

### A  AU GUICHET DU CINÉMA

CLIENT   *Deux places pour 'Rocky 3', s'il vous plaît.*
EMPLOYÉ  *Orchestre ou balcon?*
CLIENT   *Orchestre, s'il vous plaît. La prochaine séance commence à quelle heure?*
EMPLOYÉ  *A 21 heures.*
CLIENT   *Alors ça se termine vers 23.45?*
EMPLOYÉ  *C'est exact.*
CLIENT   *C'est en version anglaise avec des sous-titres?*
EMPLOYÉ  *Non, c'est en version française doublée.*
CLIENT   *Merci bien, monsieur.*

**Activity**

1  One further item of information which could be of interest to you when going to the cinema in France might be the *type* of film (e.g. horror, science fiction) if you weren't familiar with the title. How would you phrase a question in French to find this out? How would you ask whether there was an interval?

2  The conversation here goes very straightforwardly. What might your reaction be in French if the person in the box office said either of the following things to you?

(a)   '... *désolée, madame, mais c'est presque complet. Il n'y a plus que des places au tout premier ou au tout dernier rang. Ça vous intéresse ou préférez-vous revenir un autre soir?'*

(b)   '... *mais vous avez raté la dernière séance complète. Le grand film a commencé il y a une demi-heure déjà ...'*

### B  ON FAIT DES RÉSERVATIONS À L'AVANCE

TOURISTE  *On voudrait réserver des places pour le concert du 18 août – mardi soir – s'il vous plaît. Qu'est-ce qui vous reste comme places?*
EMPLOYÉE  *C'est pour combien de personnes? Et vous avez un prix particulier dans l'idée?*
TOURISTE  *C'est pour trois personnes, et dans les 40 francs.*
EMPLOYÉE  *Bien ... je peux vous offrir des places à l'orchestre à 35 francs ou au balcon à 40 francs.*
TOURISTE  *Donnez-moi trois à 40 francs, s'il vous plaît.*

# Leisure

**Activity**

How would you say in French you wanted to reserve seats for Saturday's match, for tomorrow's *Son et Lumière* or the play on 15th July?

## C  APRÈS LE FILM

GUY  *Alors, ça t'a plu, Miriam?*
MIRIAM  *Ah, oui. C'était sensationnel! Mais je trouve que les films de Spielberg sont toujours impressionnants.*
GUY  *Ses films font courir les foules aussi en Angleterre, je suppose?*
MIRIAM  *Ah, oui, sûrement.*

**Activity**

Can you think of different ways of saying in French that you either enjoyed or disliked a film, play or concert? What phrases do you know for asking someone else what they think about something they've just seen or heard? How many adjectives (e.g. funny, boring, exciting) can you think of in French which would enable you to finish Miriam's sentence above with a different word from *impressionnant*?

## D  ENQUÊTE SUR LES LOISIRS

What could you find to say in French in response to the questions in the following survey?

### La télévision

Combien d'heures en moyenne passez-vous par soir à regarder la télévision?
Combien de soirs la regardez-vous par semaine?
Quel est votre genre d'émissions préféré?
Quelle est l'émission que vous avez appréciée le plus hier soir? Sur quelle chaîne et à quelle heure? C'était quel genre d'émission?
Pourquoi l'émission vous a-t-elle plu?

### Le cinéma

Combien de fois allez-vous au cinéma en moyenne par mois?
Quel est le titre du film que vous avez vu le plus récemment? C'était quel genre de film?
Est-ce qu'il vaut mieux regarder les films à la télévision (en direct ou enregistrés sur bandes de vidéo) plutôt que d'aller les regarder au cinéma?

### Questions générales

Quelles sont les choses qui vous intéressent? Télé, cinéma, musique, lecture, sport?
Qu'est-ce que vous avez fait le weekend dernier pour vous détendre?
Est-ce que vous avez des projets de loisirs pour le weekend qui vient?

A votre avis – est-ce qu'il y a suffisamment de possibilités de loisirs pour les jeunes gens dans votre ville ou dans votre région? Qu'est-ce que vous feriez pour améliorer ces possibilités?

## SKILLS PRACTICE

1  Going to the local swimming pool is always very popular with visitors to France. How many of the following signs and notices would you be able to undersand?

(a)    LES TICKETS DU MATIN NE SONT PAS RÉUTILISABLES L'APRES-MIDI (at the ticket office)

(b)    DOUCHE OBLIGATOIRE (sign in changing rooms)

(c)    BAIGNEURS – BAIGNEUSES (two signs over changing room doors)

(d)    DÉFENSE DE ... PRATIQUER DES JEUX VIOLENTS ... CRACHER ... COURIR ... PLONGER DANS LE PETIT BASSIN (all warning notices on the walls)

(e)    ENFANTS DE MOINS DE 6 ANS NON ACCOMPAGNÉS INTERDITS (notice at entrance)

2  You read the following item in a French newspaper while you are on holiday. It appears on a Tuesday morning.

**Samedi sur 100 téléspectateurs, 68 regardaient la télé.**

TF1 – 84% ont regardé « Starsky et Hutch » (Indice de satisfaction, 14/20)

A2 – 11% ont regardé « Les sept jours du marié » (Indice de satisfaction, 11/20)

FR3 – 5% ont regardé « Le songe d'une nuit d'été » (Indice de satisfaction non précisé)

**Dimanche, sur 100 téléspectateurs, 72 regardaient la télévision.**

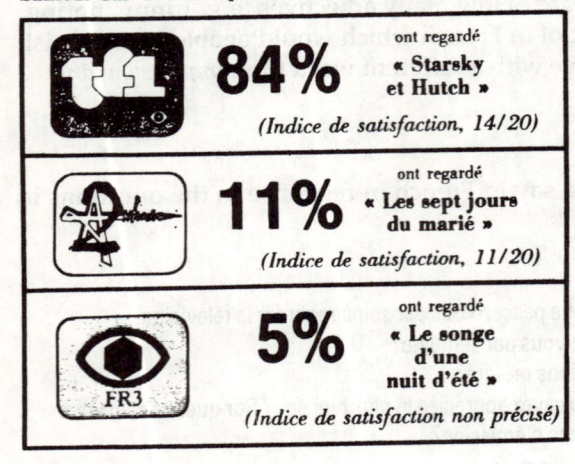

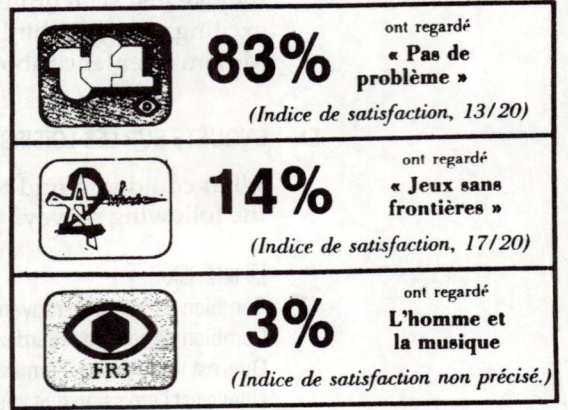

TF1 – 83% ont regardé « Pas de problème » (Indice de satisfaction, 13/20)

A2 – 14% ont regardé « Jeux sans frontières » (Indice de satisfaction, 17/20)

FR3 – 3% ont regardé L'homme et la musique (Indice de satisfaction non précisé.)

© Le Figaro 1987

(a)    Of the two evenings referred to, which had the higher number of viewers in total?

(b)    On Sunday night, which programme gave the most enjoyment to viewers?

(c)    We know that not many viewers watched FR3 on either night. What do we know about how much they enjoyed what they saw?

# Leisure

**3** You see this advert for a magazine.

**7 à Paris 2F**
TOUTE L'ACTUALITE DU CINEMA ET DU SPECTACLE

c'est l'hebdomadaire
magazine-revue
guide-programme
chaque mercredi

EN VENTE CHEZ VOTRE MARCHAND DE JOURNAUX

**CINEMA SPECTACLES**

(a) What exactly are the contents of this magazine?
(b) How often does it come out?
(c) According to the advert, where should you buy it?

**4** You see these advertisements for local exhibitions.

**Pour mieux comprendre Tchernobyl**

Une exposition sur la radioactivité.
**Explora, étage 1, à partir de mi-juillet.**
Entrée: billet explora.
En parallèle, dossier sur la radioactivité au sommaire de **Science Actualités. Etage 0.** Entrée libre.

**Les mois du long métrage**

Films scientifiques, documentaires, dessins animés, science-fiction. Tous publics, dès 3 ans. Programmes, réservations au 40.05.72.84.
**Ciné-club Louis-Lumière, étage 0.**
Entrée libre.

(a) When is the radioactivity exhibition on?
(b) What four types of film will be shown at the feature film exhibition? For what age group are they suitable? Which level of the building is the cinema auditorium? What is the entrance price?

5 You find the following tucked under the windscreen wipers of the car in a car park.

*Bienvenue en Champagne*
VACANCES 1986

Dégustez la Champagne
en
MUSIQUE

*Écoutez* **Radio Magnum 92 - 4 FM**

Guide Touristique Sonore 24 h./24 - Informations Loisirs
Renseignements pratiques - Météo - Guide gastronomique et hôtelier
...et TOUT SUR LE CHAMPAGNE !!!

(a) What are the broadcasting hours of this local radio station?
(b) Can you list the services/information which the station is offering?

6 You are trying to make your mind up about the choice of cinema film one rainy evening on your holidays. You have a copy of the film guide for the two cinemas you've got in mind.

| saint-gratien | sarcelles |
|---|---|
| **378 LES TOILES** Forum de Saint-Gratien. 989.21.89. Séances: Mer 15h, 21h; Jeu 21h. Ven 15h, 21h; Sam 15h, 17h30. 20h, 22h30; Dim 15h. 17h30, 2 1h. Pl: 16 F. Adh, Etud et – 18 ans: 11 F. C.V.: 8 F. Mer mat prix unique: 11 F. | **380 LES FLANADES** Centre commercial Sarcelles. 990.14.33 Perm de 14h à 24h. Pl: 25 F. Lun Tarif unique: 17.50F (sf Fêtes et veilles de Fêtes) – 18 ans, Etud. Milit. tlj de 17h à 19h: 17.50 F. C.V. de 14h à 19h sf Sam. Dim: 17.50 F. |
| *Meurtre au soleil* v.f. | **5 salles:** |
| *Carmen Jones* v.a. | *Emmanuelle* Int – 18 ans. |
| *Reds* v.f. | *Ben Hur* v.f. |
| Mer 15h, 21h: Jeu 21h; Ven 15h, 21h; Sam 15h, 18h30, 22h; Dim 15h, 21h. | *Opération dragon* v.f. int – 13 ans. |
| | *La Guerre des étoiles* v.f. |
| | *Le Tombeur, le frimeur et l'emmerdeuse* v.f. int – 13 ans. |

It's a Saturday night. You're torn in the end between two films. *La Guerre des Etoiles* and *Meurtre au Soleil*. Complete the table below with details for both of the films. You are sixteen years old.

**Leisure** 129

|  | M. au Sol. | Guerre Des E. |
|---|---|---|

1 Times of performances
2 Price
3 Any age restrictions?
4 Language of soundtrack

Extension: How many of the following abbreviations make sense to you? Mer mat – étud – Perm – 13 ans – milit – Pl – sf – tlj – Int – v.f. – v.o.

7 In a book shop you read these labels above various shelves of books.

SCIENCE FICTION AMOUR BIOGRAPHIES SPORT AVENTURE ART SCIENCE HISTOIRE ROMANS POLICIERS BANDES DESSINEES HUMOUR

(a) Would you understand all of these? Explain what each one is in English.
(b) Using these words as a trigger for your thoughts, jot down some sentences which you could use on a cassette letter to a French pen friend, telling her/him what your tastes are in reading and perhaps saying a little bit about something which you have read recently and enjoyed.

8 You are lucky enough to be able to use the video club membership of the French people from whom you are renting your holiday home. In the video hire shop you see the following labels above the shelves.

AVENTURE – FILMS POLICIERS – ÉROTISME – GUERRE – HUMOUR – FILMS D'EPOUVANTE – FILMS POUR LA FAMILLE

(a) Can you identify each category in English?
(b) Use the list as a trigger for a parallel activity to the one in 7 (b) above, this time relating to films not books.

9 You read the following 'blurb' about a series of popular French books.

> Elisabeth dévala les dernières marches de l'escalier, traversa le couloir en trombe et lança un coup d'œil affolé à la grande horloge du collège. Elle se répétait en elle-même: 'S'il te plaît, Todd, il ne faut pas m'en vouloir d'être en retard'. Le soir même, il devait la conduire au bal. Ce serait formidable! Arrivée dehors, elle ne vit pas Todd du premier coup d'œil mais elle l'aperçut qui marchait vers le petit cabriolet et montait aux côtés de Jessica! ... Sa propre sœur jumelle! ... Ainsi commence 'SŒURS RIVALES', un livre de la nouvelle série SUN VALLEY. SUN VALLEY, ce sont des livres où les sentiments sont toujours violents. Surtout entre les jumelles Wakefield dont la rivalité fait trembler toute la série SUN VALLEY. De rage, d'amour et de jalousie. SUN VALLEY, les livres dont les pages ont le cœur qui saigne.

(a) If someone asked you to explain what type of series this was, what would you say?

# French

10  You read this short article in a French pop magazine.

> Simon Le Bon était tout heureux il y a quelques semaines de marier son frère David à Jane Griffin. En compagnie de sa femme Yasmine et de son autre frère Jonathan, tous étaient venus souhaiter au jeune couple de longues années de bonheur et ... beaucoup d'enfants. Avec un peu de retard, nous nous joignons à eux et présentons à David et Jane nos plus sincères félicitations et tous nos vœux de bonheur.

(a) What event is referred to?
(b) Who are the four people present at the event?
(c) What do the writers of the article wish to say about the event?

11  You read the following announcement in a free sheet which is being distributed at the campsite where you are staying.

## SPORT, DÉTENTE AVEC L'A.R.V.I.F.

Pour la seconde année consécutive, l'Association des Résidents du Village Ile-de-France (A.R.V.I.F.) propose avec le concours des Club Sportifs Laonnois, de la Direction Départementale Jeunesse et Sports et de la Ville de Laon, plusieurs activités de détente, ouvertes aux adolescents.

Tir, plongée, camping et équitation sont au programme de l'été 86.

| THEME PROPOSE | CLUB PARTICIPANT | DATE/PERIOD | LIEU | FRAIS D'INSCRIPTION |
|---|---|---|---|---|
| Initation, pratique tir à la carabine, au pistolet | Société Mixte de Tir de Laon: P. Doudin L. Auburtin | Les 4 et 5 juillet, de 10 à 12 heures et de 14 à 17 heures Le 6, de 10 à 12 heures | Laon, stand de tir | 30F |
| Initiation à la plongée sous-marine | Club de plongée de Laon J. Wargnier J. L. Mathieu et animateurs | Les 22, 23 et 24 août, en matinée | Laon, piscine | 30F |
| Camping, activités nautiques, cyclotourisme | A.R.V.I.F. et autres J. L Solau et animateurs | Du 4 au 11 août | Plan d'eau de l'Ailette Chamouille et ses environs | 160F |
| Découverte, initation à l'équitation | Association Laon, de rééd. par l'équitation, handi-cheval D. Huart | Les 2 et 3 août Pique-nique le midi | Goudelancourt-les-Berrieux | 50F |

Inscriptions: Jean-Louis Solau, 6, rue des Hortensias, à Laon. Tél. 23.20.21.04

Ces activités sont bien évidemment ouvertes à tous les touristes et vacanciers résidant à Loan ou de passage.

(a) As a visitor, are you eligible to take part?
(b) How would you book a place for an activity?

# Leisure

(c) According to the section above the table, what are the four principal activities proposed?

(d) Do you need previous experience to take part in the sub-aqua diving?

**Extension:**

(a) Write down what you would say in a telephone call to the appropriate organizer. Say who you are, how long you're staying and confirm that the activities are open to tourists. Say what experience you've had of sub-aqua diving (or one of the other activities which interests you) and book for one of the sessions stated on the advert. Confirm the venue and the price.

(b) Imagine you've spent a couple of days enjoying some of the activities. Write a short letter to your pen friend who lives in another part of France, and tell her/him what you've been doing and how you've enjoyed it.

12  The following is an entry from a guide book about leisure parks, with the key to the symbols used underneath.

| | |
|---|---|
| Accueil | Sans interruption toute l'année, de 9 h 30 à 18 heures. Entrée et activités payantes. |
| Parkings | 3 parkings: 900 places. |
| Hébergement et Restauration | Salle dortoir sommaire pour 50 personnes. Cafétéria – Restauration rapide et familiale – Buvette (én été). Aires de pique-niques (plages ou clairières). Aire naturelle de camping. |
| Particularités | Pratique de la planche à voile. Location de planche et enseignement. (4 cours de tennis en 84). |

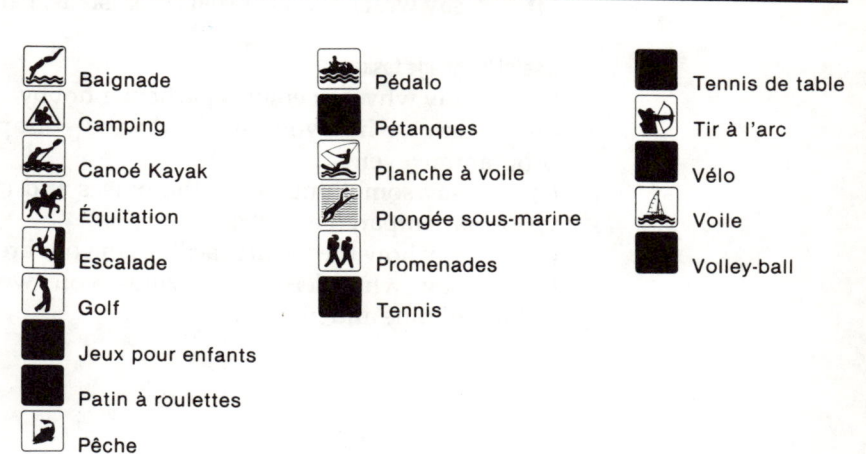

| | | | | | |
|---|---|---|---|---|---|
| | Baignade | | Pédalo | | Tennis de table |
| | Camping | | Pétanques | | Tir à l'arc |
| | Canoé Kayak | | Planche à voile | | Vélo |
| | Équitation | | Plongée sous-marine | | Voile |
| | Escalade | | Promenades | | Volley-ball |
| | Golf | | Tennis | | |
| | Jeux pour enfants | | | | |
| | Patin à roulettes | | | | |
| | Pêche | | | | |

# French

(a) What are the nine sports available at this leisure park according to the symbols to the left of the text?

(b) What information could you explain to a non French-speaking person who wanted to know about (i) facilities for eating and drinking; (ii) prices; (iii) any specialities of the centre which are referred to?

## CHECK-LIST

**Essential language tasks**

(a) say what your hobby is/what's involved in it
(b) talk about what you do in free time at evenings and weekends, e.g. radio, tv, reading, entertainments
(c) say which sports you take part in and which you enjoy watching
(d) ask about leisure possibilities in an area you are visiting
(e) tell a foreign visitor about the leisure possibilities in your area
(f) say what you think about a tv programme/film/concert/event you've seen
(g) find out someone else's opinion about a performance and show you agree/disagree
(h) find out the cost of seats for a film/show/concert/play/sports event/event
(i) find out the performance dates/times
(j) find out if there is an interval and if there are refreshments available
(k) find out what sort of play/film it is (e.g. horror, spy, adventure)
(l) in the case of a non-French film/tv film, find out if the film is in the original language or in a French version
(m) buy/book tickets for a performance/event
(n) say which kinds of seats (e.g. stalls, balcony)

**Useful language tasks**

(a) say why you enjoy a particular hobby
(b) say why you enjoyed/were disappointed by a film/programme/event
(c) say something about the pluses and minuses of French television as compared to British television
(d) say how the leisure facilities in your area might be improved
(e) say what leisure activities you would undertake given unlimited time and money.

# TOPIC TWELVE

# RELATIONS WITH OTHERS

## A  ON PRÉSENTE QUELQU'UN

M. HAMON  Alors, Monsieur Hacquard. Permettez-moi de vous présenter Keith Johnson, le correspondant anglais de Philippe.
M. HACQUARD  Enchanté, Keith. On a beaucoup parlé de vous.
KEITH  Je suis bien heureux de faire votre connaissance, monsieur.
M. HACQUARD  Vous venez de quel coin de la Grande-Bretagne, Keith?
KEITH  J'habite la banlieue de Manchester.
M. HACQUARD  Ah bon! Que le monde est petit! J'ai une cousine qui s'est mariée avec un Anglais, et eux, ils habitent Wigan qui fait partie de l'agglomération de Manchester, si je ne me trompe pas?
KEITH  Oui, c'est vrai. Je ne connais pas la ville personnellement, mais ce n'est pas tellement loin de Manchester – c'est à 35 kms, peut-être.
M. HACQUARD  Alors, le voyage s'est passé sans problèmes? Vous devez être fatigué ou non?
KEITH  Ça s'est très bien passé. J'ai pris un vol direct de Manchester à Paris et puis je suis descendu à Avignon en T.G.V.

**Activity**

The above is fairly typical of a semi-formal situation where an adult (in this case invited as a friend of the family) meets you when you are staying with French hosts. If you were meeting some people of your own age, say at a party, how might the conversation go differently, do you think? Try and re-write the dialogue, thinking of the sorts of questions that might be asked as well as thinking about how the style of the language might be different.

## B  ON ARRANGE QUELQUE CHOSE

MADELEINE  Allô . . . c'est bien Martin? Tiens . . . c'est Madeleine à l'appareil. Bonjour!
MARTIN  Salut, Madeleine! Comment ça va?
MADELEINE  Bof . . . on fait aller, quoi. Et toi?
MARTIN  Bien, merci.
MADELEINE  Dis-moi . . . est-ce que tu es libre ce soir?
MARTIN  Qu'est-ce que tu proposes? En principe je ne suis pas encore occupé.
MADELEINE  Si on allait au cinéma?
MARTIN  Merci, mais ça ne me dit pas grand'chose. J'aimerais mieux aller au café . . . si tu es d'accord.

MADELEINE   Alors... je t'invite à prendre un verre!
MARTIN   Pourquoi pas? Ce serait sympa. Mais c'est moi qui paie... j'insiste!
MADELEINE   On verra! Alors à 20.30 devant le Café de la Gare?
MARTIN   D'accord... à bientôt!
MADELEINE   A ce soir!

**Activity**

1  Using the material in this dialogue and other words and phrases you know, make a list of the different ways in French of doing the following things:
   (a)   asking/inviting someone to do something or go somewhere
   (b)   accepting an invitation enthusiastically
   (c)   refusing an invitation very politely
   (d)   saying very politely that you'd really prefer to do something else.

2  If you can find a partner to work with, the following is a good way of practising the phrases you've collected for activity 1 above. Without showing each other, you should each take a sheet of paper and divide it up into sections for days of the week, as in a diary. You should each blank off about a third of the time and write in, in French, what it is you are doing that particular evening or part of the weekend. One of you should then 'ring up' the other person and try to fix a day and time to do something or go out somewhere. The person who is being invited should say if she/he is free or not. You can negotiate with each other, as in the dialogue between Martin and Madeleine regarding the activity itself or the day and time. You should each make a note in your diary of what it is you've agreed. Run through the procedure a second time, with the roles reversed, (i.e. you are being invited this time rather than doing the inviting) again comparing notes at the end to see if you have successfully communicated with each other.

**ENQUÊTE SUR L'ADHÉSION AUX CLUBS**

What would your response be to a survey in French on club membership on the following lines?

Vous êtes membre d'un ou de plusieurs clubs?
Lequel/lesquels?
Depuis quand êtes-vous membre?
Est-ce que vous êtes obligé(e) de payer une cotisation?
Combien par mois/par an?
Quelles sont les activités du club/des clubs dont vous êtes membre?
Vous vous réunissez combien de fois par semaine/mois/an?
Où est-ce que vous vous réunissez? Toujours au même endroit ou à des endroits différents?
Qu'est-ce qui vous a attiré à devenir membre du club/des clubs que vous fréquentez?

# Relations with others

**SKILLS PRACTICE**

1. You're anxious to take presents back from your trip for your relatives and friends. The following advert catches your eye in a catalogue.

---

### Sac de plage – 139 F

Idéal pour les vacances à la mer!

Plié, un grand sac fourre-tout (40×60cm)
Déplié, un tapis de plage (115×175cm)
Utilisable aussi en cabine de bain
et en poncho imperméable!

En nylon, renforcé de robustes sangles

No 3260.4 Prix Club: 139 F
jusqu'au 30 Sept 1982 – après cette date: 149 F

---

(a) What are the four uses to which this bag can be put?
(b) In what sense is the price special?

2. You're staying in France on an exchange trip with your local youth club. The leader wants to make contact with the cultural centre in the town where you are staying. She asks you to brief her before the visit, as she speaks very little French. Here is the documentation which you have been sent in advance.

## le Centre d'Animation Culturelle et la Maison des Loisirs

La vocation du Centre d'Animation Culturelle est de permettre aux habitants de la Ville Nouvelle et du département de rencontrer la création sous toutes ses formes, par l'animation et le contact direct avec les créateurs.
Le Syndicat Communautaire d'Aménagement de Cergy-Pontoise, met pour cela à la disposition du C.A.C., un ensemble d'équipements composé de salles d'activités, de foyers, d'un petit théâtre, de salles polyvalentes, et de la Maison des Loisirs, qu'il animera en collaboration avec le Conservatoire de Musique, de Danse et d'Art Dramatique et la Bibliothèque.

**MAISON DES LOISIRS**

Son rôle: offrir un support technique en personnel, locaux et matériel à des actions socio-culturelles, socio-éducatives et de loisirs.
- *Centre de moyens*
(Impression, information, documentation, prêt de matériel).
- *Foyers* (stages, rencontres, expositions).
- *Ateliers* (vidéographes, sonothèque, etc.).
- *Petit Théâtre* (réunions, colloques, ateliers de création, diffusion culturelle, cinéma, etc.).
- *Salles polyvalentes*.

Fill in the table below to show how you would brief the youth leader.

Function of the Centre d'Animation Culturelle:
Premises/rooms available in the centre:
Function of the Maison des Loisirs:
Examples of the activities which go on in the Maison des Loisirs:

3. You read this letter on the correspondence page of a teenage magazine during the course of a visit to France.

**Christian S., Ajaccio:**
**«J'AI PERDU SON AMITIE»**

Je connais L. depuis trois ans. Au début, nous étions copain-copine. Sans plus. Cette année, nos relations sont devenues plus régulières sans dépasser, cependant, le cap de l'amitié. Je l'associais à toutes mes sorties, et idem pour L. Seulement voilà: au fil des mois, mes sentiments pour elle sont devenus beaucoup plus tendres et un jour, par l'intermédiaire d'une de ses copines, je lui ai fait savoir que je souhaitais flirter avec elle. A ma grande déception, elle a répondu par la négative, et, le pire, depuis nous ne nous voyons quasiment plus ... Elle trouve toujours un prétexte pour annuler nos sorties. Je vous en prie, dites-moi ce que je dois faire pour retrouver son amitié et que tout redevienne entre nous comme avant. Merci.

**La réponse de OK!**

Un ami, un vrai, c'est beaucoup plus difficile à avoir qu'un flirt. Et 99% de nos lectrices regrettent de ne pas en avoir un avec qui elle pourrait sortir et parler sans arrière-pensée. Ainsi, L. avait la chance – rare – d'avoir un ami. Toi. Et elle a dû être choquée – ou plus exactement troublée – en apprenant, par une intermédiaire en plus, que tu voulais flirter avec elle. D'un côté, L. a dû être flattée que tu aies des sentiments tendres, très tendres, pour elle. Mais de l'autre, elle n'a pas dû comprendre – puisque vous vous connaissez bien – que tu te sois confié d'abord à sa copine. C'est certainement cette intervention d'un tiers qui l'a contrariée. D'ailleurs, tu ignores en quels termes ta «déclaration d'amour» lui a été rapportée par cette amie ... Pour que tout redevienne «comme avant» entre vous, il faut absolument que tu aies une conversation avec L. Au nom de votre «vieille amitié» (insiste sur ce fait), elle ne refusera pas de te rencontrer.

(a) What has been the difference between this, the third year of their relationship, and the previous two years, as far as frequency of going out together is concerned?
(b) How have Christian's feelings towards his girl friend changed over the last months?
(c) What did this change lead him to do?
(d) What was the girl's reaction to what he did?
(e) What advice precisely is Christian seeking?
(f) According to the magazine's reply, what was it that upset the girl?
(g) What advice is offered exactly?

4   You read the following article in a serious magazine.

### Avoir 20 ans Aujourd'hui

*Toutes les enquêtes, tous les sondages le montrent: la préoccupation majeure des jeunes d'aujourd'hui (la génération des 16-25 ans) est et demeure l'emploi. Quels que soient la tranche d'âge (les 16-18 ans, les 18-21, etc.), l'origine sociale, le niveau d'instruction, tous, à des degrés divers, expriment en priorité leur espoir de «trouver du travail» ou leur crainte d' «être au chômage».*

**Inquiets sur l'état du monde**

Qu'ils soient étudiants, lycéens ou élèves d'écoles professionnelles, près du 50% des jeunes (soit deux fois plus qu'en 1978) considèrent que les études qu'ils font ne préparent pas bien au métier qu'ils aimeraient exercer. Amère constatation qui en dit long sur les griefs qu'ils peuvent formuler à l'encontre de notre système éducatif, et qui condamne sans appel la «réformite» aigüe dont semblent souffrir tous les ministres de l'Education nationale de ces dernières décennies, toutes «sensibilités» politiques confondues.

Lorsqu'il est question non plus d'exercer une profession, mais de «se débrouiller dans la vie», les chiffres sont souvent plus négatifs encore.

Envisagé sous cet angle, l'avenir n'apparaît donc pas des plus roses: dans l'enquête SOFRES- «Figaro-Magazine» d'avril 1984 portant sur les 16-22 ans, 37% (contre 31%) d'entre eux estimaient que leur vie serait «moins heureuse» que celle de leurs parents. Toutefois, à la même question. 46% (contre 19%) des 19–23 ans interrogés en octobre de cette même année répondaient «plus heureuse» (enquête SOFRES-« Le Nouvel Observateur – Radio France). Au delà de cette apparente contradiction, un fait est certain: les jeunes craignent que les lendemains ne chantent pas. Outre le chômage, ils redoutent une guerre mondiale, ou un conflit nucléaire, le terrorisme et la violence, ils sont inquiets devant des phénomènes comme la faim dans le monde, la crise économique, les atteintes à l'environnement; pour eux-mêmes, ils appréhendent le manque d'argent, les accidents, la mésentente familiale et la solitude...

(a)   What is the main point which this article is making about young people's principal worry?
(b)   What do young people have to say about the effectiveness of the French education system in preparing them for a job?
(c)   What was the question which was put to young people in the two opinion polls referred to, in April and October 1984?
(d)   Make a list of the national and international problems which worry young people.
(e)   Make a list of the personal problems which worry them.

**Extension**

Using some of the vocabulary and ideas in this article, plus other things which may occur to you, jot down some sentences in French about the things which make you happy or worried about the future.

5   If you are ever staying with French people it is likely that you may sit down and watch the television news together, or that you will hear the family reacting to things they hear or read in the news. It may well be that you are asked to react too. The key things to revise are the language functions which refer to emotions, e.g. approval, disapproval, fear, worry, relief, surprise, interest, disgust etc. When you are nearer to the examination and you feel confident in all those language functions, read through the short news items below and think what your reaction might be in French to hearing or reading that particular piece of news. You would only be expected to say something brief, not give a long, complicated political commentary!

### Israël: URSS

Des représentants israéliens et soviétiques sont actuellement en contact pour envisager une reprise des relations entre les deux pays au niveau consulaire, a rapporté vendredi un porte-parole du ministère israélien des Affaires étrangères. L'URSS, qui avait rompu ses relations diplomatiques avec Israël en 1967, aurait pris l'initiative de cette reprise.

### Nicaragua: véto US

Jeudi au Conseil de Sécurité de l'ONU, les États-Unis ont opposé leur veto à une résolution les appelant à arrêter leurs «*activités militaires et para-militaires jugées illégales*» et leur soutien aux «contras» du Nicaragua. Le texte de la résolution, s'appuyait sur le récent arrêt de la Cour internationale accusant les États-Unis de violer le droit international: il avait été approuvé onze voix contre une.

### RDA: mur

Un Allemand de l'Est déguisé en soldat soviétique a réussi mercredi à passer à l'Ouest en franchissant le mur de Berlin. Heinz Braun, 48 ans, avait maquillé sa voiture personnelle pour qu'elle ressemble à un véhicule militaire soviétique. Grâce à trois mannequins «habillés» d'uniformes, il a ensuite passé sans encombre la zone de l'In-validenstrasse, entre les parties orientale et occidentale de Berlin.

---

## CHECK-LIST

**Essential language tasks**

(*a*)    say which clubs you belong to, what you do and how often/where you meet
(*b*)    talk about any friends/acquaintances in France
(*c*)    say hello to people you meet and respond to their greetings
(*d*)    break off the conversation when you wish to leave and say goodbye
(*e*)    introduce yourself and show you're pleased to meet someone else
(*f*)    give and receive gifts politely and gratefully
(*g*)    find out what someone else wants to do as a leisure activity
(*h*)    express your own preference of activity
(*i*)    agree amicably on what to do if there is disagreement
(*j*)    invite someone out to pictures, disco, youth club etc.
(*k*)    respond politely to what other people suggest
(*l*)    discuss with someone whether an activity is possible or impossible
(*m*)    discuss whether something is probable/doubtful
(*n*)    say you're grateful and you're sorry
(*o*)    show how you feel about something e.g. delighted, disappointed, surprised
(*p*)    fix a time and place to meet someone by agreement.

**Useful language tasks**

(*a*)    introduce someone else
(*b*)    ask someone you've just met about their journey/health and

# Relations with others

possible mutual acquaintances with people/places (e.g. a French person might have heard of the town you're from)

(c)     say why you prefer a particular activity when discussing what to do

(d)     react to the objections which other people may make to your suggestions about possible activities

(e)     react to comments made by other people about current events in the news e.g. a terrorist attack or a speech from the British Prime Minister.

# SCHOOL AND CAREER

### A  EXTRAIT D'UNE LETTRE

... tu sais qu'on est en train de faire un dossier sur la vie scolaire en Angleterre. C'est pour ça que je t'écris. On s'intéresse surtout à des détails de la vie réelle. Est-ce que tu pourrais m'envoyer quelques renseignements sur ton collège, sous les rubriques suivantes?

Nom du collège – privé ou de l'État? Nombre d'élèves – mixte ou non? Nombre d'enseignants. Situation – par exemple au centre de la ville? Locaux (c'est-à-dire les bâtiments) anciens ou modernes? Construit en? Nombre de cours par jour et durée de chaque cours – semaine scolaire anglaise 'normale' (c'est-à-dire du lundi au vendredi, matinée et après-midi)? Les heures et la durée des récréations et de la pause à midi – durée des vacances scolaires à différents moments de l'année.

Ça nous intéresse aussi d'avoir tes impressions personnelles sur la vie scolaire. En gros, est-ce que ton collège te plaît ou non? Est-ce qu'il y a des aspects que tu aimes et d'autres qui te plaisent moins? Tu as des matières préférées? Tu pratiques un sport au collège? Est-ce que tu participes de temps en temps aux séjours organisés qui ont lieu pendant les vacances scolaires? Est-que les élèves de ton collège ont beaucoup de difficulté à trouver un emploi?

### Activity

1. How detailed a reply could you manage in French in response to the request for all this information?
2. Imagine a group of French youngsters is going to be in your school for a few days as part of an exchange visit programme. You have to interview one of the group for the school magazine. You feel you will get more information out of your interviewee if you conduct the interview in French. Make up a list of questions which you would ask, based on the material in the extract from the letter which you have here. Don't forget that the letter asks for the information very much in written 'note' form. You will need to think how to word the questions differently in a way which would be natural in everyday spoken French.

# School and career

**B  ENQUÊTE SUR LE CHOIX D'UN MÉTIER**

Est-ce que vous avez une idée claire de l'emploi que vous aimeriez prendre? Quels sont les facteurs qui influencent votre choix? Classez-les sous une des rubriques, 'très important', 'relativement important' ou 'peu important'.

|  | très important | relativement important | peu important |
|---|---|---|---|
| 1 Salaire |  |  |  |
| 2 Conditions de travail |  |  |  |
| 3 Sécurité d'emploi |  |  |  |
| 4 Satisfaction du travail |  |  |  |
| 5 Possibilité d'avancement |  |  |  |

Ou est-ce que vous trouvez que le seul facteur d'importance est celui de disponibilité d'emploi?

C'est-à-dire que vous vous trouvez obligé(e) de prendre n'importe quel emploi, parce que le chômage est si élevé?

## SKILLS PRACTICE

1   The following is an extract from a brochure published by the Lycée Français Charles de Gaulle in London.

> Le choix des sports pratiqués au Lycée est le suivant: football, rugby, athlétisme, natation, patin à glace, tennis, volley-ball, handball, basket-ball, cricket, escrime, squash et danse rythmique. Dans nombre de ces spécialités, le Lycée Français Charles de Gaulle obtient de très bons résultats dans les diverses compétitions inter-scolaires britanniques.
> Les sports dits 'de base' sont gratuits mais pour certaines specialités telles que le patin à glace ou l'escrime, une contribution supplémentaire est demandée.

(*a*)   According to this extract, which sports are given as examples of specialities?

(*b*)   What comment is made about the school's record in the sporting field?

**Extension**

Using this extract as a 'trigger', write down some comments on the choice of basic and speciality sports in your school. Comment on particular achievements for the school or you personally. Remember that in the examination you might either have to talk about this in the general conversation in the oral test, or it might come in as part of a reply to a letter.

2  The following is an extract from a letter which you receive from your pen-friend in July.

> Ensuite je vais travailler pendant un mois pour me faire de l'argent de poche. Je vais vendre des glaces dans la rue. Ça n'est pas trop désagréable et on gagne assez d'argent. Ainsi je pourrai après partir en voyage à l'étranger avec trois amis. Nous voulons aller camper en Grèce. Nous irons d'abord en train, puis à pied. Je prendrai plein de photos, comme ça je pourrai te faire voir. Si je réussis mon bac, l'année prochaine, je vais entrer à l'université pour étudier la physique et la biologie. Les études durent quatre ans. Je voudrais plus tard travailler dans un laboratoire. C'est ce qui m'intéresse. Et toi? Quelle carrière vas-tu poursuivre l'année prochaine? Sais-tu quel métier tu aimerais faire? Jusqu'à quand es-tu en congé? Pour moi la rentrée sera le premier octobre. Je te souhaite de bien t'amuser cet été. J'attends de tes nouvelles avec impatience. Je t'embrasse bien fort. Amitiés.

(a)  How long is your friend going to work during the summer holiday period?
(b)  What is the job and what are the comments made about it?
(c)  What is the holiday destination after the job and what are the means of travel?
(d)  What type and what length of university course is your friend hoping to follow?
(e)  What are the two questions which you are asked about (i) your career and (ii) your holidays?

## School and career 143

**Extension**

Write down what you would say in the section of your next letter where you reply on this topic to your pen friend. Give information and comments about any holiday job you have and any other plans for the summer period. Give information and comments also on what you plan to do in September and what your long-term job plans are, if any.

3   Your pen friend knows you are toying with the idea of getting a job for a couple of months in the summer holidays in France. In March she/he sends you this cutting from the evening paper.

> Vendeurs-euses
> Vente – bord de mer
> Débutants acceptés.
> Tel. 42 36 13 19

(*a*)   Write down what you would say when you telephoned the enquiry number. Explain who you are and why you are ringing. Give details of any *relevant* qualifications or skills. Give details of any part-time jobs you've already done. Say why you think an English girl/boy might be especially suitable for this particular job.

(*b*)   Assume the person to whom you speak is encouraging and asks you to put your application in writing. Put down all the information you gave in (*a*) above in written form, thinking carefully how the style and wording might differ from your spoken comments.

4   The following article catches your eye when you see it in a local newspaper while on holiday, because it refers to an English group.

> **Ils sont partis, les jeunes correspondants anglais de Hutton**
>
> Après un bon mois passé au terrain de camping, les élèves anglais du collège de Hutton avec leurs directeurs ont pris le chemin du retour en Angleterre. Jeudi après-midi, après un dernier repas pris au «Val de Loire», car dans la matinée tout le matériel avait été rangé dans le car ainsi que les valises, nos amis britanniques ont embarqué non sans quelque nostalgie.
>
> Il faut dire que cette année avait été un peu particulière, puisque c'était la 20ᵉ année consécutive que des élèves de ce collège anglais venaient camper à Meung. D'ailleurs, à cette occasion, une petite cérémonie avait été organisée par M. Tachon et la municipalité dans l'orangerie du château, cérémonie que nous vous avons commentée à l'époque.

(*a*)   How long has this group been staying in the area and where?
(*b*)   From your reading of the first paragraph, what must 'Val de Loire' be?
(*c*)   What is special about this year's visit?

## French

5   A French visitor to your school heard your class hold a heated argument about school life, during which they drew up the following comments and complaints:

- ☐ The pupils' working day is too long.
- ☐ Too much time is spent in writing.
- ☐ More time should be given to music and drama.
- ☐ The school buildings are not equipped well enough for science.
- ☐ Teachers should change their teaching methods.
- ☐ Pupils should be able to choose their teachers.
- ☐ The standard of school meals should be improved.
- ☐ There are too many different subjects on the school time-table.
- ☐ There are not enough recreational activities in school.
- ☐ The school is too large.

### TÉMOIGNAGES

## "Écrire, toujours écrire…"

**Vingt et un élèves de la classe de troisième 1 B du collège d'enseignement secondaire de Séméac-Aureilham (Hautes-Pyrénées) nous ont envoyé un témoignage collectif sur leur vie quotidienne.**

LE métier d'élève n'est pas aussi enviable qu'on le dit. Pour certains d'entre nous, la journée est longue. Par exemple pour celui qui vient avec un car de ramassage. Debout à 6 heures, il prend le car à 7 heures et revient chez lui à 19 heures. Il finit ses devoirs, mange et doit se coucher à 21 heures. Il ne s'« appartient » pas. Le lendemain, la journée sera la même. Prisonnier de l'enseignement, l'élève est enchaîné à sa chaise durant la journée, et ne peut la quitter que pour subir un « interrogatoire » au tableau. Le « métier » d'élève est d'écrire, toujours écrire.

Nous demandons que les élèves participent au choix des emplois du temps en début d'année, et que les horaires soient équilibrés pour plaire aux élèves et aux professeurs.

Nous demandons une scolarité entièrement gratuite. En ce moment, la scolarité est gratuite, mais les faux frais la rendent chère. Il faudrait que l'équipement pour les matières comme le dessin ou le travail manuel soit gratuit, ainsi que les voyages organisés, qui sont une partie de l'enseignement assez négligée.

Il faudrait dédoubler la classe pour les cours de travail manuel, les sciences et le français, comme les années précédentes.

Nous voudrions plus de rapports amicaux entre maîtres et élèves ; moins de droits des profs sur les élèves. Il faut changer la manière d'enseigner, parce qu'elle est trop banale, aussi bien pour les professeurs que pour les élèves.

Nous voulons : avoir le droit de choisir les professeurs ; changer le règlement scolaire ; du plein air pour toutes les classes des jeux et du sport pour tous les demi-pensionnaires ; un changement des horaires de la journée (par exemple, la journée continue) ; ne pas mettre deux heures de langues différentes à la suite.

Nous voulons aussi : plus de vacances plus de loisirs au C.E.S. ; une salle de classe stable pour chaque classe, comme à l'école primaire ; le droit de peindre notre salle avec la couleur qu'on aura choisie ; la suppression des heures de colle plus de technologie pour les filles qui le désirent.

Nous souhaitons : créer nous-mêmes un nouveau règlement ; qu'il y ait un club de ski gratuit le mercredi après-midi pour apprendre à tous les élèves à skier, car nous sommes à quarante kilomètres des pistes de ski, et il n'y a pas le tiers des élèves qui sachent skier.

Nous demandons un goûter pour les demi-pensionnaires, comme dans les autres C.E.S. ; une machine à boissons chaudes changer la discipline ; avoir le droit d'exposer notre avis pour les grandes décisions à prendre.

After the French visitor returned home, he sent you this article about life in a school in France which he thought might add weight to your arguments. You decide to use this article in further class discussions. To help you do so, read the article and then answer the questions below *in English*.

**a**   Who wrote the article? _____

## School and career 145

**b** According to the first paragraph of the article, what is the daily routine of a French pupil who travels to that school each day?

_____
_____

**c** Look again at the comments and complaints listed above. Which of the same points are made in the article? Show this by putting a tick in the box next to any point in the list above which is included in the article.

**d** Find any 3 other changes that the writers of the article would like to see affect their particular school and mention these briefly below:–

Change i _____

Change ii _____

Change iii _____

*Source: York Reading Extended Question 7*

### CHECK-LIST

**Essential language tasks**

(a)    talk (and find out from someone else) about your school, e.g. number of teachers/students, age of buildings, location of school, school year and holidays, facilities, trips and events

(b)    talk about the school day/week, i.e. starting and finishing times, number of lessons in day and their duration, number and times of breaks throughout day, arrangements for meals, homework

(c)    talk about your educational programme, i.e. what year you are in, what subjects you study, how many periods of each subject per week, which subjects you like/dislike, the out of school activities you take part in.

**Useful language tasks**

(a)    talk about your educational career, i.e. which schools you have been to, where you intend to go next or whether you are going to try getting a job

(b)    explain the examination/qualifications you are aiming for

(c)    talk about any special events in the school, past, present or future, which a French person might be interested in

(d)    talk about your hopes/fears for employment prospects in the future, especially what your plans are for the summer after you have taken your GCSE examination

(e)    talk about your choice of job, giving reasons and explaining what the job involves.

# LANGUAGE

### A  AU BUREAU DE POSTE

TOURISTE   *Excusez-moi, madame . . . je ne parle pas très bien le français. Je voudrais téléphoner en Angleterre, mais sans payer maintenant. Je voudrais appeler mes parents – eux, ils vont payer. Je ne sais pas la bonne expression en français pour tout ça.*

EMPLOYÉE   *C'est une communication en p.c.v., monsieur. Vous avez le numéro?*

TOURISTE   *Pardon, madame. Je n'entends pas très bien à cause de la grille et du bruit des autres clients. Voulez-vous bien parler un petit peu plus fort et un peu plus lentement, s'il vous plaît?*

EMPLOYÉE   *Alors je répète: est-ce que vous avez le numéro?*

TOURISTE   *Ah, oui. Je l'ai écrit sur cette feuille de papier. Je trouve que les numéros sont toujours très difficiles en français.*

EMPLOYÉE   *Vous vous débrouillez quand même, monsieur. Vous apprenez le français depuis quand, monsieur?*

TOURISTE   *Depuis deux ans, seulement. Mais je fais des progrès parce que je suis chez des amis. Alors je parle beaucoup de français et on me corrige d'une manière vraiment sympathique.*

EMPLOYÉE   *Alors, allez dans la cabine 9, s'il vous plaît.*

TOURISTE   *C'est bien '9' que vous avez dit, madame?*

EMPLOYÉE   *Oui, monsieur.*

**Activity**

Go through the dialogue and list what you feel are the key phrases which are useful when coping with problems to do with your knowledge (or lack of knowledge!) of the French language. Which ones do you feel are missing? For example, could you say in French: What's the French for this? Can you write that down? How do you spell that? I've forgotten the French word for this.

### B  ENQUÊTE SUR LES LANGUES

Quelle est votre première langue?
Quelle est votre deuxième langue?
Vous l'apprenez depuis combien de temps?
Est-ce que vous connaissez d'autres langues?
Comment est votre profil linguistique? Essayez de dresser une liste de vos compétences en différentes langues en utilisant le schéma suivant:

# Language

|  | 1ère | 2ème langue | 3ème |
|---|---|---|---|
| Parler couramment<br>　　relativement bien<br>　　　un petit peu | ___ | ___ | ___ |
| Écouter　sans problèmes<br>　　　avec quelques difficultés<br>　　　en comprenant un petit peu | ___ | ___ | ___ |
| Lire　sans problèmes<br>　　avec quelques difficultés<br>　　en comprenant un petit peu | ___ | ___ | ___ |
| Écrire　facilement<br>　　　avec quelques difficultés<br>　　　quelques mots seulement | ___ | ___ | ___ |

### Activity

Try asking some of your friends to do their linguistic profile, when you have completed yours. You may find yourself surprised by the linguistic talent which is there, given there are so many bilingual and trilingual people in Great Britain.

## SKILLS PRACTICE

1   The following advert in a magazine catches your eye.

## Tous les Européens qui traitent leurs affaires en Français ne sont pas Français

Hors de France, 750 000 responsables utilisent le français comme langue d'affaires.

Plus d'Espagnols, d'Italiens, de Belges et de Suisses traitent leurs affaires en français qu'en anglais*.

Pour atteindre un plus grand nombre d'hommes d'affaires européens : vous devez aussi leur parler français.

Prenez...                                                    * Sources PES 3

**L'EXPRESS**

　(*a*)　　To which group of French speakers does this advert refer?

(b)     In the last full line of the text, what is stated as being the advantage of speaking French?
(c)     What comment would you make about sexism in this advertisement?

2   The following is an advert for a French language course based on video.

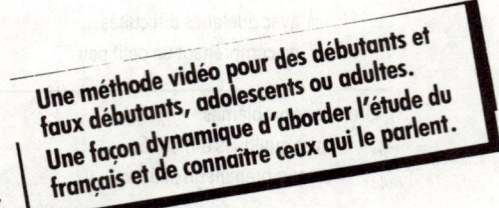

Une méthode vidéo pour des débutants et faux débutants, adolescents ou adultes.
Une façon dynamique d'aborder l'étude du français et de connaître ceux qui le parlent.

**Niveau 1**
4 cassettes vidéo,
1 livre de l'élève,
2 cassettes sonores (pour le livre élève),
1 cahier d'exercices,
1 cassette sonore (exercices),
1 guide d'utilisation.

Pour tout renseignement, s'adresser aux:
CLASSIQUES HACHETTE
Export Livre
79, bd Saint Germain
F - 75288 PARIS CEDEX 06

(a)     Is the course for young or old learners? For advanced students only or for others?
(b)     How many audio cassettes are there altogether in the pack for level 1.

**Extension**
Using some of the vocabulary from the advert, jot down some comments on the course book you've been using in French. How dynamic is it? Has it helped you to get to know the people who speak French as well as the French language? Do you like the audio cassettes? Do you like the pupil's book? Do you like doing exercises? Have you seen any videos in French?

3   Look at the advertisements for language courses shown opposite and on page 150. Imagine that you are considering enrolling for a course and you want to compare certain features (numbered 1 to 5 on the table) of the two language centres. Find the necessary information in the advertisements and complete the table on page 151.

# UNIVERSITÉ D'AMIENS

## Cours d'été pour étudiants étrangers
en juillet
*Centre de liaison et d'échanges internationaux*

**INSCRIPTION**
Toute personne âgée d'au moins 18 ans et possédant une connaissance de la langue française au moins égale à celle que requiert une inscription à l'Université.
Frais de cours et d'accueil (logement, repas, excursions) : 2 000 F dont 50 F à verser dès l'inscription, non remboursables.

**COURS**
Tous les matins sauf le dimanche et les jours d'excursion deux heures de cours; un après-midi sur deux, deux heures de travaux pratiques. Séances en laboratoire de langues
Trois niveaux :
  A - **Supérieur.** Langue et civilisation. Littérature française des XIX° et XX° siècles. Civilisations (institutions, histoire et géographie, art). Stylistique.
  B - **Moyen.** Grammaire et civilisation. Compréhension et expression. Littérature. Civilisation.
  C - **Élémentaire.** Phonétique et grammaire. Linguistique appliquée.

**PROFESSEURS**
Les cours sont assurés par des professeurs de l'Université et leurs collaborateurs.

**LOGEMENT ET REPAS**
En cité universitaire (chambres individuelles).

**EXCURSIONS**
La côte de la Manche.
Les églises et châteaux de Picardie.
Les usines et centres d'activités économiques typiques de la région.

**SPORTS**
  Tennis;
  piscine;

**ACTIVITÉS CULTURELLES**
  spectacles, bibliothèque,
  discothèque.
  Centre national d'animation musicale.

Pour tous renseignements, s'adresser au
**Centre de liaison et d'échanges internationaux**
*Cours de vacances*
18, place Saint-Michel,
80-Amiens.

## Chambre de Commerce et d'Industrie de La Rochelle
# Cours de vacances pour étrangers
organisés par l'Institut d'Études Françaises de La Rochelle

Deux sessions : 7 juillet-3 août
4 août-31 août

Logement et pension dans des Familles.

Age minimum : 16 ans.

### Étudiants - Professeurs

- Cours destinés aux étudiants n'ayant aucune connaissance de la langue française : sections élémentaires
Méthode audio-visuelle
- Cours destinés aux étudiants n'ayant qu'une connaissance imparfaite de la langue française : sections moyennes
- Cours destinés aux étudiants ayant une bonne maîtrise de la langue française écrite et parlée : sections supérieures

— *Orientation « Littérature »* : Littérature classique - Théâtre contemporain - Poésie contemporaine - Roman contemporain - Méthodologie.

— *Orientation « Linguistique »* : Phonétique - Stylistique - Linguistique générale - Grammaire structurale - Laboratoire - Conversation.
— *Orientation « Civilisation »* : Histoire de l'Art - Civilisation - Sociologie - Conversation - Traduction - Laboratoire.
Traduction dans les sections moyennes et supérieures en 8 langues : allemand - anglais - espagnol - italien - japonais - suédois - norvégien - danois.
— *Orientation économique* :

Économie générale : problèmes intérieurs français - problèmes internationaux - problèmes commerciaux. Ces cours s'adressent plus particulièrement aux professeurs, étudiants économistes, techniciens, cadres commerciaux.

### Section de perfectionnement pour professeurs étrangers de français
Stages intensifs de quatre semaines (brochure détaillée sur demande).

### Loisirs et distractions
— sports (natation - voile - équitation)
— cinéma
— excursions chaque week-end

RENSEIGNEMENTS - INSCRIPTIONS
S'adresser à l'Institut d'Études Françaises, 12, rue Arcère, 17000 LA ROCHELLE.

# Language 151

|   | LA ROCHELLE | AMIENS |
|---|---|---|
| 1 dates courses available: | | |
| 2 minumum age of students: | | |
| 3 kind of accommodation: | | |
| 4 sports available: | | |
| 5 other entertainments: | | |

*Source: Midland Reading Higher Part 2, Exercise 3, Questions 11 to 15*

## CHECK-LIST

**Essential language tasks**
(a) say you can/cannot understand
(b) ask someone to repeat/explain something
(c) ask someone to spell something out for you, e.g. a name or place
(d) ask if a person speaks a particular language
(e) say how much/little French you know
(f) say how well you speak/understand French
(g) ask how you say something in French (i.e. 'what's the French for . . .?)
(h) ask what something means in French
(i) ask someone to speak a little more slowly
(j) tell someone you can't hear them very well
(k) say you don't know/you've forgotten.

**Useful language tasks**
(a) say how long you've been learning French and any other languages you study
(b) say what you like best about learning French
(c) say a little bit about how you're taught in French, i.e. what kinds of things you do in class and for homework
(d) ask someone to write something down for you
(e) ask someone how a word is pronounced
(f) ask someone to correct you if they don't understand what you've said.

# MONEY

### A  AU MAGASIN DE SOUVENIRS

TOURISTE  *Vous avez des livres de poche sur la région, en plusieurs langues, dans la vitrine. Combien sont-ils?*

COMMERÇANT  *Vous aimeriez acheter un livre en quelle langue, madame?*

TOURISTE  *En anglais, s'il vous plaît, monsieur.*

COMMERÇANT  *La version anglaise est à 30 francs.*

TOURISTE  *Ah bon . . . c'est un petit peu trop cher pour moi. Vous n'avez rien de moins cher?*

COMMERÇANT  *Malheureusement, non. Mais j'ai cette très belle série de cartes postales de la région. Ça, c'est vraiment bon marché . . . 10 francs les 15 cartes.*

TOURISTE  *Ça doit être joli. Je voudrais bien les voir. Voulez-vous bien me les montrer, monsieur?*

COMMERÇANT  *Avec plaisir, madame. Attendez un moment. Je n'en aurai pas pour longtemps.*

**Activity**

Make a list of what you feel are the key words and phrases in this dialogue which are to do with money/price. Are there any basic phrases missing which you would require when paying by cash? (Other forms of payment are coming later.) What do the shopkeeper's very last words mean?

### B  AU MAGASIN D'ÉLECTROMÉNAGER

EMPLOYÉE  *Alors, monsieur, c'est bien cette cafetière-ci que vous prenez? Vous avez de la chance . . . c'est la dernière de ce type qui reste.*

TOURISTE  *Ah oui . . . c'est beaucoup moins cher que chez nous. Mais il y a un petit problème. C'est que je n'ai pas assez d'argent français sur moi. Est-ce que je peux revenir un petit peu plus tard après être passé à la banque pour toucher des chèques de voyage?*

EMPLOYÉE  *Vous n'avez pas d'Eurochèques, ou des cartes de crédit, monsieur?*

TOURISTE  *Pas sur moi, non.*

EMPLOYÉE  *Alors, ça ne présente pas de problèmes majeurs, monsieur. Mais on vous demanderait normalement de verser un petit acompte en espèces.*

TOURISTE  *Ah, oui, bien sûr. 50 francs . . . ça suffit?*

# Money

EMPLOYÉE  *C'est parfait. Je vous donne un reçu, monsieur. C'est en quel nom?*
TOURISTE  *Smith. S–M–I–T–H.*
EMPLOYÉE  *Voilà. Quand vous reviendrez, voulez-vous bien passer directement à la caisse, s'il vous plaît?*
TOURISTE  *Merci, madame. A bientôt.*

### Activity
Using the material in this dialogue, can you work out how to say: Do you accept credit cards/travellers' cheques/Eurocheques? Do I have to pay a deposit? May I have a receipt? Where is the cash point/cash desk?

From your memory of situations which involved payment in other topics (e.g. 4, 8 and 9) are you able to say these things: Do I have to pay in advance? I've nothing less than a 100-franc note. Do you have 50-franc notes and 10-franc coins?

### C  ENQUÊTE SUR L'ARGENT DE POCHE

Combien d'argent de poche recevez-vous par semaine?
Est-ce que vous aidez à faire le ménage ou à faire les courses pour 'gagner' votre argent de poche?
Est-ce que vous avez un emploi à temps partiel pour gagner de l'argent?
Quand/où travaillez-vous?
Combien d'heures par semaine?
Qu'est-ce que vous faites exactement?
Comment est-ce que vous dépensez votre argent de poche?
Est-ce que vous mettez de l'argent de côté chaque semaine?
Avez-vous l'intention d'acheter quelque chose de spécial?
Est-ce que vous vous considérez plutôt riche, à court d'argent ou à sec?

### Activity
Think of some responses to the survey questions relating to your personal finances.

## SKILLS PRACTICE

**SIGNS AND NOTICES**  1  Would you be able to explain the following signs and notices which are all connected with this topic?
(a)  LES CHEQUES NE SONT PLUS ACCEPTÉS POUR LES ACHATS INFÉRIEURS A 100 F (sign at till in hypermarket)
(b)  PAIEMENT EN ESPECES UNIQUEMENT (sign at petrol station)
(c)  TOUTES LES CARTES DE CRÉDIT SONT ACCEPTÉES (sign in shop)
(d)  PRIERE DE PRÉSENTER UNE PIECE D'IDENTITÉ (sign at foreign exchange counter in bank)
(e)  PAR MESURE DE SÉCURITÉ NOTRE APPAREIL VOUS PHOTOGRAPHIE AU

MOMENT OU VOUS ÉTABLISSEZ VOTRE CHEQUE (sign at cash point in large store)

2  You see the following in the financial column of a newspaper.

**Le change**

Le 1 août 1986
| | |
|---|---|
| Dollar | 6,77 |
| Ecu | 6,87 |
| Mark | 3,25 |
| Franc belge (100 FB) | 15,71 |
| Florin | 2,88 |
| Lire (1000 lires it.) | 4,74 |
| Livre sterling | 10,11 |
| Franc suisse | 4,07 |
| Peseta (100 P) | 5,01 |
| Yen (100 Y) | 4,42 |

*Compte non tenu des commissions bancaires (de 1.5 à 2%)

(a)  How many French francs would you expect to get in exchange for £10 on that particular day? Would commission for the bank be included in this figure?

**Extension**

This document can be a useful basis for practice of numbers! Try to find a partner to work with. She/he should be the clerk with the list of exchange rates. You should be the customers of different nationalities. You mustn't look at the book! Quiz your partner about the rate for various currencies – Le dollar est à combien? Le franc suisse est à combien? She/he gives you the rate in French: Six soixante-dix-sept, quatre zéro sept etc. You write down the figures you're given in each case. Compare what you've written down with the list in the book in order to see how successfully communication has taken place.

3  You see this item as part of a leaflet issued by the French Post Office promoting their travellers' cheque service.

> Avec les chèques de voyage, vous pouvez retirer de l'argent liquide auprès des banques ou payer dans des milliers de magasins, hôtels ou restaurants à travers le monde.

(a)  What are the two things mentioned here which travellers' cheques enable you to do?

4  In the same leaflet there is something about their Postchèque service for travellers.

> **La facilité Postchèque**
> Pendant votre voyage, vous rencontrez un maximum de facilités:
> -la Poste est universelle, elle est présente partout, dans les petits villages comme dans les grandes villes;
> -partout la Poste est bien connue, les habitants sauront toujours vous indiquer le bureau le plus proche;
> -vous pouvez utiliser vos Postchèques dans plusieurs pays au cours d'un même voyage.

What are the three advantages of this facility which are listed here?

# Money

**5** The leaflet also has something to say about credit cards.

> **Pour vos paiements chez les commerçants**
> Pour régler vos achats chez les commerçants, la Carte Bleue est un moyen pratique et simple. Vous n'avez plus besoin d'argent liquide, ni de chèque, ni de pièce d'identité. De nombreux commerçants acceptent aujourd'hui cette forme moderne de paiement. Ils sont 300 000 en France, reconnaissables par le panonceau **CB** (grands magasins, hypermarchés, restaurants, stations-service, commerces de détail, hôtels...). Ils sont 4 millions répartis dans plus de 160 pays et reconnaissables par le panonceau **VISA**.
> Il vous suffit de présenter votre Carte Bleue. Vous signez la facture établie par le commerçant après l'avoir vérifiée. Le commerçant vous rend votre Carte Bleue avec un double de la facture. C'est simple, c'est rapide.

(a)   In the first paragraph, what are the three things mentioned which you can do without if you use credit cards?
(b)   In the second paragraph, which sign are you told to look for in France to show that the Carte Bleue card is accepted?
(c)   What are the six outlets mentioned which are most likely to accept the card?
(d)   According to the last paragraph, what are the exact steps involved, in order, for paying by credit card?

**6** Here is some advice from a different leaflet on possible snags.

> Certains commerçants et agents de banque peuvent ne pas être encore familiarisés avec la Carte Bleue Internationale. A la moindre hésitation de leur part, dans quelque pays que vous vous trouviez, demandez-leur d'appeler le 'Centre d'Autorisation Local' (Local Authorization Center). C'est efficace, rapide et sans frais.

(a)   What are you advised to do if your card is queried?
(b)   What will this step cost you in time and money?

7 You are interested in the following article which appears in the holiday period in France.

## Le hit-parade des stations

|  | St-Tropez | Nice | Deauville | Biarritz | La Ciotat | Étretat | Argelès | St-Malo |
|---|---|---|---|---|---|---|---|---|
| Baguette | 2,70 | 2,80 | 2,55 | 2,50 | 2,40 | 2,30 | 2,55 | 2,45 |
| Ricard (en terrasse) | 10 | 12,50 | 8,50 | 9 | 12,50 | 15 | 6,50 | 7,50 |
| Perrier (1/4 en terrasse) | 12 | 8 | 8,50 | 12,50 | 9,50 | 10 | 7,10 | 7 |
| Coupe de glace (3 boules en terrasse) | 20 | 19 | 20 | 18 | 16 | 25 | 9 | 14 |
| Pellicule Kodak 24 poses couleur | 33 | 32 | 30 | 32 | 33 | 30 | 35,50 | 28 |
| Maillot de bain homme (slip) | 200 | 200 | 140 | 150 | 110 | 100 | 120 | 100 |
| Maillot de bain femme (deux pièces) | 300 | 250 | 180 | 180 | 160 | 200 | 170 | 125 |
| Ambre solaire (petit modèle) | 40 | 40 | 30 | 23 | 29 | 20 | 21,50 | 20,50 |
| Parasol sur plage (journée) | 25 | 34 | 45 | 33 | 28 | 20 | 28 | 18 |
| Pédalo (une heure) | 60 | 35 | 60 | 45 | 40 | 30 | 35 | 30 |
| Discothèque (entrée avec consommation) | 110 | 90 | 90 | 80 | 80 | 60 | 45 | 55 |
| TOTAL (en francs) | 812,70 | 723,30 | 614,55 | 585,00 | 520,40 | 512,30 | 480,15 | 407,45 |

(a) If you forgot to pack the following things in your suitcase, in which resort in each case would it cost you the most to buy a replacement on the spot – small size sun-tan lotion, colour film, swimming trunks?

(b) Which resort is most expensive over all for the two drinks in the table?

(c) What group of products is it worth avoiding buying in St-Tropez which send it to the top of the prices 'hit-parade'?

# Money

### Extension

You've stayed one summer in Étretat and your French pen-friend has been with her/his parents in Nice. Imagine the dialogue which might go on between you when you compare notes afterwards on prices.

*Example:* 'Nous, on a payé 100 francs un maillot de bain homme.'
'Ben, à Nice on a payé 200 francs!'
'Mais tu sais, c'est beaucoup plus cher à Nice – c'est peut-être la station la plus chère de la France.'
'On a payé 19 francs une coupe de glace en terrasse de cafe.'
'Ah bon! Ça, c'était plus cher à Étretat! Nous, on a payé 25 francs!'
'Ça m'étonne que c'était moins cher à Nice . . .'

## CHECK-LIST

**essential language tasks**
(a)   ask about prices
(b)   ask for the cash point (i.e. where you pay)
(c)   pay for what you've bought
(d)   talk about how much pocket money you get and how you spend it
(e)   say if you have enough/are short of money
(f)   say if you think something is too dear
(g)   ask for something cheaper.

**Useful language tasks**
(a)   comment on differences between prices in UK and a French-speaking country
(b)   ask for coins of a particular value (e.g. to fit a slot machine)
(c)   ask for notes of a particular value (e.g. when being given change)
(d)   ask if it is possible to pay by Eurochèque/credit card
(e)   correct someone who has given you the wrong change
(f)   ask if you have to leave a deposit/pay in advance.

**PART TWO**

# GETTING READY FOR THE EXAMINATION

| | | |
|---|---|---|
| 2 ▶ | Listening comprehension | **161** |
| 3 ▶ | Reading comprehension | **183** |
| 4 ▶ | Speaking | **199** |
| 5 ▶ | Writing | **217** |
| 6 ▶ | Verb tables | **235** |

The authors are most grateful for the degree of co-operation shown by the Examination Associations in granting permission for extracts from sample papers to be reproduced in this section. The suggestions for tackling the questions are those of the authors, not necessarily those of the Associations.

CHAPTER TWO

# LISTENING COMPREHENSION

## CONTENTS

▶ **What the National Criteria say is expected of candidates in the listening tests**   163

▶ **What the National Criteria say about methods of testing**   163

▶ **What to bear in mind as you prepare for the examination**   163

▶ **Typical listening activities**   164

▶ **What are the different types of listening skill?**   165

▶ **Tackling the examination itself**   168

▶ **Using clues to understanding**   169

▶ **What are the possible clues when listening?**   169
Your background knowledge   171
Word patterns   171
Sound patterns   172
More complicated word patterns   173

# Listening comprehension

## WHAT THE NATIONAL CRITERIA SAY IS EXPECTED OF CANDIDATES IN THE LISTENING TESTS

An understanding of details in announcements, instructions, requests, monologues (e.g. weather forecasts, news items), interviews and dialogues within a range of clearly defined topic areas from the syllabus.

Understanding rather than powers of memory.

In addition at **higher** level:

1 to show the same skills over a wider range of topics;
2 to identify important points or themes, including attitudes, emotions and ideas;
3 to draw conclusions from ideas expressed in the listening material;
4 to identify the relationship between ideas expressed in the material;
5 to show understanding of different styles of speech, e.g. on radio and television, in the home and in more formal situations with strangers.

## WHAT THE NATIONAL CRITERIA SAY ABOUT METHODS OF TESTING

1 Assessment can best be carried out by questions **in English** with answers in the candidates' own words **in English**;
2 If multiple-choice questions are used, they should not be the only method of testing listening. Multiple-choice answers should preferably be in English but may be possible in French, in which case they should be **heard** as well as being printed on the paper.

## WHAT TO BEAR IN MIND AS YOU PREPARE FOR THE EXAMINATION

1 It is important that you find out exactly what types of listening tasks there will be in the examination papers you are taking.
2 The French that you hear will be recorded by native speakers. Frequently you will have the chance to hear things twice. This would happen in real life because people would repeat what they had said if you hadn't understood. In some cases, however, particularly in higher level papers, the item may only be heard once.
3 There may be sound effects and background noise on some of the recordings, especially in the higher tests. As the background noises will often be helpful clues to understanding there is no need to worry about this.
4 Normally there will be a limit to the length of the items you will hear

in French, so that longer pieces will be split up into smaller segments. This means that your understanding of French is what counts, not just your powers of memory.

5   That is not to say that memory is not important. As far as vocabulary is concerned the time you spend on revision of the topics will more than repay itself because the test items will consist almost entirely of the words and phrases from the published lists. There may be a small number of words which are not on the topic lists but you will still be able to score full marks providing you have revised all your vocabulary thoroughly and take care in tackling the questions.

6   Sometimes, therefore, you are going to come across words which are new to you. You are also bound to come across some words which are on the lists but which you've forgotten. For tips on how to deal with this, see pages 169–74.

7   Normally questions and answers will be in English. At basic level you will often be listening to the French then showing your understanding by transferring information into written or graphic form, e.g. completing a table of information, ticking a box, filling in a form or completing a drawing. In the higher level tests there is more of an emphasis on understanding ideas, attitudes and emotions.

## TYPICAL LISTENING ACTIVITIES

### 1 LISTENING FOLLOWED BY TRANSFER OF INFORMATION

(a)     Listen to directions and trace the route you are given on a town plan.
(b)     Listen to the description of a stranger you're to meet at the airport, then pick the person out from a choice of four photographs.
(c)     Listen to a telephone call, then fill in a memo form in French.

### 2 INFORMATION GAPS

(a)     Listen to the recording where a policeman is asking for four items of information concerning a lost passport. Write down in English the four things which you need to say so the policeman can register the loss on a form.
(b)     Listen to someone requesting information, such as the price of a ticket, then show your understanding by writing down the price.

### 3 LISTEN AND RESPOND

(a)     Listen to an announcement from a radio broadcast concerning a traffic problem. Write down what action you would take if you heard it in a car as you were approaching the outskirts of Avignon.
(b)     Listen to a recording of a doctor giving advice about a patient. Write down exactly what the advice is, so you could explain as an interpreter for a sick relative what the doctor had said.

# Listening comprehension

(c) Listen to a recording of a telephone conversation, where a French person is ringing up the holiday villa your family has rented, asking to speak to the owner who is away. Jot down the number and a simple message about ringing back later in the week.

## 4 LISTEN AND IDENTIFY MAIN POINTS, MAIN THEMES, ATTITUDES, KEY IDEAS, OPINIONS AND EMOTIONS

(a) Listen to what comes out of a radio loudspeaker as someone is trying to tune it in across a waveband. Mark down the order in which you hear snippets of different types of programmes such as quizzes, news items, advertisements.

(b) Listen to the introductory news headlines and write down the gist of what each of the main stories is about.

(c) Listen to a conversation which two people are having about a news item. From the printed news headlines you have in front of you tick the story which you think the two people are discussing.

(d) Listen to someone talking about an incident which has really stuck in his/her memory. Answer some questions on the four main points.

(e) Listen to the conversation and pick the word which best describes the attitude of one of the speakers – helpful? courteous? aggressive?

(f) Listen to the conversation and pick the word which best describes what one of the speakers is trying to do – explain? apologize? accuse?

## WHAT ARE THE DIFFERENT TYPES OF LISTENING SKILL?

1. Notice that the examples of activities involve **different** types of listening skill. It is generally true that for detailed listening a knowledge of **single** word items of vocabulary can make all the difference between getting the answer correct or not. You need to bear in mind that it's also the case very often that you can have a good idea of the **form** in which the information will appear so that you are listening for something quite specific, e.g. a time, a date, a number or a price.

2. There will be other tasks where you will not know beforehand the form in which the relevant information will appear. If you read this question on your examination paper:

   If you were on holiday with friends, driving along the N26, what should you tell the driver to do if you heard this item of traffic news on the car radio?

   [English version of script] *Major blockage on N26... you're advised to avoid area if possible.*

   You have no way of knowing what to expect as far as the **exact** words which are going to be used, although you might have some idea of the possibilities in such a situation (e.g. bad weather, traffic jam or road accident). It helps to think about those possibilities before you actually start listening. In other words, you can use the clues to understanding which may well be there in the wording of the question, the topic and the setting.

3  Certain tasks will ask you to show you've understood the **gist** of what you have heard, rather than asking about specific individual details. You don't have to understand anything like every single word in order to get the gist of a message. As long as you understand the main points it won't matter if there are other words you haven't understood which perhaps give extra details which are not such an essential part of the message.

**Activity**
Study carefully these two listening comprehension questions from a sample paper produced by SEG and from a 16+ examination on GCSE lines set by the JMB and YHRE. Which is the one testing *detailed* listening and which is testing *gist* understanding? To get the first one right, what key item of vocabulary must you be able to understand? The second question is more difficult but do you need to understand every single word? What would you say are the key words?

> (i) You hear an announcement in a department store. In which department are the reduced prices?

[Script: *Venez vite! Prix choc au rayon vêtements enfants!*]

> (ii) Listen to a French person explaining how to prepare mayonnaise and work out which order these pictures should be in.

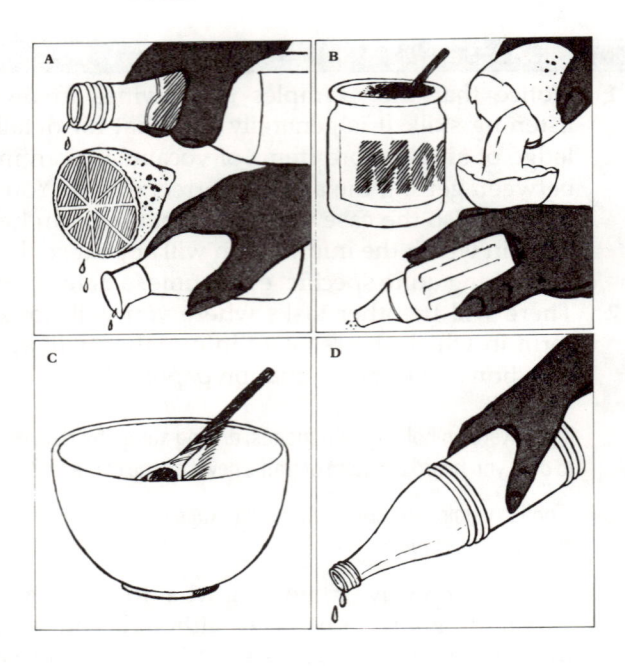

# Listening comprehension 167

[Script: *Tu peux très bien faire une mayonnaise sans mixeur. Tu prends un bol et une cuillère en bois. Tu mets une cuillère à soupe de moutarde dans le bol, une grosse pincée de sel et un jaune d'œuf. Puis tu verses l'huile goutte à goutte en tournant avec la cuillère en bois. Quand tu as une quantité suffisante de mayonnaise, tu peux ajouter une cuillère de vinaigre ou d'jus de citron ou même de whisky.*]

*Answer:* The correct order is C, B, D, A.

4  It should be clear by now that a number of different types of skill are used when listening. Thinking of real life, we listen in different ways with quite different purposes on different occasions. Compare the way you might listen to the football results with the way you listen to a radio play, to casual everyday conversation or to precise instructions on how to leave a plane which has just made an emergency landing! It is important therefore, to try to get in as much practice as possible in **different** types of listening skill in French.

5  Your school, college or Adult Centre may be able to lend you materials which you could listen to at home on cassette. There are quite a number of sources of French on network television and radio. Many on television are designed for the ordinary viewer, i.e. feature films and with sub-titles. Others are designed for language learners and come in a multi-media format with accompanying books, cassettes and computer software. If you listen to France Inter on 1800 metres LW you should get quite good reception (depending on how far north you live) of news bulletins on the hour. The French will be very fast and hard to understand at first, but you will probably get used to it especially if it's concerned with items you have already heard or seen on British radio or TV.

6  The best type of listening practice is 'normal' French i.e. language which is meant to be heard *in real life*, not something specially written for an examination or something which is designed to be *read silently* and then gets read out aloud masquerading as 'listening' material.

7  Listening to French at normal or near normal speed is important too. If what you hear is slowed down significantly compared with normal speech it can actually be *more* difficult to understand, or so all the research shows. The material in the tests in GCSE will be at normal speed, so you have to train yourself to get used to this in preparation.

8  When you first hear 'normal' French you will need to get used to some of its features which are different from the written version, in two major aspects. Firstly, a lot of words get run together. Here are a few examples:

|  |  |
|---|---|
| c'est pas vrai | (ce n'est pas vrai) |
| t'as fini? | (tu as fini?) |
| j'suis désolé(e) | (je suis désolé(e)) |
| y'en de bons | (il y en a de bons) |
| je t'l'ai donné | (je te l'ai donné) |

| | |
|---|---|
| t'es fou! | (tu es fou!) |
| j'sais pas | (je ne sais pas) |
| qu'est-ce tu fais? | (qu'est-ce que tu fais?) |
| c'est pas moi | (ce n'est pas moi) |
| t'aurais dû... | (tu aurais dû...) |
| t'en as besoin? | (tu en as besoin?) |
| à vot'service! | (à votre service) |

Secondly, people will tend to hesitate, fill in the spaces with certain words (see page 214 in the Speaking section) and repeat themselves. In real life people also start off a sentence and never finish it because their train of thought changes. All this can be quite helpful to you, because it gives you time to think as well as to hear some of the information twice. Here is a typical example of these features transcribed from a message left by someone on a telephone answering machine:

> mardi soir Janine il est euh six heures bon ben salut c'est Michel je sais pas si tu rentres ce soir m'enfin j'aimerais bien que tu m'appelles euh demain dans la journée de toutes façons j'suis là toute la journée merci bien au revoir

9  The tapes which you will hear in the GCSE tests might seem a bit more coherent than the last example but they will still sound very much like real people talking so you need to get used to this type of thing. Don't forget that quite often you will be listening to announcements, short news items etc. which are scripted and therefore not likely to have hesitation and changing sentence patterns.

10  The cassette accompanying this course will give you a good chance to practise listening.

## TACKLING THE EXAMINATION ITSELF

1  Easier said than done, but try to keep calm! Doing a test from a tape recording is nerve racking but getting into a flap isn't going to help your performance. Even if you're sure in your mind that you've got something wrong or haven't given a full answer, there is no point in worrying about this as your concentration for the next item may well suffer.

2  Remember the question itself is bound to have important clues to help you understand the French. If a question has a number of items, it is most important to read them *all* before you listen to the tape. You need to have a clear idea of exactly what information you are listening for.

3  If, as should be the case, you're allowed to make notes on scrap paper, you may well find this helpful, especially if dates, times, prices etc. are involved. To save yourself valuable time, work out beforehand your own 'shorthand' of abbreviations for common words or even think of symbols. For example, 'to' could be → and 'from' could

# Listening comprehension

be ←– anything which will help you to write something down in note form quickly and clearly.

4   Most of the items will be played twice, so you have a chance to concentrate on the second time round on the points of information which you may have missed on the first occasion. As a general strategy, most people find it helpful to jot down notes on the first hearing so they can concentrate specifically on the parts of the tape which contain information required by the questions but not fully understood the first time round. The first hearing is always the difficult one but you should feel happier by the second one.

5   There may be words which you don't understand but that doesn't necessarily mean that you won't be able to answer the questions correctly. The word may not be crucial for a question on detailed understanding nor may it hinder your gist understanding if that is what is being tested. Even if the word in question is a vital one, you've already had examples of the way that human beings repeat themselves. The same item of information may come up again later in the recording but expressed in a different way – in words you may find easier to understand this time.

6   If you're *really* stuck, make a sensible guess at the answer. This will give you some chances of scoring positively, whereas a blank cannot gain any marks.

## USING CLUES TO UNDERSTANDING

Understanding a foreign language is in some ways like detective work. You need to think positively, using any information which you have as a possible clue which may help you to understand what seems unclear at first. It isn't just a case of **what** you know but rather **applying** what you know in a way which often can lead you to work out the meaning of a word or phrase.

## WHAT ARE THE POSSIBLE CLUES WHEN LISTENING?

1   The *context* or *setting* in its broadest sense: the layout of the questions you have to answer or the task you have to complete; any title which is given; the background noise on the tape; the number of speakers; the tone of voice or register; the length of the item. All these are potential clues to meaning before you even start to think about the actual words on the tape.

2   The *verbal context*: often you can work out the meaning of an unknown word, by educated guesswork, from other words in the sentence which you have understood. We often do this in our own language, so there is no reason why the same skill cannot be applied to the foreign language.

3   *Grammar* This will probably be of more help to you when *reading* a text, rather than when listening, because you have the time and the

facility to study the words on the printed page at length. Your grammatical knowledge can give you clues, however, when listening. You are certainly more likely to work out the meaning of an unfamiliar word if you are aware of its grammatical function. Is it a noun, a verb, an adverb or an adjective for example? As a comic example from English, the sentence, 'Giant waves down funnel' can have two different meanings depending on whether 'giant' is a noun or an adjective. You won't have to cope with ambiguous sentences like that in the examination but pinning down the grammatical function of an unknown word can help you towards understanding its possible meaning.

As a simple example, you could hear a word which is very familiar to you (**regardé**) but you're not aware in the first instance how it fits into the sentence. To get the exact meaning you have to do a bit of rapid analysis!

The **-é** ending on **regardé** is potentially misleading simply because it may not be **-é** that you are hearing but **-ez** or **-er** which all sound the same. The important thing here is to remember that language does not consist of a collection of totally isolated sounds. All the sounds are interlinked, so that the words depend on each other for their meaning. Your grammatical knowledge can help you to unravel the meaning.

If you think you've heard **regardé**, for example, you know that somewhere close to that word there should be part of the verb **avoir** such as **tu as regardé le match à la télé?** or **je l'ai regardé hier soir**. So the meaning here is 'watched'.

If there isn't any part of **avoir**, then perhaps what you heard was **regarder**, the infinitive **to watch**. Again, there will be grammatical markers or clues which will help you to make the decision on the meaning. This could be a verb which is followed by an infinitive (e.g. **aller: tu vas regarder le match;** or **vouloir: tu veux regarder le match?**) or a verbal phrase like **avoir l'intention de: moi, je n'ai pas l'intention de regarder le match.**

Or perhaps what you heard was **regardez**! In which case you would expect simply the word **vous** to precede as it would be the present tense of the verb: **vous regardez souvent la télé?**

What would be the meaning if you *thought* you had heard **Regardez**! all on its own without any pronoun like **vous** in front of it?

This may sound very complicated but these are the sorts of decision which you will make quite easily with practice in listening. Reading these examples here, in isolation, is much harder than dealing with a proper piece of listening when you have the whole context to support your understanding.

Don't forget that the grammatical clues with which you are familiar in your *own* language won't always coincide with the clues in French, especially when you are listening to the language. As a simple example, you are used to plural words in English ending in -s in most cases. If someone asks you to pass 'the glasses' you know that you have to hand over the two or three glasses on the table. In French you would hear **tu me passes les verres** with the word **verres** sounding identical to **verre**. In the two sentences **tu me passes le verre** and **tu me passes les verres** the only way in which you know you have to pass the glass or the glasses is through the grammatical markers **le** (singular) and **les** (plural).

It's also worth remembering that there are other marker words which can help your sort out verb tenses in particular. Some of them are listed on pages 229–30 in the section on letter writing.

**YOUR BACKGROUND KNOWLEDGE**

The time which you devote during your course to learning about life in French-speaking countries helps you in real life to prepare for a visit abroad but it is also valuable in the examination. If you didn't already know, for example, that it is quite normal to buy postage stamps in a tobacconist's in France, it could lead you to misunderstand something which you hear on one of the tape-recorded tests. Another example of an item of background knowledge which could reinforce your comprehension might be the late starting time for the last complete performance in a French cinema. You would expect to hear 9.30 p.m. in a French context whereas you wouldn't if someone were talking about a visit to a British cinema.

**WORD PATTERNS**

There can sometimes be useful clues to meanings which you will hear at the beginning and ending of words. Here are just a few examples. Why not make your own lists? Train yourself into noticing how words are divided up into different parts rather than treating them always as one single block.

**Beginnings**

(i) re- will normally contain the idea of 'again' (as it does in English in 're-paint', 're-allocate'). What will **refaire**, **retourner** and **recycler** mean?

(ii) pré- will often indicate 'fore-' or 'pre-'. What must the word **prénom** mean?

(iii) in- or im- will often correspond to English 'im-' as in 'impossible', un- as in 'unacceptable' or -less as in 'fruitless'. What might **insupportable** and **inutile** mean?

(iv) para- or par(e) will have the idea of 'against' or 'protection against'. What might the word **pare-chocs** be on a car?

**Endings**

(i) -er (masculine) or -ère (feminine) will often indicate the person occupying a job. What must **un douanier** be?

(ii) -ette has the idea of a small version of something. What might une **camionnette** be?

(iii) -aine is often found at the end of a number indicating 'approximately', 'around'. What must **une vingtaine** mean?
(iv) Don't forget that the *middles* of words can also give you clues because you can often spot a word within a word. If you see the word **congélateur** (freezer), you've got a clear clue to the meaning from *-gél-* if you think of **geler** (to freeze) or **le gel** (frost).

[**Answers** re-do/do again; return; recycle; first or forename; intolerable/unbearable; useless; bumper; customs officer; van/small truck; twenty or so]

**SOUND PATTERNS**

When listening to French it is not easy to apply any set of rules on sound patterns, since stress, intonation, liaison (as in **les oranges**), the telescoping of words (as in **t'as compris?**) and agreements (**une petite fille**) all alter what you hear according to the combination of the words in a sentence on a particular occasion in a way which doesn't happen when words are printed on the page.

When you are listening there will be words which are either identical or nearly identical in spelling to English words (but perhaps not identical in meaning!) but of one thing you can be quite certain – they will *not* sound like English. You only need to think of a simple word like 'train' to become aware of this. As you become more experienced in French it will become easier for you to work backwards from the sounds to the spelling, so that you can get a picture in your mind's eye of how the word might look in print. One way of developing this skill is to look at English words which you see printed in text books or magazines and say the word out loud to yourself with a French pronunciation.

Here are some examples of key differences in the sounds of the two languages. You should collect further examples to incorporate in lists of your own.

the nasal sounds (e.g. English bomb and French **bombe**)
'r' (e.g. English region and French **région**)
'qu' (e.g. English quit and French **quitter**)
'ch' (e.g. English charming and French **charmant**)
'-ion' (e.g. English hesitation and French **hésitation**)
'h' (e.g. English history and French **histoire**)

The important point is that whereas you would have no difficulty at all recognizing the words above when you saw them written down you might be 'thrown' by some of them when you heard them because of differences in pronunciation. Be on your guard against this.

# Listening comprehension

**MORE COMPLICATED WORD PATTERNS**

You can sometimes make a reasonable guess at the meaning of a French word if you try switching letters around in certain *patterns*. This is an extension of the idea of looking at the beginning and ending of words. A few examples are given in the table below. It takes a lot of practice to try this out when listening but it can be helpful when reading, when the text is in front of you.

See if you can spot other patterns of this nature as you read and make a collection of such similarities between the two languages, which mean that a lot of French words are only thinly disguised versions of words you know in English. It won't always work though!

|  |  | *Ending of French word* | *Ending of English word* |
|---|---|---|---|
| (nouns) |  | **-é** or **-ée** | -y |
| (adverbs) |  | **-ment** | -ly |
|  |  | **-ant** | -ing |
| (adject.) |  | **-aire** | -ar or -ary |
|  |  | **-eux** | -ous |
|  |  | **-f** | -ve |

*Beginning of French word* — *Beginning of English word*

**dé-** — dis-

*Middle of French word* — *Middle of English word*

**-ô-, -â-, -ê-** — -os-, -as-, -es-

**Activity**

What is the English for: **fraternité**; **magnifiquement**; **encourageant**; **imaginaire**; **scandaleux**; **massif**; **décourageant**; **hôtesse**?

[**Answers** fraternity; magnificently; encouraging; imaginary; scandalous; massive; discouraging; hostess]

You can see that there are ways of coping when you're faced with words you don't understand at first. Don't forget the most important piece of evidence though, which was highlighted at the beginning of this section – *context*. Unless you use context as a way of checking any guesswork, you could be misled in two possible ways:

1. By coming up against a **faux ami** (false friend), so called because it looks very familiar, having an identical or near identical spelling to an English word. However, its meaning can be quite different, as the examples below show. Whilst you need to be aware of **faux amis** (and again make your own collection of ones you come across), don't forget they are in the minority. The similarity between French and English words is helpful more often than not. In the following examples the similarity *does* mislead you, however.

| French word | English meaning |
|---|---|
| **assister à** | to be present at |
| **caméra** | cine camera |
| **cave** | cellar |
| **chance** | luck |
| **large** | wide |
| **librairie** | bookshop |
| **pétrole** | oil, paraffin |
| **photographe** | photographer |

2   By *mis-hearing* a French word, so that the spelling of it which you have in your mind's eye is the wrong one – in fact the spelling of another word which has a different meaning. For example, when you hear the word *rue* (street), what you think you have heard is *roue* (wheel). Here are some other words which can cause problems:

| **argent** | money | **agent** | policeman |
|---|---|---|---|
| **cousin** | cousin | **coussin** | cushion |
| **dans** | in | **dont** | of which, whose |
| **magasin** | shop | **magazine** | magazine |
| **vous** | you | **vu** | saw |

The *context* should really prevent you from getting words mixed up. In the few examples above the pairs of words are actually pronounced differently from each other. In French, as in English, there are also words which are pronounced the same, may or may not be spelt differently, and have different meanings! Two examples:

| **le livre** | book | **la livre** | £ sterling or lb |
|---|---|---|---|
| **prêt** | ready | **près** | near |

Now is your chance to think how you would apply some of the tips in this chapter to some sample examination questions. The ones that follow immediately are from the NEA, the first at basic level and the second at higher level. The scripts are printed, so to try out the questions you really need to get someone to record the words for you on cassette. Work through the questions then read through the commentaries when you've finished.

A   The recording you are about to hear involves the sort of situation you will find yourself in, if you visit France or look after a French-speaking visitor in England.

This is what you should do for each question:
1   Read the instruction and question in English.
2   Listen carefully to the French conversation.
3   Read the questions again.
4   Listen to the conversation again, to find the answers to the questions.
5   Answer the question IN ENGLISH.

**A young woman is about to leave a youth hostel where she has been staying.**

## Listening comprehension

The form below shows the sort of things the warden needs to know, to work out how much to charge. Complete the form, using only the information you learn from the conversation.

This is what you should do:
1. Read the form carefully.
2. Listen carefully to the conversation.
3. Read the form carefully again.
4. Listen again to the first part of the conversation.
5. Fill in 'Part A' of the form.
6. Listen again to the second part of the conversation, and fill in 'Part B' of the form.
7. Listen again to the third part of the conversation and fill in 'Part C' of the form.

**Part A**

*Number of nights:* ☐          *Dormitory number:* ☐

**Part B**                      **Part C**

                                TOTAL COST  ☐

*Facilities used*        (Tick if used)   *Payment made by:*
Hire of sleeping bag         ☐                                    cheque           ☐
Hire of sheets               ☐        (tick as appropriate)       credit card      ☐
Use of sports facilities     ☐                                    cash             ☐
Cooked meals taken in hostel ☐                                    paid in advance  ☐

[Script for A.

(*First part*)

© Female voice: *Bonjour, monsieur*
Male voice: *Bonjour mademoiselle. Vous partez aujourd'hui?*
Female voice: *Eh oui. Je peux payer maintenant?*
Male voice: *Oui, oui. Ça s'est bien passé votre séjour ici?*
Female voice: *Très bien.*
Male voice: *Alors, voyons. Dortoir 4. Ça fait trois nuits, n'est-ce pas?*
Female voice: *Oui, trois nuits.*

(*Second part*)

Male voice: *Avec sac de couchage?*
Female voice: *Pardon?*
Male voice: *Vous avez loué un sac de couchage, n'est-ce pas?*
Female voice: *Ah oui, c'est ça.*
Male voice: *Et vous n'avez pas pris de repas à la cantine?*
Female voice: *Non, j'ai mangé en ville.*
Male voice: *D'accord.*

# 176  French

*(Third part)*

Male voice: *... Je crois que c'est tout. Alors, ça fait 60F.*
Female voice: *Bon. Voilà 50 et 10 qui font 60.*
Male voice: *Merci bien. Et voilà votre passeport. Au revoir mademoiselle, et bon voyage!*
Female voice: *Au revoir, monsieur. Merci.*]

B  [Instructions as for A above.] Write neatly and put down all the information you are asked to give.

**While you are staying in an hotel in France, you get tooth-ache.** You go the hotel receptionist. You have the following questions in your mind, as you listen to what she has to say.

Tick in the appropriate box to show:
– how the receptionist answers the questions that are in your mind

or – that the information is not given.

|  | Yes | No | The receptionist is not sure | Information not given |
|---|---|---|---|---|
| (a) Is there a dentist's nearby? | ___ | ___ | ___ | ___ |
| (b) If so, is it open at this time of day? | ___ | ___ | ___ | ___ |
| (c) Do I need an appointment? | ___ | ___ | ___ | ___ |
| (d) Do I have to go there to make an appointment? | ___ | ___ | ___ | ___ |
| (e) Will it be very expensive? | ___ | ___ | ___ | ___ |
| (f) Will I have to pay on the spot? | ___ | ___ | ___ | ___ |

[Script for B.

© Female voice: *Un dentiste? Ah oui, il y a un dentiste pas très loin d'ici et ... je pense que c'est ouvert. Mais, en général, bien entendu, il faut avoir un rendez-vous. Euh, si vous voulez, je peux téléphoner et prendre un rendez-vous pour vous, monsieur. Mais attention, vous savez qu'en France, en général, il faut payer quand on va chez le dentiste, et ... ensuite vous pouvez vous faire rembourser par la Sécurité Sociale.*]

**Commentary: Script A**

Let's think first of all what *knowledge* you need to score well on this question. The key topic areas are accommodation and money, the latter amounting very much to numbers. Spend some time going over the questions and script and write down the key words which you needed to understand in order to get all the information down correctly. You'll be surprised at how few there are and at how many words there are in the conversation which you don't actually need to understand. Your *background knowledge* will also help you to confirm

# Listening comprehension

your understanding of the price. 60 francs is reasonable whereas 6, 16 or 600 would not be.

Think also how you needed to apply your listening *skills*. Before you heard the first part of the tape you knew you had two pieces of information to get, both of them numbers. If you don't get the dormitory number (4) first time around then you have to concentrate on that on the second listening. The number of nights (3) is mentioned by the man, then repeated by the woman so even on the first hearing you have two chances of picking that item up. For the second part of the tape you have to listen for four things to see if they are mentioned. You have to go further than that becasue you must tick whether or not the girl used any of the four facilities mentioned. This could be a good example of a *two-stage approach* – on the first hearing identify which of the four are mentioned and then concentrate just on those you have identified to see what is said about them. the man refers to 'sleeping bag'. (twice in fact, as the girl says **pardon**?) and the girl answers 'yes' to his question about having hired one. The man refers in the negative (**vous n'avez pas pris . . .**) to taking meals in the canteen. The girl confirms this in two ways – **non** and **j'ai mangé en ville**. In the third part you know you have to listen for a figure in francs and for signs of how the payment is being made. The figure is given to you in three forms, by the man (60F) and twice by the woman who is obviously counting out the money (**50 et 10 . . . qui font 60**) so you have plenty of confirmation. The word **voilà** as she hands it over also makes it clear that she is paying cash there and then. Why couldn't it possibly be 'paid in advance'?

**Commentary: Script B**

Firstly, let's think about *knowledge* required. The *topic areas* which are likely to give you the vocabulary fo this one are health/welfare, money and social relations (arranging meetings). You also need to understand '(not) far away' which will have come in under travel or geographical surroundings. This is a good example of how any one question can ask you to call upon vocabulary from five or six topics. Write down a list of the key words which you *must* understand in order to put down all the information correctly. Your *background knowledge* about medical and dental services in France is again of great help here as it confirms what you hear, namely that you pay for treatment first and claim back later. What do you notice about the amount of repetition of information in this script compared with Script A? Why should there be a difference in the amount perhaps? In what ways does the style of the language seem different from the script for the basic level question? Notice the *pauses* and the *hesitations* as well as the *gap-fillers* which you read about in this chapter and the chapter on Speaking (see page 214).

When we come to think about listening *skills* required, this question is harder. We have six pieces of information each of which has to be classified as a clear yes/no, an 'unsure' or a 'not mentioned'. The technique of picking out the items you're more confident about the first time around then homing in on ones you're doubtful about the second time comes into its own here. For (*a*) the hotel receptionist is quite definite (**Ah oui . . . il y a un dentiste pas très loin d'ici**) and at the end she says in two ways that you have to pay on the spot (**il faut payer quand on va . . .** and **ensuite vous pouvez vous faire rembourser . . .**) so you might pick those up on the first hearing. For (*b*) she says **je pense que c'est ouvert** so she's not absolutely sure. She seems more confident that you need an appointment (**en général . . . bien entendu**) and offers to make one for you. Although she warns you about paying on the spot, she doesn't actually say that it will be expensive, so you need to tick the 'information not given' box for f). Even if you think (or know) that dental treatment in France is expensive you must only answer the question from the information which is actually on the tape. In other words, your background knowledge should back up and confirm what you hear. It doesn't *replace* what you hear.

Finally, two questions of a different format to look at, both taken from the York Level 5 examination paper in 1985 which was very much on the lines of GCSE, conducted by the JMB and the YHREB. Both questions were at higher level. Write down for yourself *how* you would tackle each one, using any of the techniques you remember from this chapter. In other words, try to construct a commentary for yourself along the lines of the ones provided for the first two questions above. What do you notice about the speech patterns in the second script, by the way?

A   Listen to these people talking and choose from List 1 below the phrase that best describes what they are doing. In each case, write only the letter (e.g. **A**, **B**, **C** etc.) of the phrase you choose.

Find out as well what the person is talking about. Choose from List 2 below and in each case, write in the second box provided the letter of your choice (e.g. **R**, **S**, **T** etc.)

# Listening comprehension

**LIST 1**
**What the person is doing**

A  Asking for information
B  Complaining
C  Congratulating
D  Correcting
E  Asking permission
F  Apologising
G  Showing pleasure

**LIST 2**
**Topics**

P  A train arriving late
Q  A birthday party
R  Booking a tennis court
S  Passing a driving test
T  A trip to the country
V  Bumping into someone
W  Leaving work early
X  Working conditions
Y  How to get somewhere
Z  Playing in a match

a  A man talks to someone in the Metro.
   He is ☐
   He is talking about ☐

b  A woman is talking to her boss at work.
   She is ☐
   She is talking about ☐

c  A man talks to someone in the street.
   He is ☐
   He is talking about ☐

d  A man is talking to his boss in the office.
   He is ☐
   He is talking about ☐

e  A man is talking to a friend at home.
   He is ☐
   He is talking about ☐

f  A man is talking to a friend at the sports centre.
   He is ☐
   He is talking about ☐

[Script for A:

© (a) *Oh, je vous demande pardon. Je ne vous avais pas vu. Je suis vraiment désolé.*

(b) *Bonjour, monsieur, excusez-moi de vous déranger. Je voulais vous demander une autorisation. Euh, pourrais-je partir tout à l'heure deux heures plus tôt que d'habitude du bureau? J'ai effroyablement mal aux dents et le dentiste ne peut pas me recevoir plus tard que cinq heures.*

(c) *Pardon, monsieur. Pourriez-vous m'indiquer la route pour Quimper, s'il vous plaît?*

(d) *Monsieur le Directeur, je ne peux pas continuer à travailler dans ce bureau. Le chauffage ne marche pas, la fenêtre ferme mal, c'est insupportable.*

(e) *Ah c'était merveilleux. Cette nature, sous le soleil, tous ces gens joyeux, je me suis amusé et j'ai trouvé ça merveilleux.*

(f) *Bravo, Michel. Tu as très bien joué, c'était formidable.*]

**B** Look at the headlines (shown opposite) from the front page of a French newspaper and listen to these French people talking about one of the articles.

Write down which article they are talking about. (Put the letter only.)

*Answer:* _____

[Script for B:

ⓒ Male voice: *Ben, moi je suis tout à fait d'accord. Je trouve qu'il était temps que quelqu'un fasse quelque chose parce que c'est, la situation commençait à devenir, euh, intenable. Euh, on s'ennuie à longueur de journée. Les émissions sont tout le temps les mêmes, 'y a pas de, de variété. Moi, je trouve que, euh, ils ont tout à fait raison.*
Female voice: *Ah, je sais pas, je crois quand même, tu es un petit peu sévère, hein. Ça a toujours été à peu près comme ça, ça dépend des chaînes aussi, je crois.*
Male voice: *mais enfin, 'y a trois chaînes et on, on peut pratiquement jamais trouver un programme intéressant. Moi, il m'arrive des soirs où je suis là, assis à la maison en train de boire un verre, et, euh, j'veux regarder une émission euh intéressante, euh, c'est impossible . . .*]

**A** Sabotage ? Renault porte plainte

**B** Marie, la seule Française qui torée à cheval

**C** 120 millions pour sauver des sables le Mont-Saint-Michel

**D** TOUT DOIT CHANGER A LA TELE

**E** Foire de Paris : un château de 500 pièces

**F** Et toujours du soleil

CHAPTER THREE

# READING COMPREHENSION

**CONTENTS**

- What the National Criteria says is expected of candidates in the reading comprehension tests — 185

- What the National Criteria say about methods of testing — 185

- What to bear in mind as you prepare for the examination — 185

- Typical reading activities — 186

- What are the different types of reading skill? — 187

- Tackling the examination itself — 188

# Reading comprehension

## WHAT THE NATIONAL CRITERIA SAY IS EXPECTED OF CANDIDATES IN THE READING COMPREHENSION TESTS

An understanding, from a restricted range of clearly defined topics, of public notices and signs (e.g. menus, timetables).

An ability to extract specific information from texts such as simple brochures, guides, letters and forms of imaginative writing appropriate for a sixteen year old.

In general to show understanding, not to write summaries of texts. In addition, at *higher* level:

1. to show the same skills but over a wider range of topics;
2. to show understanding of a wider range of texts, e.g. magazines and newspapers appropriate for a sixteen year old;
3. to show the ability to identify important points or themes in a text;
4. to draw conclusions from a text;
5. to show they understand the connection between different parts or ideas in a text.

## WHAT THE NATIONAL CRITERIA SAY ABOUT METHODS OF TESTING

1. Assessment of reading comprehension can best be carried out by means of questions set *in English* to be answered in the candidates' own words *in English*.
2. Multiple-choice tests, preferably with questions in English, are acceptable as long as they are not the only method of testing this skill area.

## WHAT TO BEAR IN MIND AS YOU PREPARE FOR THE EXAMINATION

1. The importance of *practice* in reading *different types* of material in *different ways* (see below) cannot be stressed enough.
2. Vocabulary revision will be crucial since the texts used in the tests will have words which feature on the lists provided by the Examination Associations. There may be a limited number of words which will not be on the lists but it will be possible to answer all the questions and score full marks as long as you know the prescribed words.
3. A great deal of the advice which is offered in the chapter of *Listening Comprehension* is also helpful as far as reading is concerned. It would be useful to go through that section again if you have not already done so. Ask yourself which of the hints in particular apply to reading.

4    Reading French is a skill which you develop over a number of years. Often in school or college there is insufficient time in lessons to read in French but this is something which you can do on your own at home. Ask your teacher or tutor for advice about suitable materials. The first paragraphs of this chapter give some ideas on what to read and by the end of the chapter you should have further examples which can be supplemented by those in the chapter on *Revising Vocabulary*.

5    Anything you can find to read in French which is *enjoyable* (e.g. connected with one of your interests or hobbies) will be very good practice. Don't forget the real life emphasis of GCSE. What you need is reading material designed to be read by French people in everyday life.

6    Reading *handwritten* letters in French is likely to be one of the skills tested somewhere on the reading papers, as well as featuring in the writing tests where you will read a letter and respond to it. It is particularly important that you practise this since it is quite different from reading a typewritten letter. If you have friends who have pen pals in France or a French-speaking country, why not swap letters if they're not too intimate? You could even do your own analysis of the differences in the formation of the letters between French and British handwriting. It's hard to generalize as styles are individual but there are some key differences with which you need to become familiar if you are not to panic when you see real French handwriting in the examination.

### TYPICAL READING ACTIVITIES

**1 Understanding public signs, notices, labels etc.** which you might come across on a visit to a French-speaking country. Multiple-choice questions (choose the best answer from A, B, C or D) set on this type of reading material should only occur where you would have a choice in real life, for example 2- or 4-star petrol; a drinks dispenser; a menu; different windows at a post office.

**2 Extracting key points or items of information.** For example you would read a letter and then jot down the key points you would wish to relay to someone who can't understand French. or you might be asked to read a page from a TV guide and then be asked to write down what time you would want to watch that evening, if you were interested in soap operas.

**3 Identifying important points** from a longer piece of writing. For example you might be given a newspaper headline and short article and then be asked to write a few sentences which explain the main theme. Or you might have in front of you the results of a survey (e.g. on holidays) and have to explain the five questions which were asked and write down what was the most popular reply to each. On

# Reading comprehension

occasions you might be given two newspaper articles which cover the same incident (e.g. an outbreak of football hooliganism) and then have to write down the differences you can spot between the two accounts.

You can see from these examples that question types become increasingly harder. You would therefore expect to meet more of the first and second types in basic level examination papers and more of the third type in higher level papers.

## WHAT ARE THE DIFFERENT TYPES OF READING SKILL?

The examination will test *different* types of reading skill because in real life we read in different ways for different purposes.

1. We sometimes *skim* through a page of a newspaper. Here we certainly don't attempt to understand the *detail* of any article but we try to gain an *overall impression*, perhaps to see if the article is of any interest before taking the trouble to read more closely. We're not looking for any particular items of information.
2. We also *scan* through print when we're looking for something quite *specific*. When we scan we generally know what we're looking for. An example of this might be looking for a particular heading in a table of contents in a book, or looking for the title of a television programme in the list of the evening's programmes to see what time it begins.
3. We may also *search* through a page of a book or a page of a newspaper, looking for a particular piece of information. This is slightly different from scanning because when we search we may not know exactly what form the information will be in. When we scan we are generally looking for one key word or group of words.
4. We also read for *overall comprehension*. For example when we read through a letter from someone we want to make sense of what is being conveyed to us. Sometimes we may read something in very fine detail when reading for overall comprehension, especially if it is something like a set of instructions for a new electrical appliance or a legal document.

**Activity**

Make a list of all the things which you, your friends or your relatives might read during the course of a week (e.g. comics, magazines, TV Times, newspaper, bus timetable, mail-order catalogue, new insurance policy). Which of the four types of reading skill might you use in reading the different types of text? It's quite likely that you would use more than one type while reading any one particular thing.

If you're asking what has this got to do with French, the answer is straightforward. You need to be aware of these *different* types of reading skill so that you can make sure you practise as many of them as possible in French, rather than concentrating on one particular type. All four types are likely to be tested in the examination, although there will be more emphasis on scanning perhaps in the basic tests.

## TACKLING THE EXAMINATION ITSELF

As always, spend time *reading instructions* carefully. You will not score extra credit for doing *more* than the question asks. If you do not attempt to do the thing which are required then you will miss chances to gain marks.

You may feel that you do not have very much to do in the tests since the amount of writing will probably be limited. Often you will only have short answers to write in English or you may be ticking a box or completing a table. Do not be misled into thinking that this gives you plenty of time. In fact you need all the time you are allowed in order to *read* the questions and the texts really thoroughly several times, *think* about answers and then to mark them in *carefully*.

Don't forget to bear in mind your overall timing across the paper. Generally the number of marks per question will be indicated, so this gives you a good idea of what *proportion* of time to allocate to each question or section. Doing well on just a few parts won't really help. You have to make sure you are giving yourself a chance to pick up the marks which are going for each of the questions or sections.

Some people find that they work best on the lines recommended for tackling listening tests. Read all the questions on the text, then the whole of the text itself. Re-read the questions then go through the text again concentrating on the relevant parts necessary for answering. In other words, *read with a purpose*. This technique really does come into its own on longer texts but you need to take care on short items too.

Don't forget the idea of clues to meaning. When you are listening background noises can be clues. When you are reading there can be helpful clues in the *type-face, layout, illustrations and title*. Don't forget that there can be important clues in the *questions* too.

Don't panic if there are words you've forgotten or think you haven't seen before. The tips for coping with this were given in the chapter on *Listening Comprehension*. They are much easier to apply when reading, simply because you can go back over a printed text several times in a way that is impossible with a tape-recorded listening item in an examination.

Now is your chance to apply some of the tips to some sample questions produced by the Examination Associations. Try each question yourself, then go through the commentaries provided.

## Reading comprehension

**A** Here is a school timetable. Answer the questions which follow.

**Lycée: Louis Philippe**  **Nom: Leblanc Pierre**

|  | **Lundi** | **Mardi** | **Mercredi** | **Jeudi** | **Vendredi** | **Samedi** |
|---|---|---|---|---|---|---|
| **0815** | Français | Math. | CONGÉ | Dessin | Travaux Manuels | Math. |
| **0915** | Math. | Géographie |  | Géographie | Anglais | Français |
|  |  |  | RÉCRÉATION |  |  |  |
| **1030** | Anglais | Travaux Manuels | CONGÉ | Français | Math. | Sciences Naturelles |
| **1130** | Histoire | Latin |  | Musique | Latin | Travaux Dirigés |
|  |  |  | DÉJEUNER |  |  |  |
| **1400** | Sciences Naturelles | Dessin | CONGÉ | Espagnol | Espagnol | – |
| **1500** | Éducation Physique | Français |  | Math. | Éducation Physique | – |
| **1600** | Instruction Civique | Anglais |  | – | Histoire | – |

(a) What is the name of the school? *(1 mark)*
(b) Name one language other than French and Latin which is studied. *(1 mark)*
(c) On which school day is there no French lesson *(1 mark)*

*Source: SEG Basic Question 9*

# French

B  **Exercise 2: Questions 16–22**

**Camping**

You are touring France with a friend by car and you decide to stop for a night at the 'Camping du Puits d'Enfer'. You arrive at half-past seven in the evening (19.30 h).

Look at the following questions and answer them in English by referring to the camp site notice below.

---

**CAMPING DU PUITS D'ENFER**

85100 – LE CHÂTEAU – D'OLONNE

Tél: (51) 32-73-19

Terrain Classé * NN – 500 emplacements *

| | |
|---|---|
| OUVERT: | du 1er JUIN au 30 SEPTEMBRE |
| | Aucune réservation n'est possible. |
| TARIFS: | *Redevances journalières:* |
| | Adulte............................. 5,00 F |
| | Enfant de moins de 7 ans.... 3,00 F |
| | Emplacement pour la tente  2,50 F |
| | Véhicule......................... 2,00 F |
| | Le tarif journalier est calculé pour une période de 24 heures, **de midi à midi.** |
| BUREAU: | ouvert de 8 à 20 heures |
| COMMERCES: | Épicerie libre-service: ouverte de 8 à 13 h. et de 17 à 19 h. |
| | Boissons, Glaces, Alimentation, Bouteilles de gaz . . . |
| | Plats cuisinés (froids et chauds) servis à la réception jusqu'à 20 h 30. |
| COURRIER: | Le facteur passe tous les matins à 10 h. |
| TRANSPORT: | Un autocar pour Château d'Olonne passe toutes les heures, sur l'heure. |

---

16  How much must you pay a night for
   (a) pitching your tent?           ........... F
   (b) yourself and your friend?     ........... F
   (c) your car?                     ........... F

## Reading comprehension

17  By eight o'clock (20.00 h) you are very hungry but you haven't any cooking gas left. Where are hot dishes available on the site? _____

18  You want to make an early start the next morning to visit Château d'Olonne. When will you be able to buy some fresh bread for breakfast? _____

19  You are finishing your breakfast at 8.30 a.m. and decide to go by bus to Château d'Olonne. When can you catch a bus? _____

20  You post a card to your mother that evening. When will the postman collect it from the letter box? _____

21  What will you have to do if you stay until after midday the following day? _____

22  You want to return to the Puits d'Enfer next year. During which period is the camp site open? _____

[9]

*Source: MEG Basic Section 2, Extended 2, Questions 16–22*

C  You are going to visit a friend who lives in Paris. He sends you the map and instructions for finding his flat (below).

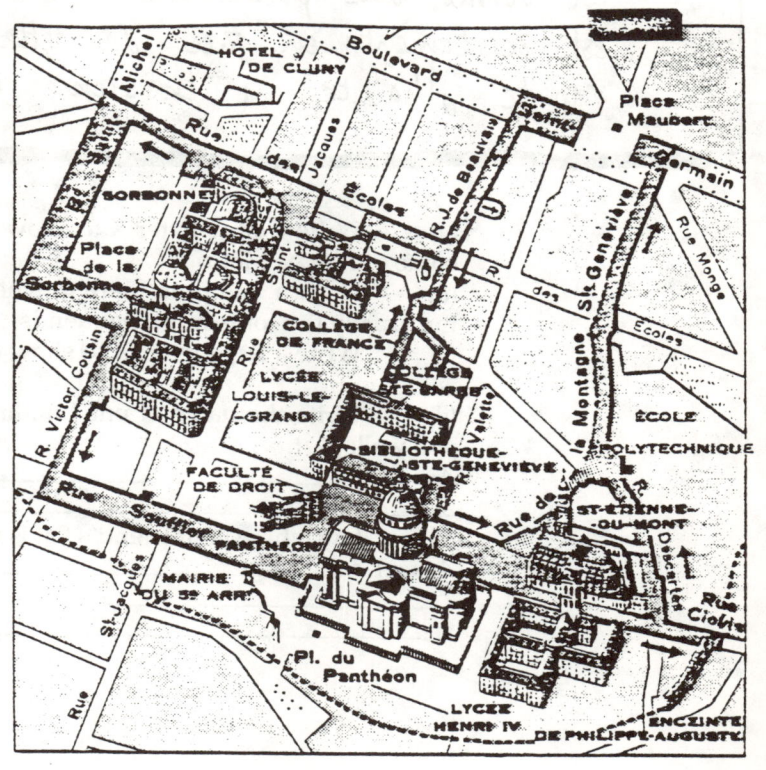

# French

> Voici les explications nécessaires pour trouver ma maison.
>
> Prends le métro et descends à la place Maubert. La sortie de métro est sur le boulevard Saint-Germain. Traverse le boulevard et prends la rue de la Montagne Ste. Geneviève. Tu continues tout droit et tu arrives devant un grand monument. Tourne à droite et fais le tour du monument. Tu arriveras dans la rue Soufflot. Descends la rue Soufflot et prends la première rue à gauche. C'est la rue où j'habite. Marche tout droit et au bout d'environ cent mètres, tu verras une petite rue à droite. Mon immeuble est exactement en face de cette petite rue. Monte, j'habite au troisième étage.

(a) Write a large letter X to show on the map where you should come out of the Métro.

(b) Draw a line from there to where your friend's flat is, following **exactly** the route he recommends.

(c) Write a large letter X to show exactly where your friend's flat is.

(d) Write the name of one building named in the map that you will walk past.
Answer: _____

(e) Say where your friend's flat is in the building.
Answer: _____

Source: NEA Higher Question 2

## Reading comprehension

**D    Exercise 2: Questions 6–10**

Read the passage below and then answer questions 6 to 10.
For each question, tick one of the boxes to show the correct answer.

Cette année encore vous serez très nombreux à partir à la «chasse à la chambre en ville» avant le début des cours.

Vous rêvez d'une chambre tout confort avec coin bibliothèque pour ranger vos livres et vous vous retrouvez devant une pièce obscure, meublée très simplement et avec une vue panoramique sur . . . les W.C. (extérieurs bien sûr).

«Inutile de commencer à faire la tournée de tous les gardiens d'immeuble de Paris trop tôt, j'ai bien le temps» vous dites-vous. Début septembre ça peut encore marcher, mais si vous pratiquez ce sport-là fin septembre vous risquez de ne rien trouver.

Vous pouvez toujours mettre des petits messages chez les commerçants ou dans les supermarchés du coin, mais ce n'est pas toujours très efficace.

Restent les petites annonces des journaux. Mais alors là prenez garde aux propositions séduisantes telles que: «à cinq minutes du métro». Cinq minutes comment? A pied? En vélo? En bus? Vérifiez vous-même la géographie de votre future hutte.

Méfiance aussi envers les subtilités des «possibilités» en tout genre. Avec «possibilité douche» ne rêvez pas trop. Un grand bac et un tuyau d'eau peuvent être une possibilité! De même avec «possibilité cuisine». Ça ne veut peut-être pas dire coin-cuisine équipée mais plus simplement un petit meuble pour mettre votre camping-gaz et un clou pour accrocher votre casserole.

Tout cela, non pour vous décourager mais, au contraire, pour vous aider à affronter les annonces des agences ou des particuliers. En conclusion, faites attention, mais ne vous montrez quand même pas trop difficile, sinon la chambre risque de vous passer sous le nez!

**Questions 6–10**

6   The article is intended to help you to
    ☐    choose your reading material.
    ☐    organise your lodging.
    ☐    use your time sensibly.
    ☐    get around Paris.

7   In which paragraph does the author suggest an idea which might have little success?
    ☐    paragraph 4 (Vous pouvez . . .)
    ☐    paragraph 5 (Restent les petites announces . . .)
    ☐    paragraph 6 (Méfiance aussi . . .
    ☐    paragraph 7 (Tout cela, non pour . . .)

8   The author thinks that advertisements in newspapers are often
    ☐    difficult to understand.
    ☐    totally dishonest.
    ☐    misleading.
    ☐    impartial.

9   Which of the following is most likely to help you find what you need?
    ☐   a precise idea of what you want.
    ☐   plenty of energy.
    ☐   ability to assess potential for development.
    ☐   willingness to accept something less than the ideal.

10  The author's style of writing may be described as
    ☐   amusing but unhelpful.
    ☐   casual and friendly.
    ☐   official and formal.
    ☐   off-hand and superior.

*Source: MEG Higher Question 2*

**Commentary: test A**
The *knowledge* you require for this question is centred very much on the topic of school, in particular the names of subjects. You also need the names of the days of the week, although common sense and the lay-out of the timetable should enable you to work them out even if your memory suffered a complete relapse! Your *cultural knowledge* prepares you for the idea of Saturday being on the timetable. You'll also be aware enough culturally to remember that on this French timetable 'English' is a foreign language just as much as Spanish.

*Scanning skills* are required – you have to *search* for the school name, for a language other than French or Latin as well as scanning each of the days to identify the one without French on the timetable. One small instance worth noting of the dangers of scanning too quickly without thinking – you can make a wrong connection between two words or ideas. In question (*a*) you're looking for 'name of school' but be careful you don't head straight for **nom** at the top right. The name you have there is that of the pupil. The school's name is the Lycée Louis Philippe. Not something you're likely to get wrong (because your cultural knowledge tells you that schools generally get named after historical figures like Louis Philippe rather than being called the French equivalent of White, Peter!) but it illustrates the possibility of pitfalls.

Here are the *answers:* (*a*) Louis Philippe (*b*) English or Spanish (*c*) Friday.

**Commentary: text B**
Looking back on this question, what *knowledge* is required? The main *topic area* for vocabulary is accommodation, but others come in as well – money, shops, food, even transport. When you reach the end of the commentary and have checked your answers, make a list of all the words you needed to understand to score full marks. It won't be as long a list as you think given the total number of words in the text. Numbers, dates and the 24-hour clock are also required knowledge, and an understanding of **tout** is another useful piece of grammar.

What reading skills are involved? What should be happening is that the questions send you *scanning* for the information. Question 16 directs you to the price list, but then you need to go back carefully to the question so that you know *exactly* what to look for. You then read off the price for two adults, the price for the tent pitch and the price for a vehicle. Similarly question 17 should set you looking for a reference to hot food; question 19 sets you looking for Château d'Olonne. In some cases you will not be sure of the exact word or words to look for. In question 18 you are looking for a connection with bread and the opening time of a shop. You might hope to find **boulangerie** but in fact the information you need is under **épicerie** as the camp has a grocer's shop open at 8.00 a.m.

Did you apply the important tip about reading the instructions *carefully*? Notice that it tells you that you arrive at 7.30 p.m. This doesn't really affect the questions but it clears up any uncertainty you might have about the price as the daily rate is from noon to noon the following day.

Did you use some of the techniques for working out the meaning of words? If you'd forgotten **emplacement**, did you look for **place** (space;room) in the middle of the word? **Redevances** (rate – and also TV licence!) is quite hard but it is connected with **devoir**, to owe. **Journalières** must be connected with **jour**, so that the whole phrase means 'daily rates'. The big heading in the left hand column, TARIFS confirms this. You still have to work out **le tarif journalier est calculé** . . ., but a reasonable guess could lead you to the English 'calculate'. The **-é** ending on a verb is generally a past participle ending in -ed or -t in English so then you have 'the daily rate is calculated . . .'. Similarly **cuisiné** gives you 'cooked' in the references to dishes available at reception.

Notice that TARIFS is not the only word there which looks very much like an English word which has an identical or near identical meaning. What are the others? Make a list.

Here are the *answers*: Qn 16 2,50, 10,00, 2,00; Qn 17 at reception; Qn 18 8.00 a.m.; Qn 19 9.00 a.m.; Qn 20 10.00 a.m.; Qn 21 pay for another day; Qn 22 1st June – 30th September.

**Commentary: text C**

Note the *French handwriting*. What problems did this cause you if any? This style is fairly clear compared to some you may have seen in letters from French pen-friends!

The key *knowledge* here is the topic of travel (understanding directions) with some vocabulary from geographical surroundings and house/home. Make a list of the words which you *must* be able to understand to get the questions right by going through the text and questions again when you have checked your answers against the ones in the book.

This is a good example of a real-life task. If you were in this situation and had to find this person's flat, *how* would you read the letter? Would it be *skimming* to get the *gist* of the main argument (as in the fourth question you tried out on student accommodation)? Or would you want to understand every detail? If so, why?

The map is of great help because it enables you to check your understanding of the letter. Where the letter says you come right up to a large building, you are able to confirm this on the map thanks to the drawing of the Panthéon. When you come out of the métro you get your bearings because the letter gets you searching for the Boulevard Saint-Germain on the map so you can begin tracing your route.

Notice as usual that you musn't be too hasty in your reading. Question (a) asks you to show where you should come out of the métro. If you read the letter too hurriedly and pick up . . . *descends à la place Maubert* you might put your X somewhere on the square itself rather than on the Boulevard Saint-Germain, which, as the letter goes on to say, is actually where you emerge from the métro station (**La sortie de métro est sur . . .**).

Here are the answers: For (a), (b) and (c) see the amended map below.

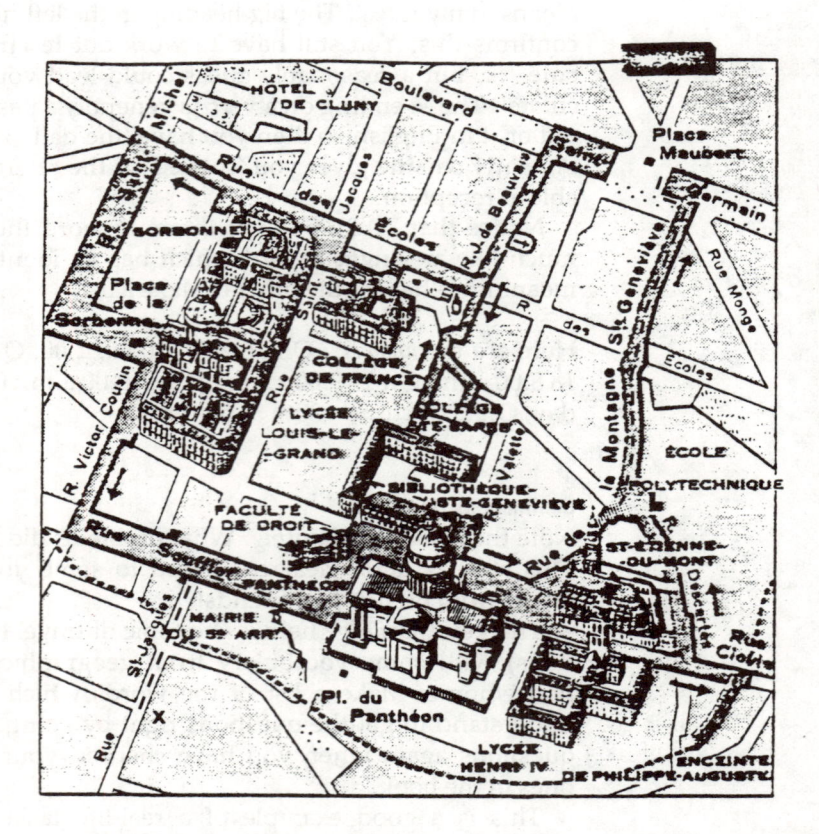

(d) Ecole Polytechnique, St Etienne du Mont, Panthéon, Faculté de Droit, Mairie.

### Reading comprehension

**Commentary: text D**

Let's start with *knowledge*. The two key *vocabulary areas* here are accommodation and house/home but there are many words which come in from other areas.

The text deals with *ideas and attitudes*, not so much with facts and figures as in the two basic level questions. A wider range of reading skills is involved. You will certainly be *skimming* as two of the questions (6 and 10) are asking you to make a *judgement* about the text as a whole rather than directing you to specific lines or specific paragraphs. Question 7 asks you to make a decision about particular paragraphs. Question 8 should lead you to *scan* the text to pick up the reference to newspaper adverts in paragraph 5.

It is quite important in this text to identify the *shape and flow* of the *argument*. Certain phrases identify *key* ideas, e.g. **Tout cela...** (all this) which signals that the author is going to sum up what he's said and **En conclusion...** which gives the closing idea which holds the answer to question 9.

Notice how the author sets up one idea and then follows it with 'but...' ('**Début septembre ça peut encore marcher, mais si vous pratiquez ce sport-là fin septembre vous risquez de ne rien trouver.**') and a contrasting idea. (Can you find another sentence on a similar pattern?) **Début** contrasts with **fin** and 'it may still work' contrasts with 'you've a good chance of finding nothing'. In the last but one sentence in the last paragraph **non pour vous décourager** contrasts with **au contraire pour vous aider....** This particular sentence should help you to decide that the style is helpful. There are other clues that it is informal and casual rather than being official and formal. What are those clues, do you think?

Did you use some of your *decoding skills* on words that may not be in prescribed vocabulary lists? If you didn't know **chasse à la chambre ...** (hunt for rooms/accommodation) did you think of the verb **chasser**, to chase or hunt? Did you work out **propositions** from the English word or from **proposer**, to suggest? Did the **-é(e)** ending on **équipée** give you the clue to an English past participle in -ed or -t – equipped? Did you make the guess from **subtilités** to 'subtleties'? (-é ending on a noun giving a -y ending in English).

Notice some of the *dangers*, too. The reference to a library corner (**coin bibliothèque**) in paragraph 2 might mislead you into choosing the first option in question 6. Equally the references to transport in paragraph 5 (**A pied? En vélo** ...) might mislead you into choosing the fourth option in question 6 unless you've got the gist of the whole article (which is all about organizing your lodging) not just odd sentences or paragraphs.

Here are the answers: Qn 6 Organize your lodging; Qn 7 Paragraph 4; Qn 8 Misleading; Qn 9 Willingness to accept something less than the ideal; Qn 10 Casual and friendly.

CHAPTER FOUR

# SPEAKING

## CONTENTS

- What the National Criteria say is expected of candidates in the speaking tests — 201

- What to bear in mind as you prepare for the examination — 201

- Typical speaking activities — 202

- Differentiation in the oral tasks — 204
  Basic   204
  Higher grades   204

- What are the implications of differentiation? — 205

- Tackling the examination itself — 206
  Role play   206

- Questions on a visual stimulus — 208

- General conversation — 210

- Role-play tasks involving narrative — 211

- Why do people find the oral test so daunting? — 212

- How will you be assessed? — 214

# Speaking

## WHAT THE NATIONAL CRITERIA SAY IS EXPECTED OF CANDIDATES IN THE SPEAKING TESTS

The answering of unprepared questions on a restricted range of clearly defined topic areas.

An ability to perform role-playing tasks which involve asking as well as answering questions in formal and informal settings (i.e. talking to strangers and friends).

A facility to pronounce French sounds well enough for a sympathetic native speaker to understand.

In addition, at **higher** level:

1. to show the same skills over a wider range of clearly defined topic areas;
2. to take part in a longer unrehearsed conversation on one or more of the subjects on the syllabus;
3. to pronounce French sounds accurately enough for a native speaker to understand without difficulty;
4. to come much closer to the way a French person would speak as far as stress and intonation are concerned.

## WHAT TO BEAR IN MIND AS YOU PREPARE FOR THE EXAMINATION

1. You are going to be questioned on **more** topics if you try the higher test. That is why it will last longer. Remember that there is actually only one oral examination paper. The higher test is really an extended version of the basic test. As a very rough guide, you could be with the examiner for about ten minutes for the basic test plus a further seven minutes if you are taking the higher test, making seventeen minutes in all.

2. The *basic* test doesn't include a full conversation as such, although you are bound to be asked about you and your family, including what you do and what you've done. In the *higher* test the conversation will be much more wide ranging, bringing in any of the topics on the syllabus. When you've given an answer you may well be asked to give your *reason* for a particular opinion. You could well be asked about what you used to do or what you *would* do in a particular situation. The role-play tasks in the higher test will also be more complex and more demanding.

3. In the basic test your French accent certainly doesn't have to be perfect as long as your message gets through to the examiner. Nor

does it have to be perfect for the higher test but it is expected that it will be much closer to the way a French person speaks.

4. Perhaps more than in the case of the other three skills, it is a fact that oral fluency has to be developed over a long period of time. It is not something which is turned on and off like a tap or which you can improve drastically at the last minute, however many hours in the day you might be prepared to revise. Nonetheless there are two things which you ought to bear in mind which might be helpful.

5. Firstly, speaking is not a skill isolated from the others. If you feel you are making good progress in reading, listening and perhaps writing there will be definite spin-offs for your speaking. The more opportunities you create for yourself for *reading and listening to real French*, the better. Even if you find the things which you listen to very difficult at first, you are probably sub-consciously absorbing some of the sounds and the intonation which will help your own French.

6. Secondly, you may be lucky enough to have a contact with a French-speaking person in the form of a language assistant if you are at a school or college. If not, do any of your friends or neighbours have any contact with someone who speaks French? Alternatively you have to fall back on your own resources and practise your French with a friend, especially in the role-play type exercises, which you can easily make up for yourselves.

7. Make sure that you are quite clear about the exact requirements for the particular examination papers which you will be taking. What are the *topics* (e.g. family, home, school), the *settings* (e.g. town, countryside, seaside) and the *language tasks* (e.g. giving information about yourself, finding the way, buying tickets) which the syllabus states will be tested? You should find that the syllabus corresponds very largely with what is in this book, but there may be some differences.

8. Careful revision should then give you a great deal of confidence. There are no 'catch' questions. If you have done your 'homework' thoroughly, there should be no unpleasant surprises for you. If you try to follow the advice in the section of this book on *Revising Vocabulary* (see page 21) you will have prepared *something* to say on each of the items on the check lists. You can be certain of one thing. If you are unable to say anything on a particular topic before the examination, when you are revising in a relaxed way at home, it is most unlikely you will think of something on the day itself if the examiner asks you. You can assume it will definitely not be 'all right on the night'!

## TYPICAL SPEAKING ACTIVITIES

**1 Role-play,** where for example, the examiner takes the role of the enquiry desk clerk at a railway station and you take the role of a holidaymaker who needs to find out the time of a particular train. You study a card to prepare this before you go into the examination room.

# Speaking

**2 Short, unprepared questions** on a stimulus (e.g. picture, photograph, diagram). For example, the examiner points at the drawing and asks, 'What has the man just done?' Generally, you don't see the visual stimulus before you go into the examination room.

**3 Conversation,** which is meant to be genuine and unrehearsed. You will not know in advance the exact questions you will be asked, but since the topics are very clearly defined in the syllabus it is not difficult for you to work out well beforehand in detail what sort of things you will be asked to talk about.

**4 'Narrative' role-play.** In this activity you may be given some information, in the form of a picture, a diagram or notes in English, about an incident or series of events such as a journey. You have time to prepare this before you go into the examination room. Then you are asked to imagine that you witnessed the incident or that you took part in the series of events. The examiner asks you in French what happened and you explain in French. The examiner may interrupt you to ask you to give a further detail or indeed may wish to help you by asking a question to remind you of something.

You can expect the first three types of activity at both basic and higher level at an appropriate level of difficulty. For example, the basic conversation will be very carefully guided by the examiner whereas the higher conversation will be allowed to develop more spontaneously, perhaps moving quite quickly from one topic to another. The fourth type of activity will only be found at higher level as a rule.

**Don't be surprised** . . . (you won't because you will have checked the details beforehand!)

**. . . if everything you say is recorded on cassette.** Recording candidates' performances so they can be played back later has been found to be one of the best ways of assessing fairly. There may even be someone in the room besides the examiner, whose job it is to work the cassette recorder, check the recording levels etc. This might seem a bit off-putting but it is definitely to your advantage because it means that the examiner can give all her/his attention to asking the questions and listening to your replies. She/he will be working very hard to bring the best out of you so you can show what you know, understand and can do. Having two people there definitely doesn't mean you're facing two 'judges' instead of one. If you are nervous about speaking in front of a microphone, try doing it at home regularly with your own cassette recorder. This can be good practice for your oral work as well as helping you to get over any nerves.

**. . . if the examiner is not your own teacher.** It might be a teacher who takes another group in your school or she/he could even be from another school. This makes things more realistic (and remember one of the important new things about GCSE was to make it close to real life) in two ways. Firstly, if you were in French-speaking country you would have to introduce yourself and engage in conversation with lots of strangers whose voices you would obviously not have heard before. Secondly, a conversation between you and someone who doesn't know you is actually much more genuine than one between you and a teacher who knows you really well – perhaps since you were eleven! For one thing the teacher who doesn't know you will be curious to find out about you and will be all the more interested in what you have to say. For another, she/he will want you to do really well just as much as your own teacher. So there is certainly no need for you to worry just because it's not your teacher with you in the examination room.

**... if there is some kind of picture or diagram to look at** as part of one of the tasks set. For example, in a role play set at the lost property office you might be asked to describe your suitcase and its contents having been shown a photograph of the case and what was in it. Always look for clues and help on any document which you're given. Something on it could be very helpful in reminding you about what to say.

## DIFFERENTIATION IN THE ORAL TASKS

Obviously the oral tests designed for candidates seeking higher grades will be more demanding. The following table gives you some idea of the different levels of difficulty in role-play and conversation tests.

**BASIC**

Straightforward role plays with the dialogue following a fairly predictable pattern, often involving requests for goods, services and information.

Guided conversation involving short answers to relatively simple everyday questions. The answers will be more than one word but will not be in the form of long sentences.

**HIGHER GRADES**

Role play with some unpredictable elements. For certain of the tasks the candidate may need to write down information which the examiner has given in reply to an equiry.

Answers to conversational questions in more depth, for example giving reasons for a choice or a preference when asked about hobbies or holidays.

Language at a more complex level including tenses other than the present and perfect.

Initiative shown by the candidate, so that if there is a pause, for example, she/he gets the conversation going again, not necessarily the examiner.

## WHAT ARE THE IMPLICATIONS OF DIFFERENTIATION?

Don't forget that the assessment is *positive*, based on the evidence you give of what you *know, understand and can do* in spoken French. It is up to you to use the opportunities which the examiner will give you to demonstrate your skills. The evidence has to be there either on the day or on the tape recording which the person making the assessment of your performance will be playing back later on. Don't be tempted to go to extremes in playing things safe. If, for example, you have been confidently using a range of different tenses in oral work which you have been doing in class as part of your course, make sure that you *show* your competence in this area in the test itself in the general conversation. The person assessing the oral doesn't know about your class work. She/he can only credit what is there.

It is true that a lot depends on the examiner. She/he has to ask the 'right' questions which will give you the chance to show what you know. This is a skill which examiners will be trained in for the GCSE, so this should not be a problem. However, don't forget that *you* can take the initiative in a conversation and change the direction. There is no real reason why the examiner has to have the *absolute* monopoly and control every single detail of what you talk about within the framework of a particular topic. Think about situations in your own language when you wish to change the flow of a conversation. What sort of phrases do you use in order to do this politely? Could you say anything similar in French?

You will remember that the idea of *predictability/unpredictability* was an important one in the design of the tests, with the higher-level situations in the role-play tasks being much less predictable than the basic ones. Here are two examples (from real life just as much as from an examination) to illustrate this:

1. You go into a hotel, announce your name and say you have reserved a single room for the night.

   **Predictable reply**: That's correct. Do you prefer a bath or a shower?

   **Less predictable reply**: I'm sorry. I have no reservation in that name. We're pretty well booked up for tonight.

2. You arrive at a garage with your exhaust-pipe hanging off and ask if they do repairs to British cars.

   **Predictable reply**: Of course. What make is it exactly?

**Less predictable reply:** No, and in any case we're about to close for the weekend.

**Other examples**

(a)     You ring someone up but the voice at the other end says you've got the wrong number;

(b)     you go to a counter at the post office for stamps and you're told that position is shutting and you have to go to another one;

(c)     you ask for five 100-franc notes in a transaction at the change office and you're told there is a shortage of 100-franc notes. Will you accept ten 50-franc notes?

These are all things which happen to us in real life. Notice that what is happening is that you are being given new information to which you must respond in some way, e.g. apologizing, noting which counter you are directed to and accepting or rejecting an offer in the case of the last three examples.

The important issue is that of *listening* to what the examiner is saying to you. You might think you are able to predict what she/he is going to say with the result that you 'switch off' and miss something which you weren't expecting.

Notice that the first two examples of less predictable replies in role plays, which are given above, (hotel room and garage repair) would lead to *negotiation* between the two people taking the roles. In other words, instead of a straightforward transaction (buying something; requesting information or a service) it would be necessary to persuade, bargain and discuss possible options. In the case of the first one you might need to persuade the receptionist to fit you in somehow or perhaps to recommend another hotel. In the case of the second you might need to plead a special case as your ferry leaves in two hours and you haven't enough money left to pay for an extra night's accommodation in France. Obviously this is much more demanding than straightforward transactions. If you are aiming for higher-level grades it is particularly important that you practise *negotiating* skills as well as *transactional* ones.

## TACKLING THE EXAMINATION ITSELF

**ROLE PLAY**

In your preparation time just before the test, when you study the card with the instructions, don't get bogged down by trying to translate word for word from English into French. The task is to convey a particular *meaning*. There may be several different ways of communicating that meaning in French which are all perfectly acceptable. Here is an example of this:

1    The instructions explain you are in a café, then ask you to perform several tasks of which the third is, 'Ask how much the bill comes to'.

2    At first you panic because you've forgotten the word for 'bill'. Then

# Speaking

you realize this doesn't matter because there are several different ways of saying this which occur to you, all of which convey the meaning appropriately:

> **Ça fait combien en tout, monsieur?**
> **Je vous dois combien, monsieur?**
> **On vous doit combien, monsieur?**
> **Combien on vous doit, monsieur?**

The important thing then is not to think in terms of single words, but *items* which you have to communicate as part of a message. It can be good practice to look at a set of role-play instructions and ask yourself how many different ways the message could be expressed in English. This can be a powerful reminder that you may have more than one way of expressing something in French, even though you are bound to be much less fluent in the foreign language. That way you will be in the frame of mind for the moment in the examination when you read the role-play instruction and start to prepare.

Don't let examination nerves lead you to mis-read very simple things in the instructions. It's surprising how many candidates slip up, for example, by asking for three postcards instead of four. This is not because they didn't know the French for basic numerals but because of tension.

Look carefully at the *tenses* used in the instructions. Does it ask you to say where *you've been* on holiday (perfect tense) or where *you will be* going (referring to the future)?

When preparing from the card, check that what you intend to say is going to convey all the items required, *no more and no less*.

Psychologically you need to try to *anticipate* what the examiner is likely to say in reply to you. In the case of the basic role play you can be reasonably certain that everything you are going to have to cope with is on the card, but this will not necessarily apply to higher level role plays.

Listen to every word which is spoken by the examiner, remembering two things in particular in the case of the higher level test:

> (i) You may be given a *new piece of information* or told about *changed circumstances* which alter the situation as far as you understood it from what was on the instruction card. You need to react to the new situation.
>
> (ii) You may be offered one or more options to which you must respond by making a choice. When you have a choice between two or more things it is no good responding by saying 'yes'!

Don't forget that the idea of *appropriate* language is a key one. This means that the *tone* and *style* have to be suitable for the setting which is stated. If you are supposed to be talking to a long established pen-friend while staying at her/his home, then clearly you are going to use the 'tu' form and a fairly chatty style. If the setting is highly formal, such as reporting the theft of traveller's cheques in a police station, then 'vous' and a much more formal style meet the requirements.

**Activity**

Here is an example of an extended role play from the N.E.A.'s sample papers for 1988:

You are on holiday in Paris and you decide to go on a coach excursion to la vallée de la Loire. You go to travel agent's to obtain the information below; write the information you are given on the answer sheet provided. Your teacher will play the part of the travel agent. Write the information given in English.

1. When is the next coach excursion to the Loire Valley?
2. How long does it last?
3. How much does it cost?
4. Which meals are included in the price?

Prepare for the role play in the way suggested in this section. Will the tone be formal or informal? Which vocabulary topics and which items of grammar do you think you might need to revise in order to be able to say your part and to understand the examiner's likely replies?

## QUESTIONS ON A VISUAL STIMULUS

You will not see the picture or diagram beforehand so you have to think on your feet! Fortunately the questions (which the examiner has printed in front of her/him and cannot alter in anyway) are fairly short.

The examiner might point to a particular part of the drawing but equally might only refer to it in French. You need to be sure you understand the English for expressions like **à gauche**, **à droite**, **au centre**, **au fond** if this type of test is going to be set for your syllabus.

Prepositions (**devant**; **à côté de**; **derrière** etc.) and pronouns (**lui**; **elle**; **eux** etc.) can also be crucial for understanding the examiner's question about the picture in the first place.

Listen carefully also to the *tense* of the verb in the question.

**Activity**

The following question is from an S.E.G. sample oral test for 1988. To try it out you should get someone else to ask you the questions *without* your seeing them but with the picture in front of you. Remember that you will certainly not see the questions written down in the examination. They are printed out for the examiner only. Note the more difficult ones marked with an asterisk intended for higher level. When you have tried the test, analyse what it is that makes the asterisked questions more demanding, in your judgement as a candidate. As part of your preparation for the examination, why not practise setting and answering easier and more difficult questions

# Speaking

209

and pictures with a partner. You could use cartoons or pictures from magazines.

**Examiner's sheet – not to be seen by the candidate**

### Questions on a visual stimulus

1 Le monsieur à droite, qu'est-ce qu'il donne à la femme?
2 Pourquoi?
3 Que fait la dame derrière lui?
*4 Qu'est-ce qu'elle vient de faire?
5 Que fait la dame à gauche?
*6 Alors, qu'est-ce que le charcutier a fait?
*7 Qu'est-ce qu'il fera maintenant?
8 Le monsieur au centre, qu'est-ce qu'il veut faire?
*9 Pourquoi le chien ne peut-il pas entrer?
*10 Comment savez-vous que les chiens ne sont pas admis?
*11 Quelle est la réaction du monsieur?

Questions marked * are for Extended Level only – all those not so marked MUST be asked, and most of the remainder, or similar questions of appropriate relevance and level of difficulty should be asked.

## GENERAL CONVERSATION

In some instances the starting point for this may be a picture, a photograph or some other document or it may simply be an opening question on one of the prescribed topics which then leads you into conversation with the examiner. In any event it is supposed to be unrehearsed and two sided, not a long, uninterrupted speech which you have prepared and memorized in advance. Listening carefully to the opening question from the examiner is crucial if you're to get off to a good start.

Don't forget that the balance of the conversation between you and the examiner has got to be right. Obviously you should be doing most of the talking (you can't score any marks during the time that the examiner is speaking!) but you must be prepared to respond to what the examiner says, rather than pressing on regardless.

The examiner is going to 'chip in', asking you a question about something you've said or requesting you to explain something a little more clearly or in a little more detail, especially in the higher test. Just as in a real conversation, something she/he says can alter the course of the conversation. This might well come as a relief to you if you are struggling! This is certainly allowed, but it should be to move you on to a slightly different *area* of the same topic, not to change to a totally different topic.

It used to be said in the past that the examiner was only there to find out if you could say certain things in French and couldn't care less about *what* it was you were trying to communicate. Often teachers gave advice to candidates on the lines of 'don't bother about telling the truth' so that if you didn't know how to say the name of your favourite sport in French you simply said any sport which you did know the French for, even if it happened to be your most hated sport! This advice clearly goes against the spirit of GCSE French.

This does not mean that you will be expected to talk about any subject under the sun. You will be expected to operate within the topics and vocabulary prescribed in the syllabus. Don't forget though that there will be certain things which you personally will want to say which may not apply to anyone else in your group. For example, your mother may have a profession which is not listed in the syllabus or you may have a hobby which is unusual. It is up to you to find out those sorts of word and to learn them, as they could very well crop up in the course of the conversation in the oral test.

**Activity**

The vocabulary section of this book sets you lots of conversation questions on the various topics, generally in the form of a survey. To give you the flavour of what might happen in the examination, however, try out the following easier and more difficult 1988 sample questions from the SEG oral. You must get someone to ask you the questions. The printed version is for the *examiner* to see, *not* the candidate. How would you respond without giving yourself too

## Speaking

much time to think? Again, try to analyse what it is that makes the higher-level questions more demanding.

### Guided conversation

Personal information. To include topics: personal identity/age/family/home/school/interests.
   Sample questions, e.g.:

> Vous avez des frères ou des sœurs?
> Où est-ce que vous habitez?
> (Est-ce) c'est près de l'école?
> Parlez-moi de votre école . . .
> Qu'est-ce que vous avez fait hier soir?
> Qu'est-ce que vous aimez faire au week-end?
> Avez-vous visité la France? (quel pays, quelle région de l'Angleterre avez-vous visité?)
> Racontez-moi votre visite . . .

### Conversation

This conversation will begin with the questions from the corresponding section of the General Level Oral test, and will then cover any topic or demand the use of any structure included in the syllabus. A typical sequence of questions might be:

> Alors, vous avez dit que vous habitez à Hambrook Park.
> C'est à quelle distance de l'école, ça?
> Cinq kilomètres! C'est loin! Alors comment venez-vous à l'école le matin?
> Ah, vous avez de la chance! Et pour rentrer le soir, c'est la même chose?
> Pourquoi votre père ne vous conduit-il pas le soir?
> Ah bon. Quel travail fait-il, votre père?
> Vous aimeriez être ingénieur, vous aussi?
> Pourquoi pas?

## ROLE-PLAY TASKS INVOLVING NARRATIVE

The basis for this type of task could be a single picture or series of pictures, a photograph or set of photographs, an annotated diagram (e.g. of a journey) or an outline of a story. Study the material very carefully in any preparation time you are given. Make use of all the clues and ideas on the material, especially if any of them are already in French.
   Read any instructions carefully. Often you are asked to tell the 'story' as though it happened to you and your friends. This means that you have to use the 'je' and 'on' forms.

### Activity

There is advice on writing accounts of incidents in the chapter on

*Writing* on page 217. The technique could be adapted for a narrative task in the oral examination which you prepare just before you go into the examination room. When you have studied that section, ask yourself what will be different about talking about an incident compared with writing about it. Jot down the differences in order to make them clearer in your own mind. Try telling the picture story on page 231 of the *Writing* chapter under examination conditions.

## WHY DO PEOPLE FIND THE ORAL TEST SO DAUNTING?

Examination nerves do bring about problems. It is easier said than done to remain calm but you ought to try to reassure yourself that you will have been speaking for years on the same sorts of topic as in the text. There is no reason why the oral part of GCSE should be any worse an ordeal than any of the other parts. Nerves can play on you in two ways though.

Firstly you lose your *concentration* on what the examiner is saying and you retain in your mind just the *last few words* of the question which has been asked. You then repeat those words, in a way which doesn't make sense, in the first words of your reply. Here are some examples:

| *Question* | *Wrong reply* | *Mistake* | *Correct reply* |
|---|---|---|---|
| **Tu aimes nager?** | Oui, tu aimes nager. | wrong person | **J'aime nager.** |
| **Tu y es allé avec ta famille?** | Oui, j'y suis allé avec ta famille. | wrong pronoun | **J'y suis allé avec ma famille.** |
| **Qu'est-ce qu'il a fait?** | Il a fait quitter la salle. | wrongly repeating *fait* | **Il a quitté la salle.** |
| **Qu'est-ce que tu ferais à sa place?** | Je téléphone à la police. | wrong tense | **Je téléphonerais à la police.** |
| **Où vas-tu passer tes vacances cet été?** | J'ai passé deux semaines en France. | wrong tense | **Je vais passer deux semaines en France.** |
| **Tu joues au tennis en été?** | Oui, j'ai joué au tennis en été. | wrong tense | **Oui, je joue au tennis en été.** |

Secondly, panic can cause you to dry up because you haven't understood the question, you've forgotten the French for a particular word or phrase to begin your answer or you start off a sentence which you can't finish because you're stuck for a word.

Here are some suggestions for getting yourself out of difficulty:
  If you really haven't understood the question at all there is little point in trying to launch into a reply. *Ask for help in French* – **Je n'ai pas tout à fait compris** or **Voulez-vous bien répéter ça, s'il vous plaît?**

## Speaking

– so that you at least keep things going in the foreign language. This is much better than breaking into English, even if you do not score as many marks as someone who responds more quickly without having to ask for help.

What you have to try to do, difficult though it may seem, is to forget that the examiner can speak any English at all. Try to imagine that you are speaking to a person who understands only French. If you were really keen to get your message across, how would you try to communicate something which you wanted to say in English but didn't know the exact words for in French?

The following strategies may help:

(i) If you forgot the word for 'toe' (when trying to say your toe hurts) you could make a general statement about pain (**Ça me fait mal** – that hurts) and point to your toe.

(ii) If you wanted to say 'our car's been stolen' and you forgot the word for 'stolen' you could try simplifying and saying **notre voiture n'est plus au parking.** This can't be as good as **on a volé notre voiture** but it keeps open the lines of communication and is obviously much better than remaining silent. The examiner should be playing the role of a reasonably sympathetic native speaker, so she/he would help you by perhaps asking a question which would enable you to explain more fully what you mean.

(iii) Sometimes you may forget a specific word but you can get very close to it by using other words you know which are very similar in meaning. You may not remember **un immeuble** (an apartment block) but you get round it by saying **un grand bâtiment** (a big building).

(iv) You might be able to get across a word for which you've forgotten the French by saying its opposite or by using a negative. For example you could get across the idea of 'near' by saying **ce n'est pas loin** (it's not far) or you could convey the idea of colder by saying **moins chaud** (less hot).

(v) Sometimes you can explain a word you've forgotten by defining it. For example, if you had forgotten the French for 'spare wheel' you could refer to **la roue pour remplacer un pneu crevé.** If for some reason you forgot the word for key then you could refer to **le machin** (or **la bidule) pour ouvrir la porte** – the thingamybob for opening the door.

(vi) You forget a particular ending for an irregular verb so you use it in the infinitive linked to a verb which you do remember how to handle.

(vii) Some of these techniques are also mentioned in the chapter on *Writing* (see page 232) which you may wish to refer to now. Why will it probably be easier to use the techniques when you're writing compared with when you are speaking in the oral test?

(viii) You will see from the *Writing* section that two things are generally not worth trying, however desperate you are. The first is to invent French words from English ones. The second is to ignore a question because you have forgotten a particular word or phrase. Remember you gain marks more easily by attempting to say what you do know than by going to great lengths to avoid showing what you don't know!

(ix) In all languages people sometimes need to pause for thought. Generally the gap is filled in by a word which doesn't really have a meaning but sends out a message to the listener – 'Hang on, I'm going to say something – I haven't finished!' Here are some words and phrases of this type which French people use which could help you in your oral test:

**Eh bien, voilà . . .**
**Bon alors . . .**
**Alors pour moi . . .**
**Moi, ce que je pense, c'est que . . .** } followed by your opinion
**Finalement . . .**
**M'enfin . . .** (short for mais enfin . . .)
**Vous voyez, hein . . .**
**En fin de compte . . .**

(The following could be in the *middle* of sentences)

   **. . . alors . . .**
   **. . . et puis . . .**
   **. . . et de toutes façons . . .** (at any rate)
   **. . . effectivement . . .** (this is it)
   **. . . que voulez-vous . . .** (how shall I put it?)

## HOW WILL YOU BE ASSESSED?

The detail will vary from syllabus to syllabus but it is likely that the following general principles will apply:

1. Your performance in the tasks will be marked *positively*. In other words you will gain credit for the oral skills and knowledge which are observable during the course of the test. You do not start off with, say, fifty marks and then get a mark knocked off for every mistake you make. That does mean of course that remaining silent can't actually score you any marks! Nor can you expect to get very far with yes/no answers.

2. In the first instance marks are awarded for *successful completion of the task*. As an example, if the role play requires you to find out the times of hovercrafts from Boulogne to Folkestone, what really counts is whether the words you say in French would have been understood by the counter clerk in the passenger information enquiry office in the Gare du Nord, with the result that you get the information you wanted. You might stumble, make some grammatical mistakes and

## Speaking

pronounce words somewhat differently from a French native speaker, but if the message could have got through, even with some difficulty on the part of the person to whom you were talking, it would still count as successful completion of the task.

3 There will generally be additional marks for the *way* in which the message was conveyed. One important aspect of this would be *appropriateness*. Did the phrases you used convey the attitude you wished to convey? If you meant to be polite and helpful, did that come across? If, for example, you spoke to a petrol pump attendant in the off-hand and casual way you might talk to a friend this could very well put her/his back up. Equally using very formal language to a friend would be off-putting to the person concerned.

4 Other factors which might come under consideration when assessing how your message was conveyed could be:

(a) Were your *pronunciation*, *stress* and *intonation* (the way the voice goes up and down) very close to, or a long way away from, that of a native speaker?

(b) Did you use very *simple* or *more complicated* phrases and structures? Did you show for example that you were able to use a number of different tenses? Did you make just the odd grammatical mistake or were there quite a lot which might have made it more difficult for a native speaker to follow what you were saying?

(c) Did you *respond very quickly* to all that was asked or did you need quite a long time to think about what you wanted to say?

Bearing these criteria in mind, it is likely that you will be assessed on a scale along these lines:

**Role play:**
0 No message would get through to a native speaker;
1 message only half conveyed or conveyed in a way which would cause a native speaker a great deal of difficulty;
2 message conveyed fully (but this shouldn't be equated with 'perfect' French).

**Conversation or narrative task:**
0 No messages get through;
1 Some messages get through but at a very simple level and requiring the native speaker to try really hard to understand;
2 the bulk of the messages get through but with some effort on the part of the listener;
3 most of the messages get through but some parts are not clear, especially when more complicated language is involved;
4 all the messages get through, including the more complicated ones. There are some pauses and errors but these do not worry the listener in any way;
5 the person listening would have no problem at all in understanding everything which the candidate was asked to say. There is hardly any hesitation.

# French

Most of the examination groups will require examiners to place each candidate's performance on this type of scale. When you are practising with a partner why not assess each other on the scale and explain to each other why the score was 0,1,2 etc.

CHAPTER FIVE

# WRITING

**CONTENTS**

- What the National Criteria say is expected of candidates in the writing tests — 219

- What to bear in mind as you prepare for the examination — 219

- Typical writing activities — 219

- Tackling the examination itself — 220

- Checking your piece of writing in the higher tests — 221

- Getting the timing right — 222

- Advice on tackling specific test types — 222

- A. Useful phrases for beginning and ending very informal letters — 226

- B. Useful phrases for beginning and ending semi-formal letters — 226

- C. Useful phrases for beginning and ending formal letters — 226

- Layout and useful phrases within the letter — 226

## Contents

▶ **What if I simply don't know the French for what I need to write?**     **232**

▶ **How will you be assessed?**     **233**

# Writing

219

## WHAT THE NATIONAL CRITERIA SAY IS EXPECTED OF CANDIDATES IN THE WRITING TESTS

The ability to carry out writing tasks within a restricted range of clearly defined topic areas, such as a short letter (formal or informal) in response to a letter in simple French or to instructions in English, or short messages (e.g. postcards, lists, notes) in response to instructions in English or simple French.

In addition, at *higher* level:

Competence to write in continuous French on a wider range of topics, in response to something written in English or French, or in response to a visual stimulus such as a picture, drawing photograph or diagram.

## WHAT TO BEAR IN MIND AS YOU PREPARE FOR THE EXAMINATION

1. Well before the examination itself you will need to find out what the syllabus will require you to write in French. There seems to be more variation between the Examination Associations in the writing tests set than is the case with other papers. If you are not aiming for higher grades, the body which is entering you for the examination (or you yourself) may decide that you will not take any form of written paper.
2. Many candidates, though, will be taking a writing test at basic level or at basic and higher level. (Remember that you cannot attempt the higher without also attempting the basic.) Some practice in writing is useful for you in real life, though. You might wish to write to a French tourist office in a region you are planning to visit on holiday. You might stay in a French hotel, leave something behind and need to write to them describing what it is and where you left it in your room.

## TYPICAL WRITING ACTIVITIES

### AT BASIC LEVEL

(i) Labelling something in French.
(ii) Writing a postcard or short letter.
(iii) Writing a simple message.
(iv) Writing a simple description of a picture.
(v) Filling in some sort of form or questionnaire.

(vi) Completing a 'model letter' i.e. an outline with some blanks.

**AT HIGHER LEVEL**

(i) More complicated letters, including more formal ones.
(ii) A letter written as a follow-up to a telegram.
(iii) An account of an incident, perhaps based on some visual prompts or based on some outline notes which you have to expand.

## TACKLING THE EXAMINATION ITSELF

The following series of hints applies generally to tackling the various tasks which might be set. You will also find some specific tips listed for the different test types, e.g. letters or accounts of incidents.

1. Read extremely carefully all the *instructions* about the number of words (writing too many can disadvantage you as much as writing too few). There will generally be guidance on the paper as to what counts as a word. Use your common sense – there is not much point in trying to reach the required number of words by writing a long list of your pets' names, for example. In any case, you will probably find you need to use the full word count in order to communicate all the items in the message.

2. Note also if any *special tenses* are to be used or not used. Is there any particular standpoint from which you are supposed to be writing? For example, you may be asked to write as yourself or alternatively taking on someone else's role.

3. Make a decision about the *style* in which you are going to write. Is it going to be *informal* (e.g. a chatty letter to your pen friend of long standing) or very *formal* (e.g. a letter to a hotel requesting a brochure)?

4. The choice of style will affect the language you use, in particular the words for 'you' and 'your'. When you check your work, don't forget to look at tu/vous, ton/ta/tes, votre/vos. Have you been consistent or have you switched from one form to the other? The style will also very much affect the way you begin and end a letter in particular. Why is the style of a letter important? Can you think of reasons based on your own experience?

5. You need to be quite clear in your mind about the various *items* which need to go in the message you have been asked to communicate in French. Those items will be there somewhere on the examination paper itself, either as English instructions, or in French (e.g. points in a letter to which you have to reply) or perhaps in pictorial form.

6. When you read through what you have written, check the points which you have made against the requirements on the paper. Make a list on scrap paper of the points you have been asked to make and then tick each one off to ensure nothing has been missed. To get **full**

marks for transmission of the message you must convey **all** the items. It is no good getting in 50 per cent of them in beautifully polished French and hoping the examiner will be convinced you could have tackled the other 50 per cent given more time. The maximum she/he could award you in those circumstances would be 50 per cent.

7   Apart from telling you *what* has to go in your message, the examination paper itself might also give you some help with *how* to say certain things in French. If there is some sort of document in French which you are asked to read before you write your answer (and in real life we frequently do write in response to something we've read) you could find help with key ideas or key words. Read the French document several times, not just once. Don't re-copy large chunks, though. Do check the spellings of any words you use from the printed French. It creates a bad impression if you miscopy them.

8   Once you are clear *what* needs to go into your written message the rest of the job lies in using all the skill and knowledge you have at your disposal to *communicate* the contents in French, in the appropriate style. In certain types of task you may have some control over the contents. For example, if you are asked to describe your house, the description could be very short and simple or you could make it quite detailed and complicated. Where you have got some control, you must try to remain within your linguistic competence. If you're not sure about how to say something which is quite complicated, then it may be better not to try. Frustrating though it is, you simply cannot expect to say *everything* you would *like* to say in a foreign language.

9   For some writing tasks it can help to start with an *outline* by jotting down key words, phrases or ideas in French which can form paragraph headings. As a next stage you can add in more detail and work up the outline into a rough copy. You can then begin *checking* (see below), making improvements as they occur to you and then write up a neat copy.

## CHECKING YOUR PIECE OF WRITING (IN THE HIGHER TESTS)

When you've done your best to get across the message as required, it's worth spending time on checking through what you've written because the *way* you communicate is also important in the award of a grade in the higher tests. Rather than reading through your answer *generally* looking for wrong spellings it helps to read through a number of different times, looking at something quite *specific* on each occasion. Here are some examples of the sorts of things you might want to look for, checking for only one of these aspects at a time.

1   Does each *verb* agree with its *subject*?
2   Is the *tense* of the verb correct for what you want to say?
3   Are the *adjectives* in the right place (generally after the nouns)? Do they agree in *gender* and *number* with the *noun* or *pronoun*?

4 Are the words **le/la/les** correctly used? Are there any slips like **les garçon**?
5 Are the words **du/de la/des** and **au/à la/aux** correctly used?

You will know yourself from pieces of writing which your teacher or tutor has marked the sorts of slips which you most frequently make. The five suggestions above are just for starters. You will want to modify the list and add to it to suit your personal requirements. The best way of doing this could well be to set aside some time to go through a sample of your written course work trying to classify the mistakes which you most often make. Your teacher or tutor may well be able to help you with this.

## GETTING THE TIMING RIGHT

Timing is important in the examination. Don't forget to allow yourself time for checking. When you use the materials in this book for practice you will wish to work under timed conditions, as though you were in the examination, on occasions. It's necessary to divide up the time in a way which makes sure that you cover *all* the requirements of any single task.

The importance of covering all the points in a message for any one task has already been stressed. It is equally important that you look at the way you divide your time up *between* different tasks. There could be two or three on the paper. Generally, the number of marks per question will be indicated so this should guide you as to what proportion of time to allocate to each one. Once again, doing brilliantly in just one section is not going to give you the best chance. The old, old advice about reading the instructions still applies.

## ADVICE ON TACKLING SPECIFIC TEST TYPES

### MESSAGES, NOTES, SHORT POSTCARDS, COMPLETION OF FORMS OR TABLES

1 Think about the *receiver* of the message. Is your relationship to him/her formal or informal? This affects which words you use for 'you' and 'your'.
2 Keep to the point, checking that you've conveyed all the items in the message by ticking them off on the examination paper.
3 Check what you've written.

**Activity**
Try these examples
1 You receive this postcard from your French pen-pal who is on holiday:

# Writing

*LA FRANCHE COMTE PITTORESQUE*
39.478.17 - SAINT-CLAUDE
Capitale mondiale de la Pipe - 39200 - Jura
L'abside de la Cathédrale
(du XVe au XVIIe siècle)
A l'intérieur 38 stalles du XVe s.

Couleurs Naturelles

Me voici à St Claude. Il ne fait pas très chaud. On passe tout le temps à faire des promenades. Le matin on va à la piscine et le soir on va au café. L'auberge des jeunes est près du camping. On s'amuse vraiment bien. Amitiés,
Guy.

You go on holiday to Lytham St Annes and you wish to send a postcard in French. Say that the weather is sunny, you spend all your time on the beach and in the evenings you go to the cinema.

2   Imagine that you are staying with a French pen-friend. You have just answered the phone and promised to give a message to your friend, who is out at present. You want to go out too, so you leave a message on the message pad.

Write a note in French saying:
Who telephoned.
Where he/she would like to go this evening.
When he/she will phone again.

*Source: SEG Writing, Basic Question 1*

3   While working on a campsite in France you accumulate lost items. The pictures below illustrate your recent 'finds'.

Write out a list for the camp notice board, naming the items and giving, if possible, additional information such as where and when each was found.

The notice must be in French. Write about 30 words in all.

**CAMPING DE MEGVILLE \*\*\***

| | OBJETS TROUVÉS | AUTRE INFORMATION |
|---|---|---|
| 1 | ............... | ............... |
| 2 | ............... | ............... |
| 3 | ............... | ............... |
| 4 | ............... | ............... |
| 5 | ............... | ............... |

*Source: MEG Basic Question 1*

4  You are to entertain a French boy or girl who is coming to spend a fortnight in England. You plan a diary showing the places you will visit and the things you will do. When the diary is complete you will send it to the French person to give an idea of what you have planned.

Obviously you will not fill in every moment of the time but you want to make the visit seem attractive.

Enter **five** different activities and the places you will visit in the diary below, spaced reasonably in the diary.

Remember that your diary entries must be in French.

# Writing

```
        Avril                           Avril
Dimanche 3                    Dimanche 10

Lun. 4                        Lun. 11

Mar. 5                        Mar. 12

Mer. 6                        Mer. 13

Jeu. 7                        Jeu. 14

Ven. 8                        Ven. 15

Sam. 9                        Sam. 16
```

*Source: MEG Basic Question 2*

### LETTERS

1. Decide whether the letter you have to write has got to be informal (e.g. to a well-established friend of your own age) or formal (e.g. a letter making a booking on a camp site or in a hotel). Your decision will affect the style of the letter. The informal one will be 'chatty', sounding very similar to the way you would speak to your friend. The more formal style will use certain set phrases of the type used in business letters, especially at the beginning and the end. There is the usual issue of 'tu' or 'vous'.
2. Study any letter or document in French carefully, several times. How can the contents be helpful to you in writing your reply? Don't forget to check if you've answered all the points, putting all the information required in your letter.

# French

## A  USEFUL PHRASES FOR BEGINNING AND ENDING VERY INFORMAL LETTERS

**Receiver** of letter likely to be: a friend of your own age.

**Begin**  Cher ami or Chère amie,
Cher Christophe,  Chère Catherine,

**End**  Bien à toi or Amitiés or A bientôt or Amicalement.

## B  USEFUL PHRASES FOR BEGINNING AND ENDING SEMI-FORMAL LETTERS

**Receiver** of letter likely to be: an adult known to you, e.g. your pen-friend's parents.

**Begin**  Cher Monsieur, or Chère Madame,

**End**  Veuillez croire, cher Monsieur/chère Madame à mes pensées les meilleures/à mon amical souvenir.

## C  USEFUL PHRASES FOR BEGINNING AND ENDING FORMAL LETTERS

**Receiver** of letter likely to be: Hotel keeper; Director of Tourist Information Office.

**Begin**  Monsieur or Madame or Madame la Directrice,

**End**  Veuillez agréer, cher Monsieur/chère Madame, l'expression de mes sentiments les plus dévoués/les plus distingués.

As a quick check back, look over the phrases for beginning and ending letters and try to answer the following questions.

1  If the family name of your pen-friend was Lorne, how would you begin a letter to Madame Lorne thanking her for hospitality on a visit you made?
2  Would you use **tu** or **vous** in the letter to her?
3  Can you work out, in English, the rough equivalents for the endings suggested for the three types of letters, A, B and C, above?
4  Would you use **tu** or **vous** in the third type of letter, C, above?

## LAYOUT AND USEFUL PHRASES WITHIN THE LETTER

**INFORMAL**

(i) Top right hand corner – name of your town/village followed by date.

# Writing

(ii) Greeting slightly further over to right than you might do normally.
(iii) First words under the comma after the greeting.

*Banbury, le 12 octobre*

*Chère Marie-Anne,*

*Merci de ta lettre . . .*

Phrases: *. . . ta lettre m'a fait grand plaisir . . . j'espère que tu vas bien . . . on s'est bien amusé . . . je dois te quitter maintenant . . . ne voyant plus grand'chose à te dire . . . écris-moi bientôt.*

**FORMAL**

(i) Top right hand corner – your full address with the name of town and date of writing a little below.
(ii) Top left hand corner – name and address of the person to whom you are writing (with any title e.g. **Madame la Directrice**).
(iii) Greetings in same position as informal letter with first words of letter in same position.

*M. X. Rochard,*
*45, rue Lafitte,*
*5400. NANCY*
*France*

*366 Moston Road,*
*Moston,*
*MANCHESTER,*
*M10 4SY*
*Grande-Bretagne*

*Manchester, le 15 novembre 1986*

*Monsieur,*

*J'ai bien reçu votre aimable lettre du . . .*

Phrases: *. . . j'accuse réception de votre lettre du 23 décembre . . . est-ce qu'il serait possible de m'envoyer . . . voulez-vous bien m'indiquer si . . . je vous prie d'accepter toutes mes excuses . . .*

**Activity**

Try these letter writing tasks:

1. Write to your French pen-friend about the visit which she/he is about to pay you. You know you will be meeting her/him at your local airport. Ask your friend to let you know what time she/he arrives and what she/he is going to be wearing. Suggest some things to do in the holidays and ask her/him if she/he is interested in them. Also ask if there are any foods which she/he likes or dislikes especially. Say you are looking forward very much to the visit. Write between 100 and 130 words.

2. A youth orchestra from Caen is planning to visit your district and give

some performances. You have been asked by the organizers to help by writing (in French) to confirm arrangements.

Using the 3 documents below as a starting point, write a letter of about 100 words:

(*a*)   Acknowledge Mme. Hervé's letter and telegram,
(*b*)   Confirming that the group is now expected on Thursday 16th July at 7.00 p.m.,
(*c*)   Saying you are enclosing a programme,
(*d*)   Giving more details of the 3 activities underlined in document 3,
(*e*)   Wishing them a pleasant journey.

DOCUMENT 1                                              Caen, le 30 juin 1985

*Chers amis,*

*Je suis heureuse de vous annoncer que les préparatifs pour la visite de nos jeunes musiciens sont maintenant complets.*

*Nous espérons arriver (en car) le mercredi, quinze juillet, au début de la soirée. Je vous communiquerai l'heure précise de notre arrivée dans quelques jours.*

*Nous attendons avec impatience d'être parmi vous, et de faire la connaissance des familles qui ont gentiment proposé de nous loger.*

*En attendant le quinze, je vous remercie vivement de tous les soins que vous avez pris pour assurer le succès de cette visite.*

*Avec mes plus sincères amitiés.*
*Madeleine Hervé (Mme)*

DOCUMENT 2 – *Text of message received by telegram on 8th July*

**REGRETTONS CHANGEMENT DE PLAN INEVITABLE. ORCHESTRE ARRIVE JEUDI 16 JUILLET 19.00 HRS. M. HERVE.**

DOCUMENT 3 – *Visit of Youth Orchestra from Caen: Outline Programme*

| | | | |
|---|---|---|---|
| Thursday | 16/7 | *Evening* | Arrival at Bus Station. Evening with families. |
| Friday | 17/7 | *Morning* | Reception at Town Hall (11.30 – 12.15). |
| | 17/7 | *Afternoon* | Rehearsal (2.00 p.m.) |
| | 17/7 | *Evening* | First concert – Church Hall (7.30 p.m.) |
| Saturday | 18/7 | *Afternoon* | Coach tour and Picnic Lunch (12.00 noon – 5.00 p.m.) |
| | 18/7 | *Evening* | Youth Club Disco (8.30 – 11.45 p.m.) |
| Sunday | 19/7 | *Morning* | (Rehearsal (10.30 a.m.) |
| | 19/7 | *Afternoon* | Second concert – Arts Centre (3.00 p.m.) |
| Monday | 20/7 | | Free for shopping, sight-seeing, etc. |

# Writing

|  | 20/7 | Evening | Farewell party for visitors and families (8.00 p.m.) |
| --- | --- | --- | --- |
| Tuesday | 21/7 | Morning | Departure from Bus Station (10.15 a.m. prompt) |

*Source: SEG Extended Writing Question 1*

### INCIDENTS BASED ON PICTURES

Read all the instructions very carefully. Are you asked, for example, to pretend you are one of the characters in the pictures, in which case you will have to write in the 'je' form. Remember that you will generally be asked to say what *happened* using past tenses. Don't be tempted to use the present even though this is actually very natural when you have a picture in front of you. Try to imagine you're telling the story to someone who has never seen the actual pictures.

You should revise past tenses. In summary you will use the *perfect tense* to write down what *event* or *step* in the action took place at a particular moment. You will need the *imperfect* for describing what things, people and places *were like*, e.g. the weather at the time or the sort of mood someone was in. You will also use the imperfect to say what *was happening* or what someone *was doing* as a background to the main action.

Study each picture carefully, so you've got the details clear in your mind before you begin planning your story.

Jot down in French words or phrases *which you know* which might fit each picture. Don't forget that if you are uncertain about how to say something in French then the choice is yours to say something *different* which you are more confident about.

Flesh out these bare bones by going through the jottings and adding any further details you can in French. Question words might be useful prompts: who? what? why? where? when? what type? how?

There are certain phrases which can come in useful when telling stories, but resist the temptation to try to work them in when they really don't fit. Here are one or two suggestions.

1   For starting off

   **ce jour-là**   that day
   **l'année dernière**   last year
   **la semaine dernière**   last week
   **mardi dernier**   last Tuesday
   **un jour en été**   one summer's day

   **il y a trois ans**   three years ago
   **il y a une semaine**   a week ago
   **récemment**   recently
   **il y a deux mois**   two months ago
   **hier matin**   yesterday morning

2   For linking paragraphs

   **à ce moment même**   at that very moment
   **à ma grande surprise**   to my great surprise

**plus tard** later
**tout d'un coup** all at once
**ensuite** next
**au bout de quelques moments** after a little while
**en fin de compte** in the end
**soudain** suddenly
**puis** then
**tout de suite** straight away

Spend some time taking stock of other similar phrases which you know. Write down a list of phrases in French which could be used either to start a story or account (e.g. to set the scene in time or place) or to link sentences, ideas or paragraphs (e.g. words like 'firstly', 'in any case', 'therefore', '(un)fortunately', 'however'). It's often the short words like this which you forget. Often they don't come under a particular vocabulary topic like holidays or shopping so they can get missed out from your revision.

Time to get back to the techniques for writing your account. The next stage is to build your notes on each picture into paragraphs, trying to keep each one to roughly the same length.

Check, and keep on checking, according to the general advice on page 221.

### Activity

Try this sample question paper:

Imagine that you are one of the persons or a friend of one or both of the persons in the pictures opposite, which show an incident which happened last week. You write a letter to a French friend, in which you talk about what happened. *Do not write the whole letter* but only about this incident. Write about 100 words.

*Source: SEG Writing Extended Question 2b*

### Expansion of outlines

For this type of task you could be given an outline of a story or account. The outline could be in French or English. What you are asked to do is to expand the bare bones of a story into a number of paragraphs, with appropriate links.

Some people find the following technique helpful. Write out a possible storyline on to your rough paper, leaving large gaps between the first ideas you have about key points in the development of the story. Think as you go along how you might expand on the details.

Begin to build up your rough copy by writing in French in the gaps the vocabulary and phrases which you know which will fit in with the meaning. Remember that your final version ought to make sense to someone who has not seen the outline.

Check and check again according to the suggested procedure. Have you, for example, miscopied any words given in the outline (if it's in French) which you have used in your version?

### Activity

Try this task:

You are in Paris on a school trip but you get separated from the

# Writing

231

group. When you eventually get back to the agreed meeting point, the coach isn't there. Write an account on the episode, including the ending, to put in a letter to your French pen-friend when you are back home a few weeks later.

## WHAT IF I SIMPLY DON'T KNOW THE FRENCH FOR WHAT I NEED TO WRITE

Firstly, this shouldn't worry you as much as it worried students in the 'bad old days' when there were no prescribed topics and you really did not know what to expect.

However carefully you revise vocabulary, though, you might still have a mental block on the day and forget a really important word, which prevents you from writing what you need to say. Imagine yourself in that position in the examination, cover the rest of this page and write down on a piece of scrap paper possible things which you could do to overcome the problem. When you've finished read the rest of the page and compare your ideas with the suggestions in the book.

It's not a pleasant position to be in but you're not under the same time pressure as in the oral examination when you have to think what you're going to say pretty quickly. So don't panic! Two other things not to do.

1 If it really is a key word necessary to communicate a certain point don't ignore the issue and think it won't be noticed. You can only get credit by attempting to communicate certain items, not for avoiding communication. You don't start with a certain number of marks and then lose so many for things you get 'wrong'. You gain marks for getting certain messages across.

2 Unless you are absolutely desperate, don't invent a word which is adapted from English, e.g. **je suis exhausté** for 'I'm exhausted'.

Now some suggestions on how you **could** help yourself:

1 Think of another word in English which means the same as, or is not too far away from, the word you have forgotten the French for. Do you know the French for this alternative word? E.g. you forget the word for 'coach' so you write **autobus**.

2 If the word you are looking for is an object or a person, can you describe what it/she/he is like, does or is used for? E.g. you forget the word for 'customs officer' so you write **le monsieur ou la dame qui examine les valises à l'aéroport**.

3 Can you express the word you've forgotten by using a simpler word? This won't be ideal but it might go some way to getting the message across. E.g. you might want to say 'boiling water' but you make do with **l'eau très chaude**.

4 Can you express the word in a more roundabout way? Again, not ideal but it could still get you some marks, whereas not trying to communicate is guaranteed to gain you nothing. E.g. you forget the word for 'lost' so you say **je ne peux pas trouver** . . .

We've been thinking here about what to do if you are stuck on an individual word. Don't forget that the same tactics apply to longer phrases and ideas. There are often many different ways of saying something so that if you forget one way there can be several others which are just as good. You must remember this when you are communicating in French in speech or writing. It can be good practice to read a piece of writing in your own language (a letter, magazine or newspaper article), look at the phrases used and ask yourself how the *same* meaning could have been expressed using *different* words and phrases. Try it here and now with this paragraph. How could 'stuck', 'individual', 'tactics', 'apply to' and so on be replaced by other words and phrases without altering the essential meaning? There are many different phrases listed under the one heading. It's also very good practice, therefore, when you've written or said something *in French* to ask yourself, 'Could I have said the same thing using different words or phrases?'

## HOW WILL YOU BE ASSESSED?

It's worth remembering that your written French will be assessed by the examiners from at least two different points of view.

1. Have the 'messages' which you were asked to 'transmit' in writing been *communicated*? This is really what counts since there is no purpose in writing if the person reading the message doesn't receive the information you intend her/him to receive. If you ask someone to meet you at a railway station at a certain time, saying you'll be wearing certain clothes, what would matter would be whether the person turns up at the correct place and found you – not how grammatically correct or elegant your French was! In assessing this key aspect of communication in your writing, the *way* you have expressed yourself is ignored as long as your *messages are clear*.

2. *How* have you expressed yourself in French? In the case of a longer piece of writing, how well does it flow or is it rather disjointed? Is the style appropriate for the particular writing task which is set? Is it chatty when it should have been formal? Have you used very simple or more complex language? How many errors are there? Would the errors be off-putting for the person reading it and make it hard work to understand the content? It's probably true to say that in real life we tolerate mistakes from a non-native speaker much more when we are listening to them than when we are reading something written by a non-native speaker.

If you are taking higher level tests in writing it will probably be the case that the second aspect of the two above will become important in a greater measure but *communication* will always count in the first place.

## CHAPTER SIX

# VERB TABLES

**CONTENTS**

▶ **Regular verbs**     236
-er type  236
-ir type  236
-re type  237

▶ **Regular reflexive verbs**     237

▶ **Irregular verbs**     237

## REGULAR VERBS

**-ER TYPE**  **travailler** (to work)

**Present tense**

| | |
|---|---|
| je travaille | nous travaillons |
| tu travailles | vous travaillez |
| il travaille | ils travaillent |

**Imperfect**

| | |
|---|---|
| je travaillais | nous travaillions |
| tu travaillais | vous travailliez |
| il travaillait | ils travaillaient |

**Perfect**

| | |
|---|---|
| j'ai travaillé | nous avons travaillé |
| tu as travaillé | vous avez travaillé |
| il a travaillé | ils ont travaillé |

**Future**

| | |
|---|---|
| je travaillerai | nous travaillerons |
| tu travailleras | vous travaillerez |
| il travaillera | ils travailleront |

**Conditional**

| | |
|---|---|
| je travaillerais | nous travaillerions |
| tu travaillerais | vous travailleriez |
| il travaillerait | ils travailleraient |

**Commands**

travaille!
travaillons!
travaillez!

**Past historic**

| | |
|---|---|
| il travailla | ils travaillèrent |

**-IR TYPE**  **finir** (to finish)

**Present tense**

| | |
|---|---|
| je finis | nous finissons |
| tu finis | vous finissez |
| il finit | ils finissent |

**Imperfect**

| | |
|---|---|
| je finissais | vous finissions |
| tu finissais | vous finissiez |
| il finissait | ils finissaient |

**Perfect**

| | |
|---|---|
| j'ai fini | nous avons fini |
| tu as fini | vous avez fini |
| il a fini | ils ont fini |

**Future**

| | |
|---|---|
| je finirai | nous finirons |
| tu finiras | vous finirez |
| il finira | ils finiront |

**Conditional**

| | |
|---|---|
| je finirais | nous finirions |
| tu finirais | vous finiriez |
| il finirait | ils finiraient |

**Commands**

finis!
finissons!
finissez!

**Past historic**

| | |
|---|---|
| il finit | ils finirent |

# Verb tables

**-RE TYPE**

**vendre** (to sell)

| Present tense | | Imperfect | | Perfect | |
|---|---|---|---|---|---|
| je vends | nous vendons | je vendais | nous vendions | j'ai vendu | nous avons vendu |
| tu vends | vous vendez | tu vendais | vous vendiez | tu as vendu | vous avez vendu |
| il vend | ils vendent | il vendait | ils vendaient | il a vendu | ils ont vendu |

| Future | | Conditional | | Commands | Past historic |
|---|---|---|---|---|---|
| je vendrai | nous vendrons | je vendrais | nous vendrions | vends! | il vendit |
| tu vendras | vous vendrez | tu vendrais | vous vendriez | vendons! | ils vendirent |
| il vendra | ils vendront | il vendrait | ils vendraient | vendez! | |

## REGULAR REFLEXIVE VERBS

Endings as above according to whether **-er**, **-ir** or **-re** type. An **-er** type is given in full as an example.

**se dépêcher** (to hurry)

| Present | | Imperfect | | Perfect | |
|---|---|---|---|---|---|
| je me dépêche | nous nous dépêchons | je me dépêchais | nous nous dépêchions | je me suis dépêché | nous nous sommes dépêchés |
| tu te dépêches | vous vous dépêchez | tu te dépêchais | vous vous dépêchiez | tu t'es dépêché | vous vous êtes dépêchés |
| il se dépêche | ils se dépêchent | il se dépêchait | ils se dépêchaient | il s'est dépêché | ils se sont dépêchés |

| Future | | Conditional | | Commands | Past historic |
|---|---|---|---|---|---|
| je me dépêcherai | nous nous dépêcherons | je me dépêcherais | nous nous dépêcherions | dépêche-toi! | il se depêcha |
| tu te dépêcheras | vous vous dépêcherez | tu te dépêcherais | vous vous dépêcheriez | dépêchons-nous! | ils se dépêchèrent |
| il se dépêchera | ils se dépêcheront | il se dépêcherait | ils se dépêcheraient | dépêchez-vous! | |

## IRREGULAR VERBS

Where a tense is not given in full, assume the *endings* follow the same pattern as the ones given for regular **-er**, **-ir** and **-re** types. The column marked perfect reminds you whether the verb takes **avoir** or **être** in that tense and gives the past participle.

# French

| Infinitive | Present tense | | Imperfect | |
|---|---|---|---|---|
| être (to be) | je suis<br>tu es<br>il est | nous sommes<br>vous êtes<br>ils sont | j'étais<br>tu étais<br>il était | nous étions<br>vous étiez<br>ils étaient |
| avoir (to have) | j'ai<br>tu as<br>il a | nous avons<br>vous avez<br>ils ont | j'avais<br>tu avais<br>il avait | nous avions<br>vous aviez<br>ils avaient |
| faire (to do, to make) | je fais<br>tu fais<br>il fait | nous faisons<br>vous faites<br>ils font | je faisais<br>tu faisais<br>etc. | |
| aller (to go) | je vais<br>tu vais<br>il va | nous allons<br>vous allez<br>ils vont | j'allais<br>tu allais<br>etc. | |
| devoir (to have to, to be obliged to, 'must') | je dois<br>tu dois<br>il doit | nous devons<br>vous devez<br>ils doivent | je devais<br>tu devais<br>etc. | |
| pouvoir (to be able, 'can') | je peux<br>tu peux<br>il peut | nous pouvons<br>vous pouvez<br>ils peuvent | je pouvais<br>tu pouvais<br>etc. | |
| savoir (to know) [how to] | je sais<br>tu sais<br>il sait | nous savons<br>vous savez<br>ils savent | je savais<br>tu savais<br>etc. | |
| conduire (to drive) | je conduis<br>tu conduis<br>il conduit | nous conduisons<br>vous conduisez<br>ils conduisent; etc. | je conduisais<br>tu conduisais | |
| connaître (to know, be familiar with) | je connais<br>tu connais<br>il connaît | nous connaissons<br>vous connaissez<br>ils connaissent | je connaissais<br>tu connaissais<br>etc. | |

    reconnaître (to organize) — exactly the same pattern as connaître but with re- as the first two letters:
        je reconnais, tu reconnais etc.

    disparaître (to disappear) — exactly the same pattern as connaître but with dispar- replacing conn- as the first letters:
        je disparais, tu disparais etc.

| | | | | |
|---|---|---|---|---|
| ouvrir (to open) | j'ouvre<br>tu ouvres<br>il ouvre | nous ouvrons<br>vous ouvrez<br>ils ouvrent | j'ouvrais<br>tu ouvrais<br> etc. | |
| mettre (to put) | je mets<br>tu mets<br>il met | nous mettons<br>vous mettez<br>ils mettent | je mettais<br>tu mettais<br>etc. | |

    promettre (to promise) — exactly the same pattern as mettre with pro- as the first three letters:

| | | | | |
|---|---|---|---|---|
| prendre (to make) | je prends<br>tu prends<br>il prend | nous prenons<br>vous prenez<br>ils prennent | je prenais<br>tu prenais<br>etc. | |

    comprendre (to understand) — Exactly the same pattern as prendre with com- as the first three letters:
        je comprends, tu comprends etc.

    apprendre (to learn) — exactly the same pattern as prendre with ap- as the first two letters:
        j'apprends, tu apprends etc.

## Verb tables

| Perfect | Future | Conditional | Command | Past historic |
|---|---|---|---|---|
| j'ai été<br>tu as été<br>etc. | je serai<br>tu seras<br>etc. | je serais<br>tu serais<br>etc. | sois!<br>soyons!<br>soyez! | il fut<br>ils furent |
| j'ai eu<br>tu as eu<br>etc. | j'aurai<br>tu auras<br>etc. | j'aurais<br>tu aurais<br>etc. | aie!<br>ayons!<br>ayez! | il eut<br>ils eurent |
| j'ai fait<br>tu as fait<br>etc. | je ferai<br>tu feras<br>etc. | je ferais<br>tu ferais<br>etc. | fais!<br>faisons!<br>faites! | il fit<br>ils firent |
| je suis allé<br>tu es allé<br>etc. | j'irai<br>tu iras<br>etc. | j'irais<br>tu irais<br>etc. | va!<br>allons!<br>allez! | il alla<br>ils allèrent |
| j'ai dû<br>tu as dû<br>etc. | je devrai<br>tu devras<br>etc. | je devrais<br>tu devrais<br>etc. | —<br>—<br>— | il dut<br>ils durent |
| j'ai pu<br>tu as pu<br>etc. | je pourrai<br>tu pourras<br>etc. | je pourrais<br>tu pourrais<br>etc. | —<br>—<br>etc. | il put<br>ils purent<br>— |
| j'ai su<br>tu as su<br>etc. | je saurai<br>tu sauras<br>etc. | je saurais<br>tu saurais<br>etc. | —<br>—<br>etc. | il sut<br>ils surent<br>— |
| j'ai conduit<br>tu as conduit<br>etc. | je conduirai<br>tu conduiras<br>etc. | je conduirais<br>tu conduirais<br>etc. | conduis!<br>conduisons!<br>conduisez! | il conduisit<br>ils conduisirent |
| j'ai connu<br>tu as connu<br>etc. | je connaîtrai<br>tu connaîtras<br>etc. | je connaîtrais<br>tu connaîtrais<br>etc. | —<br>—<br>— | il connut<br>ils connurent |
| j'ai ouvert<br>tu as ouvert<br>etc. | j'ouvrirai<br>tu ouvriras<br>etc. | j'ouvrirais<br>tu ouvrirais<br>etc. | ouvre!<br>ouvrons!<br>ouvrez! | il ouvrit<br>ils ouvrirent |
| j'ai mis<br>tu as mis<br>etc. | je mettrai<br>tu mettras<br>etc. | je mettrais<br>tu mettrais<br>etc. | mets!<br>mettons!<br>mettez! | il mit<br>ils mirent |
| j'ai pris<br>tu as pris<br>etc. | je prendrai<br>tu prendras<br>etc. | je prendrais<br>tu prendrais<br>etc. | prends!<br>prenons!<br>prenez! | il prit<br>ils prirent |

| Infinitive | Present tense | | Imperfect |
|---|---|---|---|
| sortir (to go out) | je sors<br>tu sors<br>il sort | nous sortons<br>vous sortez<br>ils sortent | je sortais<br>tu sortais<br>etc. |
| partir (to set off) | je pars<br>tu pars<br>il part | nous partons<br>vous partez<br>ils partent | je partais<br>tu partais<br>etc. |
| dormir (to sleep) | je dors<br>tu dors<br>il dort | nous dormons<br>vous dormez<br>ils dorment | je dormais<br>tu dormais<br>etc. |
| servir (to serve) | je sers<br>tu sers<br>il sert | nous servons<br>vous servez<br>ils servent | je servais<br>tu servais<br>etc. |
| recevoir (to receive) | je reçois<br>tu reçois<br>il reçoit | nous recevons<br>vous recevez<br>ils reçoivent | je recevais<br>tu recevais<br>etc. |
| vouloir (to want, wish) | je veux<br>tu veux<br>il veut | nous voulons<br>vous voulez<br>ils veulent | je voulais<br>tu voulais<br>etc. |
| venir (to come) | je viens<br>tu viens<br>il vient | nous venons<br>vous venez<br>ils viennent | je venais<br>tu venais<br>etc. |
| boire (to drink) | je bois<br>tu bois<br>il boit | nous buvons<br>vous buvez<br>ils boivent | je buvais<br>tu buvais<br>etc. |
| voir (to see) | je vois<br>tu vois<br>il voit | nous voyons<br>vous voyez<br>ils voient | je voyais<br>tu voyais<br>etc. |
| écrire (to write) | j'écris<br>tu écris<br>il écrit | nous écrivons<br>vous écrivez<br>ils écrivent | j'écrivais<br>tu écrivais<br>etc. |
| dire (to say, to tell) | je dis<br>tu dis<br>il dit | nous disons<br>vous dites<br>ils disent | je disais<br>tu disais<br>etc. |
| falloir (to be necessary) | il faut | | il fallait |
| pleuvoir (to rain) | il pleut | | il pleuvait |

# Verb tables

| Perfect | Future | Conditional | Command | Past historic |
|---|---|---|---|---|
| je suis sorti<br>tu es sorti<br>etc. | je sortirai<br>tu sortiras<br>etc. | je sortirais<br>tu sortirais<br>etc. | sors!<br>sortons!<br>sortez! | il sortit<br>ils sortirent |
| je suis parti<br>tu es parti<br>etc. | je partirai<br>tu partiras<br>etc. | je partirais<br>tu partirais<br>etc. | pars!<br>partons!<br>partez! | il partit<br>ils partirent |
| j'ai dormi<br>tu as dormi<br>etc. | je dormirai<br>tu dormiras<br>etc. | je dormirais<br>tu dormirais<br>etc. | dors!<br>dormons!<br>dormez! | il dormit<br>ils dormirent |
| j'ai servi<br>tu as servi<br>etc. | je servirai<br>tu serviras<br>etc. | je servirais<br>tu servirais<br>etc. | sers!<br>servons!<br>servez! | il servit<br>ils servirent |
| j'ai reçu<br>tu as reçu<br>etc. | je recevrai<br>tu recevras<br>etc. | je recevrais<br>tu recevrais<br>etc. | reçois!<br>recevons!<br>recevez! | il reçut<br>ils reçurent |
| j'ai voulu<br>tu as voulu<br>etc. | je voudrai<br>tu voudras<br>etc. | je voudrais<br>tu voudrais<br>etc. | —<br>—<br>— | il voulut<br>ils voulurent |
| je suis venu<br>tu es venu<br>etc. | je viendrai<br>tu viendras<br>etc. | je viendrais<br>tu viendrais<br>etc. | viens!<br>venons!<br>venez! | il vint<br>ils vinrent |
| j'ai bu<br>tu as bu<br>etc. | je boirai<br>tu boiras<br>etc. | je boirais<br>tu boirais<br>etc. | bois!<br>buvons!<br>buvez! | il but<br>ils burent |
| j'ai vu<br>tu as vu<br>etc. | je verrai<br>tu verras<br>etc. | je verrais<br>tu verrais<br>etc. | vois!<br>voyons!<br>voyez! | il vit<br>ils virent |
| j'ai écrit<br>tu as écrit<br>etc. | j'écrirai<br>tu écriras<br>etc. | j'écrirais<br>tu écrirais<br>etc. | écris!<br>écrivons!<br>écrivez! | il écrit<br>ils écrirent |
| j'ai dit<br>tu as dit<br>etc. | je dirai<br>tu diras<br>etc. | je dirais<br>tu dirais<br>etc. | dis!<br>disons!<br>dites! | il dit<br>ils dirent |
| il a fallu | il faudra | il faudrait | — | il fallut |
| il a plu | il pleuvra | il pleuvrait | — | il plut |

# ANSWERS

| VOCABULARY TOPIC 1 |
| --- |

**PART 1**   C   Examples of some of the questions you would need to ask: **Vous êtes né(e) où? Vous habitez où en ce moment? Vous êtes marié(e) ou célibataire? Quel est votre repas favori? Quels sont vos passetemps?**

**PART 2**   1   Between 14 and 16 . . . interested in cinema, dancing, music, swimming, beach, parties/celebrations, fashion . . . letters in either French or English . . . include photos.

2
| Names of people involved | Colour of hair | Colour of eyes | Height |
| --- | --- | --- | --- |
| 1 Christelle | brown | green | |
| 2 Sophie | blond | brown | |
| 3 Gilbert | brown | brown | 1m75 |
| 4 Claude | | | |

Met at Méandre . . . skiing . . . Gilbert . . . to say if they recognize him.

3   (a)   Think of the heat! Don't leave your dog in the car.
(b)   As a hygiene precaution, dogs are not allowed into the park, even on a lead.

4   (a)   the percentage of households (55 per cent) with a pet of any kind;
(b)   most popular; dogs; least popular: tortoises, hamsters and rabbits;
(c)   most likely: shopkeepers and farmers; least likely: manual labourers and executives.

5   (a)   Is Snoopy a genuine Shetland pony?
(b)   It is eating too much.
(c)   A simpler diet (in a plain meadow).

6   (a)   iii.
(b)   They shop regularly . . . have money on them permanently . . . save up to buy something.
(c)   Young people travel sooner and further.
(d)   iv.
(e)   Computers . . . video and computer games . . . space shuttle . . . lasers . . . test-tube babies.
(f)   World events/war.
(g)   i.

# French

## VOCABULARY TOPIC 2

**PART 1**   A   Some examples of the questions: **A quelle heure est-ce qu'on se couche normalement? A quelle heure est-ce qu'on mange à midi? Est-ce que je peux téléphoner en Angleterre? Comment est-ce que je peux vous aider? Où est-ce qu'il faut mettre ma valise?**

**PART 2**   1   The rooms: **(salle de) bains** = bathroom; **entrée** = entrance (hall) **w.c.** = **toilet; kitch.** = kitchenette **(salle de) séjour** = living room; **chambre** = bedroom; **balcon** = balcony.
**PL = placard** = cupboard.
The size of the balcony depends on which floor the particular flat is on.

2   (a)   No prices given.
(b)   Not mentioned.
(c)   Fully equipped kitchenette (stainless steel sink; electric hob; refrigerator; kitchen units) and fitted carpets.
(d)   No.
(e)   Electric.
(f)   Electric individual heating and double-glazing.
(g)   Has wood-clad frontage.
(h)   Shops are across the gardens and beach is very near.
(i)   Yes, on the D5 road across the way from the Leisure Centre.
(j)   The Northwood Leisure Centre.

3   (a)   It's smaller than a cassette.
(b)   3 – playback, fast forward and stop.
(c)   Works off 2 × 1.5 volt R6 batteries and can be plugged into mains.
(d)   1 year.
(e)   It's 40 francs cheaper in the warehouse than the catalogue price.
Extension: **Je voudrais acheter un lecteur de cassette stéréo, s'il vous plaît. C'est le modèle 'Tom Pouce' qui m'intéresse. Est-ce que la garantie est bonne pour la Grande-Bretagne?**

4   It's a bottle bank for used glass. You're not supposed to throw in lids, corks, porcelain, bricks, pebbles, earth or rubbish!

5   (a)   He generally gets 50 F per week plus extras.
(b)   i.
(c)   iii.

# Answers

**245**

## VOCABULARY TOPIC 3

**PART 1**  A  Some examples of the questions: **Est-ce que vous habitez une grande agglomération? Vous habitez en banlieue? Comment s'appelle la région? Il y a combien d'habitants? Qu'est-ce qu'il y a d'intéressant à voir ou à faire là-bas? Qu'est-ce qu'il y a comme possibilités touristiques?**

B  If you were writing a reply for your neighbours giving similar information about your locality, it should cover: location of the town; surrounding scenery; items of interest in town centre; any nearby historical buildings; description of the climate in summer and winter.

**PART 2**
1. (a) Push.
   (b) Wet paint.
   (c) Pedestrianized street.
   (d) No animals allowed in the shop.
   (e) Don't smoke – Throw your cigarette end away here.
   (f) Don't drop any litter.
   (g) No unauthorized entry to building site.
   (h) No bill sticking.
   (i) Use the subway.
   (j) Tourist Information Office.
   (k) Henry Moore Exhibition.
   (l) Don't walk on the grass.
   (m) Snow? Ice? Rain? – Slow down.
2. (a) 16 1 48 58 33 33 – it is the telephone information service for road conditions.
   (b) Before 1st May and after 30th September. Between those two dates the office is also closed on Sunday and Monday afternoon.
   (c) 38 97 40 22 for Fire Brigade and Police.
   (d) It's only open in July
   (e) If you were interested in fishing and wanted to contact the fishing club.
3. (a) The second column gives temperatures at 8.00 a.m. Paris time on 27 July; the third one at 2.00 p.m. on the same date.
   (b) Dinard – overcast; Rhodes – sunny; Dublin – rain; Bâle – cloudy; Lisbon – foggy.
   (c) storm . . . showers . . . snow.
4. (a) Morning will be cloudy (after the storms in the night) then very cloudy. In the afternoon storms will break out.
   (a) Wind south-south-west, weak to moderate. Lowest temperatures 13–15 degrees; highest 23–25 degrees.
   (c) Sky will be cloudy to overcast. It will become rainy.
5. Setting: Forests and lake Twin towns: Le Locle in Switzerland and Waremme in Belgium.
   Population: 10 000, of which 7 700 in the urban area. Height: 666 m.

# 246 French

Market days: Thursdays and Saturdays (morning). Parking: large number of extensive, free car parks available. Lake: 2 200 m long; 750 m wide; 38.4 m deep. Origin: from a glacier.

Examples of industries: textile; wood products; granite; sand quarries; tourism.

Examples of products: agricultural – cheese; trout farming; mountain stream water; aniseed bread; honey; smoked bacon and meat.

7  (a)  iii.

## VOCABULARY TOPIC 4

**PART 1**

C  On cherche la gare d'autobus/la gare routière/la gare S.N.C.F. On peut y aller en taxi/en métro/à pied? Il y a un arrêt d'autobus/une station de métro/une station de taxis près d'ici?

D1  Un aller simple . . . il y a un train tous les combien? Il faut combien de temps pour aller à . . . Il faut changer?

D2  Deux tickets première classe . . . trois carnets . . . un billet de tourisme pour 7 jours.

E  Le train part dans combien de temps? Dans quelques instants, monsieur. C'est par ici pour les trains de grande ligne? Là ce sont les trains de banlieue – les grandes lignes sont de l'autre côté. De quel quai part le train pour Boulogne? Quai 6, voie B. Où est-ce qu'on peut laisser les bagages? Vous avez la consigne à droite et des casiers automatiques au fond. J'ai une demi-heure d'attente maintenant. La salle d'attente est en face, madame. Où est-ce que je dois descendre? Vous descendez à Tours, mademoiselle. C'est un train direct? Ah, non. Vous avez la correspondance pour Boulogne à Amiens.

F  C'est bien le train pour Pouligny? C'est quelle direction pour la voiture-restaurant?

G  Pour 150 francs d'ordinaire, s'il vous plaît – est-ce que vous pouvez vérifier l'huile, s'il vous plaît? Faites le plein, s'il vous plaît – du super, et voulez-vous bien laver les phares? Pour 100 francs de gas-oil, s'il vous plaît. Voulez-vous bien vérifier le niveau d'eau dans la batterie? Vous vendez des cartes routières?

H  Suggestions for some of the phrases needed:

C'est peut-être la batterie, mais je ne sais pas exactement. Vous allez nous dépanner sur place ou vous allez nous remorquer au garage? C'est combien par heure/par kilomètre pour nous remorquer? Vous acceptez la carte de crédit 'Access'? Il faut attendre combien de temps?

I  C'est combien le vol aller-retour à Newcastle? Ça dure combien de temps la traversée à Folkestone? Où est-ce que je dois me présenter à l'enregistrement pour un vol à Birmingham? C'est quelle sortie/quelle porte pour le vol numéro SR 181 à Londres? C'est bien le vol à Douvres?

J  Some suggestions:

# Answers 247

1 Check on the timetable for frequency of train and availability of restaurant facilities on the train. **Merci, monsieur ... je vais consulter l'horaire tout de suite.**

2 **Excusez-moi, madame. Je crois qu'il y a une erreur. C'est justement cette place que j'ai réservée.**

3 Get off the bus (it's not really the right one for where you want to get to) unless you don't mind the 15 minute walk. **Merci, monsieur. Je ne savais pas ... je ne suis pas d'ici.**

4 **Mais madame ... il faut absolument qu'on rentre ce soir. On n'a plus d'argent et on a des enfants de deux et quatre ans avec nous.**

5 **Je suis désolé(e) monsieur mais mon père a laissé les billets dans une chambre d'hôtel où on a couché hier soir. Je n'ai pas le numéro de téléphone mais j'ai l'adresse. Il y a un annuaire ici? Je pourrais leur téléphoner pour confirmer les détails sur les billets.**

6 **Excusez-moi, madame. Il y a un problème. Il nous manque une valise. On nous demande de monter en autocar pour la correspondance à Paris. Qu'est-ce qu'on peut faire?**

7 Open your case for the security check. **Oui, monsieur, avec plaisir. Je l'ai faite moi-même et je l'ai gardée avec moi tout le temps.**

8 **Je suis désolé(e) monsieur. Mon père ne parle pas français. Il va chercher ses papiers.** (Ask your father to produce licence/insurance certificate etc.) **Comme vous voyez, nous sommes des touristes anglais ... on ne savait pas qu'il y avait une limite sur cette route.**

## PART 2

1 
(a) Uneven road surface for 2 kms.
(b) Diversion – road closed 3 kms ahead.
(c) Long load.
(d) Reims via N4.
(e) Reims via motorway.
(f) Traffic lights 800 m ahead.
(g) Roadworks between St Quentin and Junction 8.
(h) Roadworks in Raon l'Etape – recommended route to St Dié via Rambervilliers.
(i) Windscreens – 1 km on the left – fast fitting.
(j) Left at the lights – Midas Exhaust Centre – fitting in 30 minutes without booking. Change your exhaust in 30 minutes.
(k) Parking not allowed on Saturdays and Fridays from 8.00 p.m. onwards
(l) Warning! This fuel is meant for vehicles equipped to run on lead-free petrol.
(m) JO stands for working days; Q=daily.

Railway journeys:
(a) Next departures.
(b) Arrivals – Main Lines.
(c) Suburban trains.
(d) To the platforms.
(e) Passenger Reception – Enquiries – Waiting Room.

# French

    (f)    Non smoking.
    (g)    Not drinking water.
    (h)    Train cancelled owing to accident.
    Métro journeys:
    (a)    Connection.
    (b)    Tickets not valid beyond this point.

2  (a)    Bike hire.
    (b)    23 francs each unless you have a tandem at 40 francs.
    (c)    No.
    (d)    Deposit of 50 francs per bike.
    (e)    Railway Station.

3  (a)    Wednesday and Saturday; outward at 8.30 and return at 11.55.
    (b)    Out from A. Chesneau Square – opposite the memorial; return from coach station.

4  (a)    Left hand column: arrival – departure – Trans European Express – sleeper berths – sleeping cars; right hand column: restaurant car – buffet car – meals served in your seat – bar – trolley sales
    (b)    To give the facilities available in each station.
    (c)    The ones listed above the table are for general telephone enquiries; the ones in the second column of the table are for seat reservations by telephone.

5  (a)    Safety.
    (b)    One is for dry conditions, the other for rainy weather conditions.
    (c)    By leaving a certain number of vehicle spaces.
    (d)    When the road is wet.

6  (a)    No.
    (b)    Read off the amount required according to the time you plan to stay. Pay by putting in the amount in 5f, 2f or 1f coins. Press the button marked 'Ticket' and wait 5 seconds. Take the ticket. Suggestion for extension: **Pardon, madame. On a mis une pièce de 5 francs dans la machine. La pièce s'est coincée et on n'a pas de ticket**.

7  (a)    Put on your hazard indicators or give warning of your breakdown by using a warning triangle. Get out of your vehicle on the right hand side.
    (b)    It's available 24 hours of the day and free. The phones are at 1 km intervals.
    (c)    Police.
    (d)    The rates are printed on the emergency phone booths.

8  (a)    Between 3.00 p.m. and 9.00 p.m. on the Friday; between 3.00 a.m. and 9.00 a.m. on the Saturday.
    (b)    The diagonal stripes indicate there is a strong possibility of hold-ups so that leaving at those times is somewhat inadvisable. The unshaded columns indicate the ideal times to leave to avoid traffic jams.

9  (a)    Low-key.
    (b)    Rhône Valley.

# Answers 249

|   |   |   |
|---|---|---|
|    | (c) | In Paris the outward routes were becoming more difficult. In the provinces the traffic was slowly sorting itself out. |
| 10 | (a) | At the station in front of the enquiry office. |
|    | (b) | Cinema and going to swimming pool with friends. |
|    | (c) | To bring swimming costume. |
|    | (d) | 10.55. |
| 11 | (a) | The two boys drove the car 'between them', one steering and one working the pedals. |
|    | (b) | They broke a window and used a spare set of keys left on the dashboard. |
|    | (c) | Two parked cars were hit, as well as a passer-by whose leg was broken. |
| 12 |     | 18 km/p.h. (Authors' mathematical skills not necessarily guaranteed!) |

## VOCABULARY TOPIC 5

**PART 1**    B    Il y a des visites guidées? Où est-ce que je peux déposer mon sac? On peut prendre des photos flash? Vous avez des livrets-guide? Extension: Some possible phrases – **Mais, monsieur ... c'est la dernière journée des vacances. Vous ne pourriez pas faire une petite exception?**

**PART 2**

1  (a) Liable to cancellation depending on time of year, weather and energy savings – please ask.
   (b) Extra departures – please ask.
   (c) Tourist Information Office – at your disposal for all enquiries.
   (d) Town visit: Visits offered from 1st July to 15th September. Group prices on request.
   (e) Regional tours: Tours offered from July to September. An entrance charge is made to historic buildings. Departures: Capitole Square in front of the Town Hall clock.
   (f) Dinner – 8.30 p.m. – formal dress required – not recommended/advisable for children under 12.

2  Miscellaneous ... Public Services ... Emergency Services ... Ambulances ... Travel Agencies ... Banks ... Exchange ... Libraries ... Cabarets/Discos ... Campsites ... Cinemas ... Clubs ... Religious Services (Catholic and others) ... Culture and Leisure ... Education ... Garages ... Accommodation ... Local Papers ... Bike Hire ... Car Hire ... Museums and Public Buildings ... Car parks ... Local Radio ... Sport and Relaxation/Leisure ... Taxi ranks ... Town Centre Hotels ... Hotels within immediate locality ... Restaurant meals at less than 50 f ... Restaurants in the price range 50 to 80 f ... Restaurants in the range 100 f and above.

3  (a) One is the full price, the other the reduced rate.

(b) A ticket that gives you entrance to all the museums in Arles.
(c) A.M. Open: 8.30. Close 12.30 p.m. P.M. Open: 2.00 Close: 7.00.

4

|   | Cruise on Seine | Cruise on Canal |
|---|---|---|
| 1 | Saturday 13/9 | Sunday 14/9 |
| 2 | 6.30 a.m. | 8.30 a.m. |
| 3 | Breakfast, lunch with drink | Lunch |
| 4 |  | Gien – Hunting Museum: Briare Vintage vehicle Museum |
| 5 | Commentary on boat | Green, rolling scenery |
| 6 | 420 F | 280 F |

5   (a) The latter is supposed to have been modelled on the former. It has three towers, of which two are thirteenth century and one fourteenth century.
(b) It was a Roman Temple. Now it's a museum.
(c) It was an arena for gladiators. Now it's used for bull fights.
(d) The port has silted up with sand.

6   (a) (i) 20 F reduced to 15 F for students and groups of 20.
(ii) 160 vehicles from 1895 to present day.
(iii) French only.
(iv) Every day from 10.00 to 12.00 and from 2.00 p.m. to 7.00 p.m.
(b) (i) Video room with slides plus commentary and films; poster collection; explanations from the owner of the collection himself.
(ii) Shop/book stall and bar.
(iii) Model car and old toy exhibition (and poster collection). Other temporary exhibitions several times per year.

7   (b) When asked. 'What accommodation will you use?', the most popular reply was, 'staying with relatives or friends.'
(c) When asked. 'Where do you intend to go for your main holiday next Summer' and 'If you're going abroad, will you go on a package tour or make private arrangements?', the most popular replies were, 'In France' and 'On a private holiday.'
(d) When asked, 'During this holiday, will you tour around or will you stay mainly in one place?' and 'If you're going to stay in the same place, will it be by the sea, in the countryside, in the mountains or in a town?', the most popular replies were, 'Staying in the same place' and 'At the seaside.'
(e) C.

### VOCABULARY TOPIC 6

PART 1   A   Extension: Some suggested phrases – **Mais, monsieur, on a réservé bien en avance. On est vraiment déçu . . . et les chambres ne sont pas à côté. Ça c'est vraiment inacceptable.** At the campsite – **Ce n'est pas**

# Answers 251

possible madame. Il doit y avoir une erreur. Vous avez écrit pour confirmer notre réservation il y a plusieurs semaines.

**C** i *a*.   ii. *b*.   iii. *a*.   iv *b,c,d*.   v *c*.   vi *c*.   vii *a*.   viii *b*.
ix *c*.   x *b*.   xi *d*.   xii *b*.   xiii *a,b,c*.   xiv *a,b,c,d*.

**E** Phrases for the possibilities mentioned – **Le chauffage central est tombé en panne. La douche ne fonctionne pas. L'aspirateur ne fonctionne pas. On a cassé deux assiettes.** (But don't forget to add the apologies rather than just conveying the information, as here!)

**F** Bill is correct. Phrases – **Il y a peut-être une erreur? Vous acceptez les cartes de crédit?**

---

**PART 2**

1  Campsite:
   (*a*)   Meeting Room ... Games Room ... Bowls Area ... Dustbins ... Washrooms/Showers/Toilets ... Reception.
   (*b*)   Not for drinking.
   (*c*)   Razor socket.

   Youth Hostel:
   (*a*)   Girls' Dormitory ... Boys' Dormitory ... Canteen ... Lounge ... Washrooms/Showers/Toilets.
   (*b*)   Smoking in dining room strictly forbidden.
   (*c*)   Keep the hostel clean. Use the waste bins.
   (*d*)   In the evening, possibility of minibus service on request (Minimum of 6 people).
   (*e*)   Meal times.
   (*f*)   Do not leave valuables in the bedrooms.

   Hotel:
   (*a*)   Emergency Exit.
   (*b*)   In case of breakdown, do not try to leave. Press the alarm button!
   (*c*)   Booth out of order.
   (*d*)   If you wish to extend your stay, ask at the reception before 10.00 a.m.
   (*e*)   Please clean my room. Please do not disturb.

2  (*a*)   6 hectares ... 800 campers ... modern and comfortable equipment, meeting and games rooms ... middle of Montgeon Forest ... excellent roads ... all 6 hectares shaded.
   (*b*)   250 hectares ... forest setting ... 25 hectares geared for leisure ... games areas ... animal enclosures ... bowls areas ... lake for boating ... lawns with flowers.
   (*c*)   Town ... beach ... port.

3  (*a*)   Do any chores you are asked to do willingly, not grudgingly, as a way of contributing to the group spirit in the hostel.
   (*b*)   They're not allowed.
   (*c*)   The evening closing time is an hour later (11.00 p.m.) in Summer. The two hostels in Paris and the one at Choisy-le-Roi close at 1.00 or 2.00 a.m.

## 252 French

    (d)    Bottom right – meals; Bottom left – accommodation.
    (e)    Drinks not included in meals prices; sheets and sleeping bags available at 11 F (from 1 to 7 nights). Extension: Possible phrases – **On voudrait rester deux nuits. Vous avez de la place? C'est combien par personne par nuit? Vous avez une cantine? On peut louer des sacs de couchage?**

4  (a)    It's rented, furnished accommodation (house or flat) in the countryside in a pleasant village or in a farm setting. You book by the week, from 4.00 p.m. Saturday to 10.00 a.m. Saturday or you can book for the weekend. Price code would be A.

    (b)

| | Property A19 | Property B3 |
|---|---|---|
| 1 | 3 | 1 |
| 2 | in each bedroom | shower |
| 3 | 6 people | 3 adults |
| 4 | fishing and hunting on the spot; tennis and swimming pool 5 kms away | fishing 1 km away; swimming pool 14 kms away; horse-riding 8 kms away |

5  (a)    Not to bring out your dustbins before 7.30 p.m. the night before they're due to collect them. If they're put out too early, then smells and dirt result from plastic bags which get ripped open or knocked over.
    (b)    There is no point in bringing out bins as there is no collection on Wednesday morning.
    (c)    **Matin**.

6  (a)    You should hang on to your room key and ask for the code number which will give you access to the hotel through the front door.
    (b)    A simplified meals service.
    (c)    From the layout (no actual prices are given) it seems that breakfast is separate from the price of the room. Tax and service are included.
    (d)    The car park is not supervised, so you should take the usual precautions and leave nothing of value in the car.

## VOCABULARY TOPIC 7

**PART 1**    B  Suggestions for 'missing phrases' – **Les boissons sont comprises? Qu'est-ce que vous nous conseillez? Pourriez-vous nous expliquer ce que c'est exactement? C'est quoi le plat du jour? Vous acceptez les cartes de crédit?**
    C  i *f*.    ii *c*.    iii *d/e*.    iv *c*.    v *c/d/e*.    vi *b/c*.    vii *d/e*.
      viii *d/e*.    ix *a*.    x *a*.    xi *c*.
    D  Extension – suggested phrases: **Je vais garder un excellent souvenir de cette soirée, madame. On a vraiment bien mangé ... tout était délicieux.**

# Answers

253

**PART 2**

1. (a) Telephone in the basement.
   (b) Non-smoking area.
   (c) Special Summer Offer – 20F 'De Luxe' menu – 'De Luxe' Cheeseburger – small portion of chips – 25 cl drink.
   (d) Never refreeze once thawed.
   (e) Grills at any time – Tea Room – Ice-Cream Parlour and Confectioner's – Open from 11.00 a.m. to 10.00 p.m. even on Sundays.
   (f) You can find take away food products available in most service stations and restaurants, e.g. groceries, delicatessen, bread, drinks.

2. (a) They are for ¼ litre, ½ litre and 1 litre bottles.
   (b) There are French beers and 'others'.
   (c) 18 F
   (d) **Deux quarts d'Évian, un jus de pamplemousse et une Orangina** (or **un soda d'orange**).

3. (a) Open any time without any breaks.
   (a) Hamburger, toasted cheese and ham sandwich, pizza, chips.
   (a) Ice-cream.
   (a) Pizza.

4. (a) Grilled pork chop with chips and lettuce; apple tart. Service is 15 per cent extra.

5. Micro-wave oven available to warm up your meal. Don't put anything metallic in it.
   (b) Get a token from the cash desk when you pay. Then go back when you've finished your meal and exchange the token for a nice hot cup of coffee.

6. (i) What you like about Flunch
   (ii) Your criticisms.
   (iii) Your suggestions.
   (iv) How often you eat in a Flunch restaurant.

7. (a) Hang the order card on the door handle the night before if you want to eat in your room.
   (b) In your room or in the restaurant.
   (c) Fruit juice, roll and croissant, butter, jam; choice of black coffee, white coffee, tea with milk, lemon tea or chocolate.

8. (a) Open during the entire journey.
   (b) No, only a simple hot dish.
   (c) At normal meal times – breakfast, lunch and dinner.
   (d) Only on certain trains.
   (e) Sandwiches, cakes/pastries, drinks, including hot drinks and croissants at breakfast.

9. Product 1: Will keep 24 hours in a fridge; 3 days in the ice-making compartment of a fridge; several months in the *** (−18°) compartment of a freezer, within the 'best eat by' date.
   Product 2: Shouldn't be kept at temperatures above +6°.

10. Preparation: Wash and scrub the potatoes. Wrap each one up in

aluminium foil. Cooking: Put them on the barbecue grill pan. Turn them over four times during cooking without piercing the paper. Testing when ready: After 45 minutes, push a skewer through the potatoes to check if they're cooked. The skewer should go in easily. Making the sauce: Add the chopped herbs to the cream or soft white cheese. Add salt and pepper. How to serve: Serve piping hot without unwrapping the foil. How to eat: Each guest splits her/his potato in two, coats it in the sauce and eats it with a small spoon.

1  (a)    No
    (b)    Fry in a pan with butter for 2 or 3 minutes. When serving, add lemon juice and a little chopped parsley.
    (c)    No.

## VOCABULARY TOPIC 8

**PART 2**

1  (a)    Don't touch the fruit.
    (b)    Please walk around – no obligation to buy (or Admission Free).
    (c)    Cash point – Sale – Special Offer.
    (d)    Please hold the handrail.
    (e)    Have you taken your trolley?
    (f)    Keep your till ticket. A check may take place at the exit.
    (g)    Please close the door.
    (h)    Open continuously from Monday to Friday from 8.30 a.m. to 6.30 p.m.

2  (a)    Postcards–toilet paper–Elastoplast–tinned pâté.
    (b)    The reference to **cabines d'essayage**.
    (c)    **Alcools ... Sécurité ... Reprise des Vides ... Clés ... Service Consommateur.**

3  (a)    Before shopping, put in 10 francs, push, then pull. After shopping, engage the mechanism in the slot and recover your ten francs.

4  (a)    **Nous sommes quatre. On va faire un pique-nique. On voudrait du saucisson et du fromage pour quatre personnes. Un demi-concombre, une demi-douzaine de pêches. On a déjà du pain et du beurre dans la caravane.**

5  (a)    **G. Pain.**
    (b)    **Rallye.**
    (c)    **Super M.**
    (d)    **Au Panier Gourmand.**
    (e)    Not too exclusive – the clothes are off the peg.

6  (a)    They're disposable, with various designs. They're 34 cm square and come in a pack of 20.
    (b)    You get two bottles out of the 8 free.
    (c)    Ready ground. It's vacuum packed. You get four separately packed 250 gm packs in one large package.
    (d)    Bin liners.

# Answers

255

(e) Washing up liquid.
(f) 2×370 gm jars for 12F50.
(g) You pay a deposit on the bottle.

## VOCABULARY TOPIC 9

**PART 1**

A  Je voudrais envoyer un paquet en Grande-Bretagne. Dix timbres à 1.50 et six à 2.20, s'il vous plaît. Alors, donnez-moi dix à un franc, si vous en avez. Où est la cabine téléphonique la plus proche, s'il vous plaît? Il faut compter combien de temps pour arriver en Angleterre? Quelles sont vos heures d'ouverture, s'il vous plaît?

B  1 Firstly at a counter other than **'poste restante'**, then at the **'poste restante'** counter itself. 2 **Téléphone**. 3 **Retraits C.C.P./Change**. 4 **Télégraphe**.

C  Suggestion for message: 'Marcel t'a téléphoné – il t'a demandé de le retrouver devant le cinéma à 9h du soir, jeudi prochain.'

D  Nous sommes à l'Hôtel des Alpes. On a renversé un verre de vin. Vous voyez la tache sur cette jupe. Nous sommes là pour une semaine encore. On peut repasser demain? Suggestions for 'disappointment phrases': On est vraiment déçu. C'est tout à fait inadmissible. On est vraiment loin d'être satisfait.

F  Est-ce qu'il faut des jetons ou des pièces pour faire marcher les machines? Il faut introduire la pièce/le jeton tout d'abord ou quoi? Quand est-ce qu'on met la lessive? Ça dure combien de temps normalement? Ça coûte combien les séchoirs? Ça dure combien de temps?

G  Qu'est-ce qui ne va pas? On peut le/la réparer? Ça sera prêt quand? Je suis vraiment reconnaissant(e).

I  Je voudrais signaler un vol. On m'a volé mon passeport et mon portefeuille. Ça est arrivé il y a dix minutes devant la banque. Un homme m'a agressé. Il était petit aux cheveux châtains plats. Il portait un pantalon noir et un tricot vert. Je suis légèrement blessé(e). Je voudrais voir un médecin quand j'aurai fini de faire la déclaration.

**PART 2**

1  (a) Last collection 6.00 p.m.
   (b) Paris – Provinces – Abroad.
   (c) Reduced postage rate – Normal postage rate.
   (d) Telephone box not working? Dial 13. It's free!
   (e) 'Lavomatique' cannot be held responsible for lost, torn, scorched or stolen clothing.

2  (a) 9.00 until noon and 2.30 p.m. to 5.30 p.m. – Saturdays from 9.00 until noon; after 9.15 as the mail leaves the post office between 9.15 and 10.15.

3  (a) 1.90.
   (b) 2.50

4   (a)    Vous avez une formule pour un télégramme s'il vous plaît? C'est quel guichet pour les télégrammes s'il vous plaît?
    (b)    Service aéroglisseur en grève. Raté dernier train Avignon. Arriverai 11.00 jeudi.
    (c)    Write in capitals the full address (street, block, staircase of flat etc.), the text and the signature (one letter in each square): leave a blank square between each word. The text and the signature (if included) should be fully legible.
5   (a)    telephoning ... sending telegrams receiving mail sending mail ... sending or receiving money.
    (b)    Your bill could well be a lot higher than the official rate (up to a maximum of 30 per cent).
    (a)    Monday to Friday 9.30 p.m. to 8.00 a.m. Sundays and French Bank Holidays all day.
    (c)    Pay a fee and produce some proof of identity (passport or other).
    (d)    In a post office, tobacconist's or from the yellow automatic machines on front of certain post offices.
    (e)    (i) Look for the sticker marked 'Change' in one of the 170 post offices with this facility
           (ii) Look for the sticker CB/VISA or EC in one of the 780 post offices with this facility.
6   (a)    Skirt – 18.80; men's trousers 21.05: shirt: 6.50; towel 1.95.
7   (a)    If the goods don't suit you or if you've changed your mind.
    (b)    Within a fortnight.
    (c)    The goods will be exchanged, or you can have your money back, without any quibble.
    (d)    Fabric/material sold by the metre.
8   (a)    £60 in each.

## VOCABULARY TOPIC 10

**PART 1**

A   J'ai mal à la tête depuis quatre heures. J'ai de la fièvre. J'ai mal au cœur. J'ai besoin d'aller aux toilettes. Je peux me coucher? J'ai mal aux dents.

B   Mon père ne se sentait pas bien il y a deux ou trois semaines. Il s'est remis complètement maintenant.

C   Vous avez des comprimés pour soigner un rhume? Je peux avoir de l'antiseptique et un pansement? Je dois prendre les comprimés combien de fois par jour? Je prends les comprimés avant ou après les repas? Je prends ce médicament déjà contre ma toux. Je dois revenir? Les indications sont sur la bouteille? Vous avez une crème adoucissante contre un coup de soleil? Je me suis coupé(e) en ouvrant une boîte. Je peux me baigner? Ce médicament vous fait endormir?

F   Il y a eu un accident. Quelqu'un s'est blessé la jambe. Il nous faut la police-secours/une ambulance/les sapeurs-pompiers. Il faut dégager le conducteur d'urgence.

# Answers

**PART 2**

1. You're being warned how easily a cigarette end thrown out of a car can start a forest fire. You're asked to use the ashtray in your vehicle.
2. Dial the surgery (38 97 43 94) and follow the instructions on the answering machine.
3. (a) The end of the patrolled stretch of the beach.
   (b) (From top to bottom) Patrolled area with no special hazards – Dangerous area for swimming but patrolled – Swimming not allowed.
4. (a) Anti-drink/drive campaigns (with severe penalties for offenders) – compulsory wearing of seat belts – compulsory wearing of helmets for motor cyclists – speed limits on roads and motorways.
   (b) The suggestions coincide with the major road safety campaigns which are being pursued.
5. (a) One relates to the outbreak of fire in your hotel room; the other to an outbreak of fire elsewhere in the hotel.
   (b) Close the door, leaving the key in the lock. Warn the person on duty. Make for the ground floor, calmly, using the stairs. Warn reception.
   (c) Leave the room calmly when you've closed the windows. Shut the door, leaving the key in the lock. Make for the exit by the staircase.
   (d) If the corridors and staircase are full of smoke.
6. (a) Sunburn.
   (b) Sunstroke.
   (c) Cut a ripe tomato in two and apply the juice to the sunburn (as a substitute for a special cream from the chemist's).
   (d) Don't leave the baby in the sun for the next two or three days without completely covering the sunburn with clothing.
   (e) If the child doesn't get over this quickly, you should call a doctor quickly or take the child to hospital.
   (f) Don't wrap the child up too well. Don't leave her/him playing in the sun for too long, especially in the hottest parts of the day. Make her/him have a rest now and again. Make sure she/he gets a drink regularly.
7. (a) Push the button – release – wait for the operator to reply.
   (b) Presumably from the A6 motorway (place call is made from); took place on the A6 motorway, level with Arbonne, on the carriageway going to the provinces, i.e. away from Paris (place of accident and direction); 1 vehicle only involved (number of vehicles involved); 2 people injured – driver only with minor injuries, passenger seriously injured (number of possible injury victims, their condition, need to remove them from vehicle). Extension: Some suggested phrases – **'Je vous appelle d'une borne de secours sur l'autoroute A6. Ma voiture vient de se renverser. Un pneu s'est éclaté. Mon passager est gravement blessé. Il faut le transporter immédiatement à l'hôpital.**
8. (a) It concerns a British coach.
   (b) The tragedy might have been avoided.

# French

(c)   The driver seems to have lost his concentration for a moment whilst getting his ticket and money ready for a motorway toll booth.
(d)   British vehicle and driver – 44 passengers – Lourdes – 3 a.m. yesterday morning – A 10 motorway, 2 kms from a toll booth – empty road, good surface, no fog – 90 kph – coach zig-zagged – no other vehicles involved – coach ran into ditch and toppled on side – 3 dead; 9 seriously injured plus a further 18 less seriously; legs and arms – emergency services arrived rapidly; fire brigade first, then ambulances (10 in number) – survivors taken to Tours air base which is nearby – tachograph recovered.

## VOCABULARY TOPIC 11

**LEISURE**

A   1. **C'est quel genre de film? Il y a un entr'acte?**   2. Some suggestions:   (a) **On va revenir un autre soir.**   (b) **Ça, c'est dommage, mais on aimerait le voir quand même.**

B   **On voudrait réserver des places pour le match de samedi, pour le Son et Lumière de demain, la pièce du 15 juillet.**

**PART 2**

1  (a)   Tickets bought in the morning are not re-usable in the afternoon.
   (b)   Showering compulsory.
   (c)   Male swimmers – Female swimmers.
   (d)   Violent horse-play, spitting, running, diving into the small pool prohibited.
   (e)   Unaccompanied children less than 6 years old not admitted.

2  (a)   Sunday.
   (b)   **'Jeux sans Frontières'**.
   (c)   No indication of their level of enjoyment is specified.

3  (a)   A review of, and guide to, cinema and entertainment programmes.
   (b)   Weekly.
   (c)   From your newsagent.

4  (a)   From mid July onwards.
   (b)   Scientific – documentary – cartoons – science-fiction; anyone over three years of age; ground floor; free admission.

5  (a)   Round the clock.
   (b)   Tourist and leisure news; practical tips; weather forecasts; guide to eating-places and hotels – everything about the region of Champagne.

# Answers

6
| | M. au Sol | Guerre des E. |
|---|---|---|
| 1 | 8.00 p.m./10.30 p.m. | Cont. from 2.00 p.m. to midnight |
| 2 | 16 F | 25 F |
| 3 | none | none |
| 4 | French | French |

Extension: Wednesday matinée – students – continuous performance – under 13 years of age – soldiers – seats – except – every day – prohibited – French soundtrack – in original language of film.

7  Science-Fiction – Romance – Biographies – Sport – Adventure – Art – Science – History – Detective Novels – Comic Strips – Humour.

8  Adventure – Detective Films – Eroticism – War – Humour – Horror Films – Family Films.

9  Story of violent passion and jealousy. Sounds like a 'bodice ripper'!

10  (a) The wedding of Simon le Bon's brother.
(b) Simon le Bon, his wife, Yasmine, and brother Jonathan, plus the groom, David, and the bride, Jane Griffin.
(c) They wish, rather belatedly, to join in sending best wishes to the couple for their future.

11  (a) Yes.
(b) Ring 23.20.21.04 and speak to Jean-Louis Solau who takes the bookings.
(c) Shooting, diving, camping and horse-riding.
(d) No – it's an introductory course.

12  (a) (Left-hand column first, top to bottom, then right-hand column) camping – sub-aqua diving – cycling – bowls – walking – wind-surfing – fishing – tennis – sailing.
(b) (i) There is a cafeteria, fast catering for families and a refreshment stall (in the summer period). There are picnic areas on the lakeside or in forest clearings.
(ii) All we know is that there is an admission charge and a charge for the various activities.
(iii) Hire of wind-surfing boards and tuition available. Four tennis courses in 1984, although this could be a mis-print for 'tennis court'.

## VOCABULARY TOPIC 12

**PART 1**

B  1. Some suggestions for phrases:
(a) Tu voudrais . . .? Alors on va . . .? Si on allait . . .?
(b) Ah oui, avec plaisir. Volontiers! Ça me plairait énormément.
(c) Ah, c'est dommage, je suis déjà pris(e). Je suis désolé(e) mais ce n'est pas possible.
(d) Si ça ne te gêne pas, j'aimerais plutôt . . .

## PART 2

1.  (a) Folded up as a large hold-all; unfolded as a beach rug; can also be used as a 'beach hut' for changing or as a waterproof 'poncho'.
    (b) It's on special offer only until 30th September.

2.  (a) Function of CAC: To enable people who live in the New Town or in the region to have first-hand experience of artistic production in various forms. Premises of CAC: Activity rooms, club areas, small theatre, multi-purpose rooms.
    Function of M des L: To give technical support in form of staff, premises and material for cultural, educational and leisure initiatives. Examples of activities: Courses; meetings; exhibitions; conferences; creative workshops; broadcasts; showing of films.

3.  (a) They have gone out much more frequently.
    (b) The relationship has become much more serious on his part.
    (c) He let her know, through a third party, that he wanted to 'flirt' with her.
    (d) She 'gave him the elbow' and has hardly seen him since.
    (e) How he can get the relationship back to where it was before he declared his intentions.
    (f) She was shocked or rather disturbed that Christian had made his 'declaration' through another person rather than saying it to her face.
    (g) Christian should insist on talking to L. for the sake of their old friendship.

4.  (a) *All* young people (whatever the age range), whatever the class background or level of education, are concerned by employment prospects.
    (b) Nearly half feel the system does not prepare them for a job they would like to do.
    (c) They were asked whether they thought their lives would be less happy than those of their parents.
    (d) Unemployment; world war or nuclear conflict; terrorism; violence; famine; economic crisis; environmental damage.
    (e) Lack of money; accidents; family misunderstandings; loneliness.

## VOCABULARY TOPIC 13

### PART 1

A   Suggestions for questions for Activity 2: **Il y a combien d'élèves? C'est un collège mixte ou quoi? Il a été construit en quelle année? Chaque cours dure combien de temps? Vous avez combien de semaines de vacances par an?**

# Answers

**PART 2**

1.   (a)   A month.
    (b)   Ice-cream salesperson; not too unpleasant and reasonably well paid.
    (c)   Greece; train then hiking.
    (d)   4 year physics and biology course.
    (e)   Do you know what sort of job you would like to do next year? You're on holiday until what date?

2.   (a)   Ice skating and fencing.
    (b)   It gets very good results in various British inter-schools competitions.

4.   (a)   A good month at the local campsite.
    (b)   A restaurant or other eating place.
    (c)   It's the 20th year in succession that Hutton School have camped in Meung.

5.   (a)   21 pupils from a 4th year (3me in French system) class from a comprehensive in Séméac-Aurelheim.
    (b)   Up at 6.00 a.m.; on the coach to school at 7.00 a.m.; get back home at 7.00 p.m.; homework, supper and in bed by 9.00 p.m.
    (c)   Those specifically referred to are: too long a working day; too much writing; need to change teaching methods; need for pupil choice of teachers; not enough recreational activities. Certain classes are felt to be too large, but there is no reference to the overall size of the school.
    (d)   There are a very large number! In brief: pupil involvement in choice of timetable; more balanced timetable; free schooling (at present there are hidden costs, e.g. materials for practical lessons, trips); split groups for certain subjects into two; better pupil–teacher relationships; the right to choose their teachers; changes in the school rules; increase in outdoor activities and recreation; change in length of school day, e.g. continuous day; avoidance of two different foreign languages being timetabled consecutively; more holidays and more recreation within school; class base for each group as in primary school; right to decorate own room in chosen colour scheme; abolition of detention; more technology for girls; develop a new set of school rules themselves; free ski club/tuition on Wednesday afternoons; afternoon tea for those who stay for school meals; hot drinks machine; change disciplinary system; have a say in major decisions.

## VOCABULARY TOPIC 14

**PART 1**

  A   Qu'est-ce que c'est en français? (Quel est le mot français pour . . .?) Voulez-vous bien écrire ça? Ça s'épelle comment? J'ai oublié le mot français pour . . .

# French

**PART 2**  1  (a) People from European countries other than France who use French as a business language.
(b) By speaking French you will reach a larger number of European business people.
(c) The assumption is that all business people are men.
2  (a) For adolescents or adults; essentially for beginners.
(b) 3 (2 for the pupil's book + 1 tape with exercises)
3

|   | La Rochelle | Amiens |
|---|---|---|
| 1 | 7 July–3 August<br>4 August–31 August<br>7 July–31 August | July |
| 2 | 16 | 18 |
| 3 | with families | at the University |
| 4 | sailing, riding swimming | tennis, swimming |
| 5 | cinema, weekend excursions | shows, library, discos |

## VOCABULARY TOPIC 15

**PART 1**  A  I won't be a moment.
B  **Vous acceptez les cartes de crédit/les chèques de voyage/les Eurochèques? Je dois verser un acompte? Je peux avoir un reçu, s'il vous plaît? Où est la caisse, s'il vous plaît? Je dois payer en avance? Je n'ai rien moins d'un billet de 100 francs. Vous avez des billets de 50 et des pièces de 10 francs?**

**PART 2**  1  (a) Cheques are no longer accepted for purchases of less than 100 F.
(b) Cash payment only.
(c) All credit cards accepted.
(d) Please show proof of identity.
(e) As a security precaution our camera is taking a photo of you as you are writing out your cheque.
2  (a) 101.10 F excluding any bank commission.
3  (a) Withdraw cash from a bank and settle bills in shops, hotels etc. all over the world.
4  (a) There are post offices all over, i.e. in small villages as well as in big cities; everyone knows the post office and can give you directions to the nearest one; you can use the Postchèque in several countries, all in the course of one trip.
5  (a) Cash; cheques; means of identification
(b) CB
(c) Major stores; hypermarkets; restaurants; filling stations; retail outlets; hotels.
(d) Show your card – sign the bill written out by the shopkeeper

# Answers

once you've checked it – get your card back and a copy of the bill from the shopkeeper.

6   (a)    Ask the shopkeeper or bank employee to ring the Local Authorization Centre.
    (b)    It is a free, prompt service.

7   (a)    St-Tropez and Nice; Argelès; St-Tropez and Nice
    (b)    Étretat
    (c)    Anything connected with the beach/sun/water!

# LISTENING EXERCISES

A cassette has been specially prepared to accompany this book and you are strongly recommended to make use of it.

The listening exercises are based on the 15 Vocabulary topics which form Part One of this book. We recommend that you use the cassette as you come to the end of your work on each topic area. In this way, you will be able to see how well you have worked to increase your understanding of the topic.

The cassette contains a number of short items on each topic. In general, the earlier items are slightly easier and the later ones correspond to the level you might expect to find at a higher grade test. Unlike the tests you will actually take, the recordings on this cassette are heard only once. We have done this so that you will get better value for money and because we know that you can use the re-wind button to give yourself a second or third hearing, if you need to.

You will find it useful to re-listen to this cassette as a last-minute refresher shortly before you take your listening test. **Bonne chance et bon courage!**

## TOPIC 1: TALKING ABOUT YOURSELF, YOUR FAMILY AND YOUR FRIENDS

**ITEM 1:**
**MARIE-CÉCILE BERNARD**

1. How old is Marie-Cécile Bernard?
2. How many brothers and sisters does she have?
3. Which brother or sister is the youngest?
4. What is the number of her house in the Rue des Capucins?
5. Which of these is her telephone number?
   - (a)  04  32  72
   - (b)  04  25  62
   - (c)  04  23  62

**ITEM 2:**
**MONIQUE**

1. How many brothers and sisters does Monique have?
2. In which arrondissement of Marseille does she live?
3. What geographical information does she give us about her home town?

4  Which of these is her telephone number?
   (a)   91  02  57  01
   (b)   81  02  37  03
   (c)   92  01  47  02

**ITEM 3:**
**DOMINIQUE AND HER BROTHER**
1  What is the name of Dominique's brother?
2  Since when have they been getting on well?
3  What did they use to argue about?
4  What criticism does Dominique make about her brother?

**ITEM 4:**
**CATHERINE AND MONIQUE TALK ABOUT THEIR PETS**
1  What domestic animal does Catherine have?
2  How old is she and how old was she when the family first had her?
3  How many litters has Nora already had?
4  Why does Catherine not find it difficult to find homes for Nora's offspring?
5  If they are sold, what is the usual price range?
6  Why does Monique not know the exact age of her pet?
7  Give the details of his arrival.
8  What colour was Rikki on arrival and what possible explanation for this is suggested?
9  What did Monique do and how can you tell she is very fond of Rikki?

**ITEM 5:**
**M. ET MME MENDEL**
1  Complete the following identity cards for M. and Mme Mendel:

   *Fiche d'identité*

   Nom de famille ................
   Prénom ......................
   Né(e) à ......................
   Domicilié(e) à ................
   Célibataire/marié(e)/divorcé(e)
   ............................
   Emploi ......................
   Enfants  Boy - loren - 8
            Girl - ........ 4½

   *Fiche d'identité*

   Nom de famille ................
   Prénom ......................
   Né(e) à ......................
   Domicilié(e) à ................
   Célibataire/marié(e)/divorcé(e)
   .......91½..............
   Emploi .Hauswife....
   Enfants  Boy - Bayer 8 years
            Girl - ............

2  Complete this statement from the alternatives given: They live in a house/flat which they own/rent for ... francs per month.

# Listening exercises

**ITEM 6:**
**M. ET MME BOINOT**

1. What is M. Boinot's main job?
2. What is Madame Boinot's main job? — Cook in School.
3. Where do they work together in the evening? Theatre
4. What hours does Madame Boinot work during the day? 8 – 10.30  3-30
5. Give three examples of what she does when she comes home from work. Prepare meal · cleans and irons
6. At what time does M. Boinot set out for work? 7.30
7. How long does it take him to get there? ~~30 minutes~~ 15.
8. Where does he have his lunch? Canteen
9. What example does he give of the way he relaxes in the early evening? Read paper
10. At what time do they both complete their evening work?

## TOPIC 2: YOUR HOME

**ITEM 1:**
**MARIE-CÉCILE AND CATHERINE DISCUSS THEIR HOME TOWNS**

1. In which of these towns does Marie-Cécile live?
    (a) Marseille
    (b) Mayenne
    (c) Moulins
    (d) Meaux
2. How many inhabitants does it have?
3. Give four examples of the recreational opportunities offered by the town.
4. Complete this statement: Catherine lives in the centre/suburbs of Paris/Lyon/Strasbourg.
5. What does her town offer as amenities?
6. What does it not yet offer?

4/6

**ITEM 2:**
**HOW M. FIASTRE HELPS AT HOME**

1. For how long has M. Fiastre been married?
2. How many children does he have?
3. What are the two main ways in which he helps his wife with domestic tasks?
4. Why is the interviewer surprised by his answer to the question about making the bed?
5. How often does he do the cooking and baking?
6. What D.I.Y. task does he admit to having done?
7. Which item of furniture have he and his wife made themselves?
8. Are the domestic burdens equally shared in the Fiastre household?

7/8

**ITEM 3:**
**M. BOINOT'S HOUSE**

1. Does M. Boinot own his house?
2. How did M. Boinot get his house built?
3. What rooms are on the ground floor?

# 268 French

4 What rooms are on the first floor? *Kitchen*
5 What is the basement used as? *Garage*

## TOPIC 3: YOUR SURROUNDINGS AND THE WEATHER

**ITEM 1:**
**FIRST WEATHER FORECAST**

1 What will the weather be like tomorrow morning? *cold. Cool. and overcast*
2 When will it start to rain? *Afternoon*
3 Will it be warmer or cooler than the seasonal average? *Average*
4 Will the sun have set by 8 p.m.? *21 hours*

**ITEM 2:**
**SECOND WEATHER FORECAST**

1 Give the general situation for this morning.
2 Which part of tomorrow is likely to be the sunniest?
3 What might the weather be like on the Atlantic Coast?
4 What is the temperature range across the country?

**ITEM 3:**
**GUIDED VISIT OF ORLÉANS**

1 Where does the guided tour start?
   (a) Rue de la République
   (b) la cathédrale
   (c) la gare
   (d) le parc
2 Whose statue can be seen?
3 What building dates from the thirteenth century?
4 What has an old building been turned into?
5 What happened to the George V Bridge during and just after the Second World War?
6 On our right in the Rue Royale, we are shown a building which
   (a) is the Town Hall
   (b) used to be the Town Hall
   (c) is the town's biggest hôtel.
7 What is next to the railway station?
8 The Parc Pasteur is particularly recommended for tourists interested in . . . ?
9 How far is the Parc Pasteur from the station?
10 Which of these sketch maps would show a visitor how to get from the station to the Parc Pasteur?

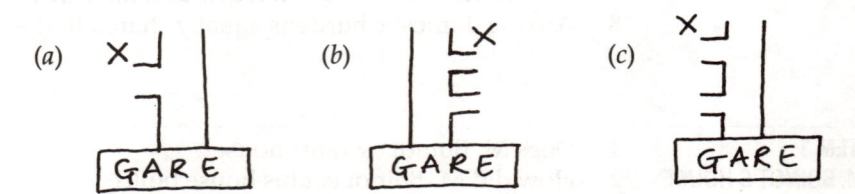

## Listening exercises 269

11  Where does the guide recommend visitors to go for further information?

| TOPIC 4: TRAVEL AND TRANSPORT |

**ITEM 1:**
**STATION ANNOUNCEMENTS**
1  What information is given about the train to Nantes and Quimper?
2  How many stops are there before Nantes?
3  How long will this train stop in Angers station?
4  Will you be able to obtain refreshments on this train?
5  What do you have to do before being allowed to travel on this particular train?
6  Why are you requested not to throw things out of the train window?

**ITEM 2:**
**ENQUIRING ABOUT BUS TRAVEL**
1  How many tickets are there in a carnet and what does a carnet cost?
2  When you get on a bus, you must put your ticket in a machine to make it valid. What colour is the machine? For how long is your ticket valid?
3  At what time does the evening bus service come into operation?
4  What difference is there in the cost of evening service travel?

**ITEM 3:**
**LEAVING YOUR LUGGAGE**
1  What is the cost of leaving items in the left luggage office?
2  When is the left luggage office closed?

**ITEM 4:**
**FINDING YOUR WAY IN TOWN**
1  To reach the town centre, you must go where and then turn which way?
2  How long will it take you?
3  What number bus would take you there?
4  How long would it take?
5  To reach the post office, you must go
   (a)     straight ahead
   (b)     to the left
   (c)     to the right.
6  Then, when you reach a square, the post office is
   (a)     on your left
   (b)     on your right.
7  From where you are now, the post office is
   (a)     nearby
   (b)     a long way away.

## French

**ITEM 5:**
**BOOKING TRAIN TICKETS**

1. When is the lady expecting to travel to Lyon?
2. How much change did she receive when buying her ticket?
3. When does the man hope to travel to Le Mans?
4. Which trains does the employee mark on the timetable for him?
5. What mistake did the employee make?
6. Where might the man have to change?

### TOPIC 5: HOLIDAYS

**ITEM 1:**
**PLANNING FOR THE EASTER HOLIDAYS**

1. How long is Catherine going to spend in Tangiers?
2. What is she going to do?
3. How many times has she already been to North Africa?
4. What is included in the package holiday price?
5. Why is Dominique, currently working in England, going back to France at Easter?
6. Where does she hope to spend her summer holidays?

**ITEM 2:**
**LAST SUMMER HOLIDAYS**

1. Give as many details as you can about Katy's holiday last summer in the Lot area of France.
2. Dominique went to Corsica. What did she spend her time doing and was she successful?

**ITEM 3:**
**A REPORT ON WHERE THE FRENCH LIKE TO SPEND THEIR HOLIDAYS**

1. What proportion of the French like to spend their holidays within France?
2. When they do go abroad, which are their favourite countries and why?
3. What two reasons are given for their reluctance to go to England?
4. What is the generally accepted French view of English weather?
5. What steps have Brittany Ferries taken to encourage the French to come to England?
6. What, however, does a census of the cars transported by Brittany Ferries reveal?

**ITEM 4:**
**M. AND MME BOINOT'S HOLIDAYS**

1. How do the Boinots travel on holiday?
2. Name three of the places they have been to recently.
3. What makes you think that they are not one of those families who always go back to the same place?

# Listening exercises

| | | |
|---|---|---|
| **ITEM 5:** | 1 | Why did she choose to go to Portugal this year? |
| **A YOUNG PERSON'S** | 2 | What is her comment on the Portuguese? |
| **ATTITUDE TO** | 3 | Although she had not yet fixed next year's holidays, in which general direction will she go and why? |
| **HOLIDAYS** | 4 | What are her two main criteria in deciding her holiday? |
| | 5 | Why does she prefer to stay mainly in one place rather than travel about? |
| | 6 | What is her attitude towards travelling? |
| | 7 | Why does she not often go to the seaside in the summer? |
| | 8 | What two kinds of holiday accommodation does she prefer? |
| | | (*a*) hotel |
| | | (*b*) youth hostel |
| | | (*c*) with friends |
| | | (*d*) an official camping-site |
| | | (*e*) casual camping |
| | | (*f*) gîte |

## TOPIC 6: ACCOMMODATION

| | | |
|---|---|---|
| **ITEM 1:** | 1 | What piece of information does the receptionist check as first priority? |
| **BOOKING IN AT A** | 2 | What problem does the young man's booking present? |
| **YOUTH HOSTEL** | 3 | Why does his bill come to 150 francs when a room costs only 40 francs per night? |
| | 4 | What is his room number? |

| | | |
|---|---|---|
| **ITEM 2:** | 1 | Give the make of car, colour of car and country of origin of Pierre Gaston. |
| **CAMPING SITE** | 2 | What is he asked to do? |
| **ANNOUNCEMENTS** | 3 | What will it cost you to go to the camp disco tonight? |
| | 4 | What time does it start? |
| | 5 | What facilities will be available? |
| | 6 | What is going to happen today at 10 a.m. in the camping site? |
| | 7 | What point is stressed by the site announcer? |
| | 8 | What is Michel Lenoir's problem? |

| | | |
|---|---|---|
| **ITEM 3:** | 1 | Why cannot the lady's booking be accepted at the Hôtel de la Gare? |
| **BOOKING IN AT A** | 2 | What is the name of the alternative hôtel suggested and how far away is it? |
| **HOTEL** | 3 | What is its telephone number? |
| | 4 | How would the owner of the Hôtel du Cheval Rouge have completed her room reservation sheet at the end of this conversation? (*see overleaf*) |

| |
|---|
| Date |
| Nom du client |
| Nombre de personnes |
| Chambres réservées: |
| à grand 4 |
| à deux lits |
| à trois lits |
| salle de bain |
| douche |
| Heure d'arrivée |
| Facture |

**ITEM 4:**
**COMPLAINING ABOUT A HÔTEL ROOM**

1. What are the three grounds for the client's dissatisfaction with her room?
2. What excuse does the manageress make when apologizing?

**ITEM 5:**
**INTERVIEW AT THE HÔTEL DU ROI RENÉ**

1. What recent change has seriously reduced the number of customers for the hôtel?
2. What criteria are used by the Commissariat Général au Tourisme in designating a hôtel as four star?
3. What is the situation in this particular hotel with reference to rooms with private baths and toilets?
4. How does M. Cruzel justify his decision not to have television and radio in his bedrooms?
5. Every room has a mini-bar. What, according to the hotel manager, would you be able to find in it?
6. What do you have to do when using the telephone in this hôtel?

# Listening exercises

**ITEM 6:**
**INTERVIEW WITH THE PROPRIETOR OF A CAMPSITE**
1. For how long has M. Durand been in charge of the campsite?
2. Where do his customers particularly enjoy eating?
3. What basic principles have guided M. Durand in the development of his campsite?

## TOPIC 7: EATING AND DRINKING

**ITEM 1:**
**MOTHER AND SON PREPARE TO RECEIVE GUESTS FOR DINNER**
1. At what time are the guests expected?
2. Who are they?
3. What will they eat?
4. How does the mother want Paul to help?
5. Why does Paul want to eat on his own in the kitchen?

**ITEM 2:**
**ORDERING DINNER IN A RESTAURANT**

1. On this menu, tick the items which the customer ordered.

*CARTE*

| | |
|---|---|
| *Hors d'oeuvre* | Potage de jour |
| | Salade mélangée |
| | 6 escargots |
| *Entrée* | Jambon sec |
| | Coquille St. Jacques |
| | Rillettes |
| *Plat principal* | Poule aux champignons |
| | Coq au vin |
| | Entrecôte |
| *Garniture* | Pommes frites |
| | Pomme vapeur |
| | Riz |
| | Yogurt |
| | Fromages |
| *Dessert* | Mousse au chocolat |
| | Pommes au four |

Service compris à 15%

2. What did he have to drink with his meal?

| | | |
|---|---|---|
| **ITEM 3:** <br> **EVERYDAY EATING** <br> **HABITS** | 1 <br> 2 <br> 3 <br> 4 | What is the man's attitude towards eating meat? <br> He likes cheese. Does he prefer goat's milk or cow's milk cheese? <br> Why does he only drink wine rarely? <br> What does he drink instead? |

| | | |
|---|---|---|
| **ITEM 4:** <br> **SCHOOL MEALS** | 1 <br> 2 <br> 3 <br> 4 <br> 5 <br> 6 <br> 7 <br> 8 | At which school are Jean-Denis and Françoise pupils? <br> What reputation does this school have, according to the interviewer? <br> Why does Jean-Denis no longer eat his lunch in the school canteen? <br> What is Françoise's opinion of the meals? <br> How many courses are there usually? <br> Give examples of what the first course might be. <br> Give examples of the main dishes which are served. <br> What special sweet is provided at Christmas? |

## TOPIC 8: SHOPPING

| | | |
|---|---|---|
| **ITEM 1:** <br> **BUYING SHOES** | 1 <br> 2 <br> 3 <br> 4 <br> 5 | What kind of shoes does the customer want and in what size? <br> Where has she seen what she particularly likes? <br> What is the problem with the colour? <br> Why does the shop assistant give her a plastic bag? <br> How much do the shoes cost and how does she pay? |

| | | |
|---|---|---|
| **ITEM 2:** <br> **SUPERMARKET** <br> **ANNOUNCEMENTS** | 1 <br> 2 <br> 3 | What is the special offer? <br> What lost property has been found and where? <br> When will the supermarket be closing? |

| | | |
|---|---|---|
| **ITEM 3:** <br> **BUYING FLOWERS** | 1 | How many flowers does the man buy and at what price? |

| | | |
|---|---|---|
| **ITEM 4:** <br> **INTERVIEW WITH** <br> **HYPERMARKET** <br> **DIRECTOR** | 1 <br> 2 <br> 3 <br> 4 <br> 5 | Although hypermarkets sell almost anything, what does M. Randouineau consider to be his main area of sales? <br> Why does the parking area outside the hypermarket have to be so large? <br> How frequently do people come to the hypermarket? <br> Why does he stay open until 10 p.m.? <br> What two main advantages of a hypermarket are referred to? |

# Listening exercises

**ITEM 5:**
**FINDING YOUR WAY ROUND A HYPERMARKET**
1 What is the customer looking for and what other products will he pass before reaching what he wants?
2 Where are the biscuits?

**ITEM 6:**
**INTERVIEW WITH OWNERS OF A SMALL SHOP**
1 Madame Bourny gives four distinct advantages for people who do their shopping at a small local shop. What are they?

## TOPIC 9: SERVICES

**ITEM 1:**
**AT THE POST OFFICE**
1 What is the cost of a letter to England?
2 What information is given about surface and air mail?
3 How many stamps does the customer buy?

**ITEM 2:**
**LOST PROPERTY**
1 What had the lady lost?
2 When and where?
3 How did she identify her belongings?

**ITEM 3:**
**IN A CAMERA SHOP**
1 What was the lady's problem with her camera?
2 Why did the shop assistant leave her to wait for a few moments?
3 What was the charge for repairing the camera?

**ITEM 4:**
**FINDING A TELEPHONE**
1 Where is the lady directed to?
2 Does she have to go far?

**ITEM 5:**
**USING A TELEPHONE IN A HÔTEL**
1 What number does the customer want?
2 What does the switchboard operator tell him to do?

## TOPIC 10: HEALTH AND WELFARE

**ITEM 1:**
**MAKING A DENTAL APPOINTMENT**
1 What is Mme Lebrun's problem?
2 How does she manage to get an appointment on a day when the dentist is very busy?

3 Why should the secretary be able to find a file with George's details on?
4 What final piece of advice does the secretary give?

**ITEM 2:**
**A VISIT TO THE DOCTOR**
1 What are Mme Durand's symptoms?
2 For how long has she had these symptoms?
3 How many operations has she already had?
4 Does she often have symptoms like these?
5 What does the doctor think might be wrong?
6 Does she recommend an immediate operation?
7 What does the medicine she prescribe taste of?
8 How often and for how long must she take the medicine?
9 The patient has to pay for the consultation. How much and to whom?

**ITEM 3:**
**WITNESSING A ROAD ACCIDENT**
1 Where has the accident taken place?
2 What has happened?
3 What injuries does the victim appear to have?
4 What instruction from the policeman does Mme Barraguin refuse to carry out and why?
5 Has the policeman written down the correct details about the witness:

Nom de famille: BARRAGUIN
Prénom: Hortense
Adresse: 50, rue du Repère, Melun.

6 At what time does the policeman interview Mme Barraguin?
7 What made the cyclist lose his balance?
8 What is Mme Barraguin's personal opinion on the responsibility of the car driver involved?
9 Is that the end of Mme Barraguin's involvement?

## TOPIC 11: LEISURE

**ITEM 1:**
**BOOKING SEATS IN A CINEMA**
1 For which part of the cinema do they decide to buy tickets and why?
2 Why must they hurry?

**ITEM 2:**
**ENQUIRING ABOUT CINEMA OPENING TIMES**
1 On what day of the week did this conversation take place?
2 Why can the manager not give the precise time at which the cinema closes?
3 On which day are they closed for the whole day?
4 Where will the enquirer find the details of the films being shown in the four different cinemas?

# Listening exercises

5 Why does he not give a precise answer to the question about the price of tickets?
6 When are reduced prices available?

**ITEM 3:**
**DISCUSSING LEISURE INTERESTS**

1 What is Monique's favourite instrument and for how long has she been playing it?
2 Her membership of an orchestra has given her the opportunity to travel in countries other than France. Which?
3 What is her favourite sport?
4 How can you tell that she does not still play?
5 Where did she travel with her sports club?

**ITEM 4:**
**M. AND MME BOINOT'S LEISURE ACTIVITIES**

1 What does Mme Boinot do on holiday while her husband is fishing?
2 What is M. Boinot's main leisure activity?
3 Why does it take up so much time?
4 Which day of the week does he set aside for fishing?
5 Here is a list of domestic tasks. Put a tick next to those undertaken by M. Boinot and two ticks next to those done by Mme Boinot:

    ironing
    cleaning the house
    external repairs
    cooking
    washing
    internal maintenance
    painting

**ITEM 5:**
**INTERVIEW WITH A CINEMA DIRECTOR**

1 Why is he not currently in charge of nine cinemas?
2 What has been the change in cinema-going habits?
3 What justifications does he give for the French practice of not allowing smoking in cinemas?

**ITEM 6:**
**INTERVIEW WITH A RUGBY ENTHUSIAST**

1 How had M. de Saint-Dô spent the previous Saturday afternoon?
2 Did he go alone?
3 In his opinion, who was the best player: Jacques Dubroca, Jean-Pierre Rives, Guy Albaladejo, Pierre Lacaze, Eric Champ?
4 How was M. de Saint-Dô involved after the match?
5 What food had been brought over specially for the occasion?
6 What personal opinion does he express about food in France?
7 How many people were at the event?
8 What did they do when the French team arrived?

# French

9   What would the atmosphere have been like if the result had been different?

## TOPIC 12: RELATIONS WITH OTHERS

**ITEM 1:**
**SHOWING A VISITOR ROUND THE HOUSE**

1   When may Michael use the hi-fi cassettes?
2   Whose are they?
3   What does she need to demonstrate to show him how to get into the garden?
4   What is always available if Michael is hungry or thirsty?
5   Where would he have to go to find a bicycle to use?
6   Where is the bathroom?
7   Where are the clean towels?
8   Where must he put his dirty washing?
9   Where can he find an extra blanket if needed?
10  What is the meaning of the lady's final remark?

**ITEM 2:**
**FIXING UP AN EVENING'S ACTIVITIES**

1   Where does the young man want to go to?
2   What is the particular attraction?
3   What family interest does he have in the event?
4   What will they do afterwards?
5   Why must they be there by 7 p.m. when it does not start until 7.30?
6   Where will they meet at 7 p.m.?

**ITEM 3:**
**SPENDING AN EVENING WITH FRIENDS**

1   Where are Annette and Jean-Pierre sitting when Marc and Marie-Claude enter the café?
2   How long is it since they last saw each other?
3   Why do they decide not to accept Marie-Claude's suggestion of going to the cinema?
4   What does Jean-Pierre suggest?
5   Why do they decide against this?
6   This also rules out Annette's suggestion. What would it have been?
7   Marc invites them all to his flat for a drink and . . . ?
8   Why does Annette reject this idea?
9   What do they decide to do in the end?
10  What is the piece of news that Annette and Jean-Pierre want to tell their friends?

# Listening exercises

| | | |
|---|---|---|
| **ITEM 4:** | 1 | Traffic news: which motorway is blocked at Savigny-sur-Orge? |
| **RADIO** | 2 | How many have been injured in the accident at Porte Maillot? |
| **ANNOUNCEMENTS** | 3 | On which part of the Paris boulevard périphérique is the traffic flowing reasonably well? |
| | 4 | News item: how many workers were at the protest meeting? |
| | 5 | What were the two main reasons for protesting? |
| | 6 | What decision was taken unanimously? |

## TOPIC 13: SCHOOL AND CAREER

| | | |
|---|---|---|
| **ITEM 1:** | 1 | Name at least three of the subjects Laurent says he does at school. |
| **INTERVIEW WITH** | 2 | Why does he sometimes get into trouble? |
| **LAURENT** | 3 | Is his teacher a man or a woman? |
| | 4 | What is his opinion of his teacher? |
| | 5 | What kind of punishment does he get when he has been naughty? |

| | | |
|---|---|---|
| **ITEM 2:** | 1 | What are Chantal's main subjects? |
| **DISCUSSION WITH** | 2 | What is the main emphasis in the baccalauréat A course that Gérard is taking? |
| **GÉRARD AND** | | |
| **CHANTAL** | 3 | What is Chantal's opinion of her course? |
| | 4 | Gérard has a different opinion. What is it? |
| | 5 | What is the meaning of the interviewer's concluding remark? |

## TOPIC 14: LANGUAGE

| | | |
|---|---|---|
| **ITEM 1:** | 1 | What invitation does Tante Monique's letter contain? |
| **CONVERSATION ON** | 2 | What is Paul's first reason for not going on his own? |
| **FORTHCOMING VISIT** | 3 | To encourage him to go, what example does his mother give of the value of learning English? |
| **TO ENGLAND** | | |
| | 4 | How could he survive in a linguistic emergency? |
| | 5 | What is Paul's second excuse for not going? |
| | 6 | How does his mother dismiss this excuse? |
| | 7 | What is his third excuse? |
| | 8 | There is no escape for Paul! His mother concludes by giving him two specific instructions. What are they? |

| | | |
|---|---|---|
| **ITEM 2:** | 1 | For whom are the language courses being arranged? |
| **CHAMBRE DE** | 2 | What is the main purpose of the courses? |
| **COMMERCE** | 3 | What two disadvantages of using interpreters are mentioned? |
| **LANGUAGE COURSES** | 4 | In what three activities would a knowledge of languages be useful? |

## French

5 What language course will be offered at what levels?
6 Under what circumstances may non-members of the Chambre de Commerce take part in the courses?

### TOPIC 15: MONEY

**ITEM 1:**
**INTERVIEW WITH A BANK MANAGER**

1 For how many hours a day is the bank open?
2 Most banks close on Saturday and Sunday but some are different. In what way?
3 What are the essential features of a document needed when changing money?
4 What three places are mentioned as possibilities for changing money when the banks are closed?
5 Why might the tourist get a worse rate of exchange at places other than a bank?

**ITEM 2:**
**CHANGING MONEY**

1 What was the customer asked to do first?
2 What was he asked to do next?
3 On what date was this conversation recorded?
4 What was the rate of exchange on that day?

**ITEM 3:**
**USING A CHEQUE BOOK**

1 Why is the customer's name not printed on this particular cheque book?
2 According to the instructions given, which of these would be the correct way of writing the date on the cheque?
   (a)   le 17 juin 1987
   (b)   le 17 – 6 – 87
   (c)   le dix-sept juin mil neuf cent quatre-vingt-sept
3 What, according to the bank assistant, is the advantage of using crossed cheques?

# ANSWERS TO LISTENING EXERCISES

## TOPIC 1

**ITEM 1**
1. 23.
2. Two brothers, one sister.
3. Anne-Sophie (13).
4. 8
5. (c) 04 23 62.

**ITEM 2**
1. None, she is an only child.
2. 14th arrondissement.
3. It is in the South of France.
4. (a) 91 02 57 01.

**ITEM 3**
1. Pierre.
2. Since Dominique left home!
3. The bathroom.
4. He spent too long getting washed.

**ITEM 4**
1. An Alsatian bitch.
2. Now 9 years old; family had her at 3 months.
3. Two.
4. She is a pedigree dog and is mated with a pedigree.
5. Between 600 and 1200 francs.
6. He is a mongrel and she found him.
7. He came into the garden one day and just sat down. The family 'adopted' him.
8. He was blue; he had probably fallen in a paint pot.
9. She washes him and looked after him. She describes him as being 'five kilos of tenderness'.

## French

**ITEM 5**

1. *Fiche d'identité*

| | |
|---|---|
| Nom de famille | MENDEL |
| Prénom | ALAIN |
| Né(e) à | STRASBOURG |
| Domicilié(e) à | DIJON |
| Célibataire/marié(e)/divorcé(e) | marié |
| Emploi | Publicité |
| Enfants | Laurent 8 ans |
| | Florence 4½ ans |

*Fiche d'identité*

| | |
|---|---|
| Nom de famille | MENDEL |
| Prénom | CLAUDE |
| Né(e) à | TOULON |
| Domicilié(e) à | DIJON |
| Célibataire/marié(e)/divorcé(e) | mariée |
| Emploi | ménagère |
| Enfants | Laurent 8 ans |
| | Florence 4½ ans |

2. They live in a flat which they rent at just over 1,000 francs per month.

**ITEM 6**

1. He is a driver for the Town Council.
2. She works part-time in a school canteen.
3. They work at the municipal theatre.
4. She works from 10.30 to 3.30.
5. The washing, the ironing and preparing the evening meal.
6. 6.30 a.m.
7. 45 minutes.
8. In the canteen at midday.
9. He reads his newspaper.
10. At midnight.

## TOPIC 2

**ITEM 1**

1. Mayenne.
2. 15,000.
3. Swimming pool, sports centre, cinema, theatre, youth club.
4. Catherine lives in the suburbs of Paris.
5. Theatre, cinema, small shopping centre, quite a lot of shops.
6. A discothèque.

**ITEM 2**

1. 1½ years.
2. None.
3. Shopping and, occasionally, housework.
4. He has only made the bed once in one and a half years!
5. Rarely.
6. Wall-papering.

# Answers to listening exercises

7 Armchairs.
8 No, his wife does much more than he does.

**ITEM 3**
1 Yes.
2 He built it with his friends, outside their normal working hours.
3 Kitchen, living room and small sitting room.
4 3 bedrooms and a bathroom.
5 Garage.

## TOPIC 3

**ITEM 1**
1 Cool and misty.
2 In the afternoon.
3 Cooler.
4 No.

**ITEM 2**
1 Cloudy with foggy patches.
2 The afternoon.
3 There are likely to be showers.
4 Twenty degrees in the North to twenty-five degrees in the South.

**ITEM 3**
1 Rue de la République.
2 Jeanne d'Arc.
3 The cathedral.
4 Town Library.
5 It was demolished in the war and rebuilt in 1946.
6 (b) used to be the Town Hall.
7 The bus station.
8 Flowers.
9 5 minutes walk
10 (c) (second on the left).
11 Syndicat d'Initiative, Tourist Information Office.

## TOPIC 4

**ITEM 1**
1 It is about to depart.
2 None.
3 Fourteen minutes.
4 Yes.

## 284 French

    5  Pay a special supplement.
    6  You could injure or even kill somebody.

**ITEM 2**
1. There are ten tickets in a carnet and it costs twenty-four francs.
2. The machine is red and the ticket is valid for an hour.
3. 10 p.m.
4. You have to use two tickets per journey instead of one.

**ITEM 3**
1. Two francs per item per twenty-four hours.
2. Never, it is open day and night.

**ITEM 4**
1. Go to the station and turn left.
2. A good five minutes' walk.
3. No. 4.
4. Two to three minutes, once the bus has come.
5. (a) straight ahead.
6. (b) on your left.
7. (a) nearby.

**ITEM 5**
1. Monday afternoon.
2. Ten francs.
3. Tomorrow.
4. She marks the through trains in the morning.
5. She marks the 8.54 by mistake – it does not stop at Le Mans.
6. Nantes.

## TOPIC 5

**ITEM 1**
1. One week.
2. Visit Tangiers and the surrounding district.
3. Never.
4. The flight, hotel room and two meals per day.
5. To sort out some problems associated with her forthcoming university exams.
6. In Scotland.

# Answers to listening exercises

**ITEM 2**
1. Rented an old farm with friends; had very good weather; went swimming and cycling; woken by the chickens in the farmyard.
2. She spent her time water-skiing and wind-surfing but was not successful.

**ITEM 3**
1. Over eighty per cent.
2. Spain and Portugal, for the sun.
3. Crossing the Channel is complicated and expensive.
4. They think it rains there all the time.
5. They have opened a new line from Caen to Portsmouth and they give away a brochure with details of bed and breakfast places in England and Wales.
6. Ninety per cent of the cars using Brittany Ferries are registered in the United Kingdom.

**ITEM 4**
1. They travel by car, taking their caravan with them.
2. Brittany, St. Jean de Luz, Barcelona and Venice.
3. She likes going to places she does not know, as if setting off on an adventure.

**ITEM 5**
1. To see the result of political changes.
2. The Portuguese were very welcoming.
3. She will go to the South in search of the sun.
4. To have a rest and to be with interesting people.
5. People interest her more than travelling around.
6. Travelling is a waste of time and is unnecessarily tiring.
7. There are too many tourists.
8. (c) and (e).

## TOPIC 6

**ITEM 1**
1. She checks that he has a membership card.
2. He wants to stay for four nights but she can only offer three for sure.
3. He is also having breakfast at ten francs each day.
4. Fifteen.

**ITEM 2**
1. Pierre Gaston is driving a red Renault, registered in Belgium.
2. He has to go urgently to the camping site office.

|  |  |  |
|---|---|---|
|  | 3 | Ten francs. |
|  | 4 | 8 p.m. |
|  | 5 | Bar and cold buffet. |
|  | 6 | The dustbins will be collected. |
|  | 7 | This collection is one hour earlier than usual. |
|  | 8 | He cannot find his parents' camping place. |

| ITEM 3 | 1 | The hotel is full. |
|---|---|---|
|  | 2 | Hôtel de la Poste, which is two minutes away. |
|  | 3 | 52 33 02. |
|  | 4 | May 28th/29th, Baker, four persons, one room with double bed, one room with twin beds, both rooms with shower only, arriving at 8 p.m., total bill 594 francs. |

| ITEM 4 | 1 | There is no soap, no towel and the lamp is not working. |
|---|---|---|
|  | 2 | She says that they are very busy and the cleaners have too much to do. |

| ITEM 5 | 1 | The opening of the autoroute has bypassed Aix so that the passing traffic no longer uses this hôtel. |
|---|---|---|
|  | 2 | They are concerned with the comfort in the hôtel, the number of rooms with private bathrooms and toilet, the sitting rooms, restaurant and facilities for the customers. |
|  | 3 | In this hôtel, all the rooms have their own toilet and three quarters have their own bathroom. |
|  | 4 | He believes it is important to respect the quietness of people in neighbouring rooms. |
|  | 5 | He mentions beer, mineral water (fizzy and non-fizzy), whisky and brandy. |
|  | 6 | You have to ask the switchboard operator who will get the number for you. |

| ITEM 6 | 1 | Fourteen years. |
|---|---|---|
|  | 2 | On the restaurant terrace around the wood fire. |
|  | 3 | He aims to give his customers maximum comfort but also wants to respect nature. |

# Answers to listening exercises

## TOPIC 7

**ITEM 1**
1. 7.30 p.m.
2. His father's colleague and wife.
3. Vegetable soup, steak and chips, salad, cheese and apple tart.
4. By laying the table.
5. He does not want to miss a particular programme on television.

**ITEM 2**
1. He ordered the salad, ham (jambon), chicken with mushrooms (poule aux champignons), with rice (riz), followed by cheese (fromages) and baked apples (pommes au four).
2. He had an aperitif, a quarter of white wine, a half bottle of beaujolais, but he did not have any coffee.

**ITEM 3**
1. He does not think it is necessary to eat meat every day.
2. He likes both.
3. He only likes good wine and this is expensive.
4. He usually drinks mineral water and occasionally beer.

**ITEM 4**
1. The Lycée Français in London.
2. It has the reputation of having very good school meals.
3. He has got bored with the same menu over many years.
4. She thinks they are balanced, filling and good.
5. Three – starter, main dish and sweet.
6. Melon, soup, ham, cold pork meats.
7. Chicken and chips, meat and beans, fish.
8. The Christmas log.

## TOPIC 8

**ITEM 1**
1. She wants size 36 sandals.
2. She has seen a pair in the shop window, on the left.
3. She wants a blue pair but they only have black or white in her size.
4. So that she can wear her new sandals and carry her old shoes away with her.
5. 185 francs; she pays by credit card.

**ITEM 2**
1. Ten per cent off suitcases.

## 288 French

|  |  |  |
|---|---|---|
|  | 2 | A pair of leather gloves near till nine. |
|  | 3 | In 10 minutes. |

**ITEM 3** | 1 | He buys six (carnations) for seven francs.

**ITEM 4**
1. Food and drink.
2. Because the customers come from a very wide area and practically all come by car.
3. Usually once a week, or once a month.
4. A lot of shopping is done by families after the husband has come home from work.
5. The cost of articles is low because of bulk buying; it is convenient to have everything under the same roof.

**ITEM 5**
1. He is looking for fish and will go past the wine and fresh products.
2. In the gangway opposite tills seven and eight.

**ITEM 6**
1. Personal contact (they can talk about their family problems); their personal tastes are known (they can be guided in their purchasing); they can buy things on credit (because the Bournys know where all their customers live); they can come on foot.

## TOPIC 9

**ITEM 1**
1. 2 francs 50.
2. All letters to England are sent by air mail.
3. Three.

**ITEM 2**
1. A pair of sun glasses.
2. On platform two, yesterday afternoon.
3. The glasses were in a red case.

**ITEM 3**
1. She could not wind the film on.
2. He took the camera into the dark room so as not to damage the film in the camera.

## Answers to listening exercises

3   Nothing.

**ITEM 4**
1   The post office.
2   No, it is in the square, on the right.

**ITEM 5**
1   Marseille 49 07 11.
2   Hang up and he will call him back.

### TOPIC 10

**ITEM 1**
1   Her son George has got a bad toothache.
2   Somebody has cancelled an appointment for 2.30 p.m.
3   He has already been to see the dentist twice before.
4   Her advice is to give him some aspirin if he is still in pain.

**ITEM 2**
1   She has a headache and stomach ache.
2   She has been feeling very unwell since she got up this morning.
3   None.
4   No, this is the first time.
5   She might be suffering from appendicitis.
6   No, she recommends a course of treatment first.
7   Strawberries.
8   Three times a day for a week.
9   Eighty-five francs, paid to the secretary.

**ITEM 3**
1   Outside the post office in the Rue du Port.
2   A cyclist has been knocked over by a car.
3   He is lying on the ground and cannot get up.
4   She refuses to move on because she is the main witness.
5   No, he has got the wrong house number – it should be 15.
6   9.45.
7   He stopped suddenly when approaching a pedestrian crossing, having apparently failed to notice the red light.
8   In her opinion, he was driving at a normal speed and was also stopping at the crossing when the cyclist fell on to the car.
9   No, the police may need to speak to her again.

# French

## TOPIC 11

**ITEM 1**
1. The balcony, so that they can see better.
2. The film is going to start in two minutes.

**ITEM 2**
1. Monday, because the cinema does not open until 5 p.m.
2. It depends on the length of the film.
3. Sunday.
4. On the posters in the entrance hall.
5. They vary according to the film and can be found at the box office.
6. For everybody on Mondays and for students all week, except Saturday evening.

**ITEM 3**
1. Clarinet, for six or seven years.
2. Germany and Italy.
3. Basketball.
4. She uses a past tense (the imperfect).
5. Mainly within her own region of the country.

**ITEM 4**
1. She knits and reads.
2. Gardening.
3. In addition to the garden round his house, he also has an orchard of fruit trees.
4. Sundays, in the fishing season.
5. M. Boinot does the external repairs and painting, Mme Boinot does the rest.

**ITEM 5**
1. Three are still being built.
2. Cinema goers are not fewer in number but they are much more selective about the films they go to see.
3. The fire risk; the hygiene factor; it is good for people's health not to smoke.

**ITEM 6**
1. He had been to Twickenham to watch the France-England rugby match.
2. No, he went with some colleagues from his school.
3. Eric Champ.
4. He organized a reception for the French supporters.

# Answers to listening exercises

5 French cheese, pork meats and wine.
6 People eat best in the south west of France.
7 350.
8 They stood and sang the French national anthem.
9 They would have enjoyed themselves just as much.

## TOPIC 12

**ITEM 1**
1 Whenever he wants.
2 They belong to the lady's son.
3 She shows him how to open the French window.
4 Fruit juice, mineral water and fruit.
5 Down to the garage in the basement.
6 Next to his bedroom.
7 In the cupboard.
8 In a basket.
9 In the bottom of the wardrobe.
10 If there is anything else he needs, he only has to ask.

**ITEM 2**
1 To the youth club.
2 There is a basketball match against a visiting team from Canada.
3 His cousin is probably playing for the town team.
4 They will go and see their friends at the café.
5 To get a good seat.
6 In front of the Town Hall.

**ITEM 3**
1 At the table by the window.
2 At least a month.
3 Two of them have already seen the film.
4 He suggests a walk along the sea front.
5 Marie-Claude has hurt her foot playing tennis with Marc.
6 She was going to suggest going to a disco.
7 To watch a film on TF1.
8 It would be boring!
9 They decide to spend the evening together in the café.
10 They are going to get married in October.

**ITEM 4**
1 The A6.
2 Four, one seriously.
3 The northern part.
4 Between 4,000 and 5,000.

# French

5  The reduction in working hours and the dismissal of 500 employees.
6  To continue the strike.

## TOPIC 13

### ITEM 1

1  Reading, spelling, history, geography, English.
2  He likes to chatter.
3  A woman.
4  He does not get on well with her because she is too strict.
5  He has to copy out lines.

### ITEM 2

1  Maths, physics and chemistry.
2  Literary studies: philosophy and two foreign languages (English and Spanish).
3  She thinks she has too much work. She would prefer to study fewer subjects but in greater detail.
4  He likes his programme of work and is quite content to study in a more specialized way at university.
5  She wishes them success in their exams in June.

## TOPIC 14

### ITEM 1

1  An invitation for Paul to spend two weeks in England at Easter.
2  He says he is no good at English.
3  She says that many job adverts specifically ask for competence in English.
4  His aunt, and, to some extent, his uncle both speak French.
5  He has things planned with his friends at home.
6  She says that his 'plans' are to stay late in bed in the morning and then spend the evening at the café with his friends.
7  He has no passport.
8  She tells him to (i) write to his aunt to thank her and accept the invitation; (ii) go to the travel agent's next day and find out about the train times.

### ITEM 2

1  For people working in commerce and industry in the area.
2  To enable members of the Chambre de Commerce to improve their export performance through a better knowledge of languages.
3  It is too complicated and too slow.
4  In reading and writing business letters; in answering telephone calls; in sending telex messages.

# Answers to listening exercises

5  English will be offered at three levels; German, Spanish and Italian will be offered at beginners' level.
6  If there is room in the classes.

## TOPIC 15

**ITEM 1**
1  Seven hours fifteen minutes.
2  Some stay open on Saturday but are closed on Monday.
3  The proof of identity must have a photograph and a signature.
4  Some shops, some railway stations and some hôtels.
5  Shops and hôtels will be expecting to make a small profit on the exchange.

**ITEM 2**
1  Sign the traveller's cheque.
2  Produce a document to prove his identity.
3  November 18th.
4  10 francs 77 to the £.

**ITEM 3**
1  It is only a temporary passport.
2  (a)
3  It prevents a lost cheque from being cashed by somebody else.

# INDICES

## INDEX OF VOCABULARY TOPICS

accidents 61, 115–16, 120–2
accommodation 73–82
　finding 193–4, 197
advertisements
　for bag 135
　for bike hire 54
　for businessmen 147–8
　for cinema magazine 127
　for exhibitions 127
　for food shop 97
　for language courses 148–51
　for local radio station 128
　for local shops 98–9
　for restaurant 89
　for supermarket 99–100
　for walkman 37
airports 62
appliances for home 34–5
applications for jobs 143
arranging leisure activities 60–1, 133–4, 224–5

banks 38–9, 110–11
bathing 117
bikes 54
book shops 129
bottle banks 38
breakdowns 50–1, 58
breakfast 90
brochures
　for French visitors to Britain 45
　on rented accommodation 79
　on school 141
　on youth hostels 78
buses 54
businessmen 147–8

cafés 83, 87, 206–7
camera shops 104–5
camping 77–8, 143, 190–1, 194–5, 223–4
career *see* school/career
career choice 141
cars 50–1, 58, 61
cassette tapes for pen-friends
　about home 34
　about identity 28
chemists 113–14
cinema 124, 125, 128–9
clothes shops 95–6
club membership 134
complaints 74–5, 84–5, 144–5

concerts 124, 228
credit cards 155
cultural centres 135–6
customs 52

dentists 176, 177–8
department stores 94
dialogues
　asking directions 47–8, 94
　at accidents 115–16
　at café 83
　at camera shop 104–5
　at chemist's 113–14
　at cinema 124, 125
　at customs 52
　at dinner party 85–6
　at doctor's 114–15
　at dry cleaner's 103–4
　at hotel 76
　at launderette 104
　at museum 64–5
　at police station 27, 105–6
　at post office 101–2, 146
　at restaurant 83–4
　at service station 50
　buying train tickets 49
　making concert reservations 124–5
　on breakdowns 50–1
　on holiday accommodation 73–4, 75
　on identity 27
　on illness 113
　on introductions 133
　on making arrangements 133–4
　on money 152–3
　on railways 49, 50
　on refunds 105
　on shopping 94–6
　on telephone 102–3
　on tourist information 64
　with pen-friend's family 33
diary entries 224–5
dinner parties 85–6
directions, asking/understanding 47–8, 94, 191–2, 195–6
discount warehouse 110
doctors 114–15
dry cleaners 103–4, 109
dustbins 80

eating/drinking 83–93

electrical goods shops 152–3
emergencies 115–16, 120–1
exchange rates 154
exchanges *see* refunds/exchanges
exhibitions 127

fire instructions 118
food *see* eating/drinking
food shops 94, 97–8, 209
friendships 136

garages 205–6
gîtes *see* rented accommodation
guides for tourists 69, 116, 131–2

health/welfare 113–23
heatstroke 119
historic buildings 66–7, 69
holidays 64–72, 208
home 33–9
hotels 73, 74–5, 77, 80–1, 90, 118, 176–7, 205
hovercraft 52

identity 27–30, 211
illness 113–15
introductions 133

jobs, holiday 142–3

labels on food 91, 92
language 146–51
language courses 148–51
launderettes 104
leaflets
　for French visitors to Britain 44–5
　on campsites 77–8
　on historic buildings 67
　on motorways 56
　on museums 69–70
　on post office 108–9, 154–5
　on sport 130–1
　on town facilities 41
　on town industries 43–4
　on trips 68
leisure 124–32
leisure parks 131–2
letters to/from pen-friends 192
　about environment 40–1
　about holiday activities 60–1

　about holiday jobs 142–3
　about school 140
　introductory 29
　postcard 222–3

métro 49, 54
money 152–7
motorways 56, 58, 89, 115–16, 120–1
museums 64–5, 69–70

news programmes 137–8
notices/signs
　at campsites 77, 190–1
　at dry cleaner's 109
　at hotels 77
　at swimming pool 126
　at youth hostels 77
　in French town 41
　on bottle bank 38
　on eating/drinking 87, 88
　on holiday 66
　on métro 54
　on money 153–4
　on parking 57
　on pets 30
　on railways 53
　on roads 53
　on safety 116, 117, 118
　on services 106–7
　on shopping 96, 97

opinion polls *see* surveys/opinion polls
orchestra, visit by 227–9

parking 57
paying for goods 95, 152–3
pen-friends, introductory details for 28, 29, 31–2
pets 30
pocket money 153
police station 27, 105–6
ponies 30
post office 101–2, 107–9, 146, 154–5
postcards 222–3
presents, buying 95, 135
problem page 136

radio stations 128
railways 49–50, 51, 53, 55, 61, 90–1

295

## French

recipes 91, 166–7
refunds/exchanges 95–6, 105, 110
relations with others 133–9
rented accommodation 35–7, 73–4, 75–6, 79–80
reservations
 for accommodation 73
 for concert 124–5
restaurants 83–5, 86, 88–9
roads 53, 58–9, 115, 117; see also motorways

safety 116–18
school/career 140–5
school life 144–5, 189, 194
service stations 50–1
services 101–12
shopping 94–100, 209; see also

money
signs see notices/signs
souvenir shops 152
sport 130–1
sunburn 119
supermarkets/hypermarkets 89, 97, 99–100
surroundings 40–6
surveys/opinion polls
 on accommodation 76
 on appliances 34–5
 on career choice 141
 on club membership 134
 on environment 40
 on holidays 65–6, 70–1
 on hypermarket restaurants 89
 on language skills 146–7
 on leisure 125

on pocket money 153
on restaurants 86
on shopping 96
on television viewing 126
on transport 52–3
on young people 137
swimming pool 126

telegrams 102, 107–8
telephoning 102–3
television 125, 126, 137–8, 180–1
timetables
 railway 55, 61
 school 189, 194
tourist information office 41, 43–4, 45, 64, 65–6, 75
traffic jams 58–9
travel 47–63

travellers' cheques 102, 110–11, 154
trips 68

unexpected, coping with 51–2

video French course 148
video hire shops 129
visitors to Britain, information for 44–5

walkman 37
weather 42–3
weddings 130
welfare see health/welfare

young people 31, 38–9, 117, 137
youth hostels 77, 78–9, 175–6

## INDEX OF EXAMINATION SKILLS

accent, French 201–2, 215
alternative ways of communicating 206–7, 213–14, 232–3
anticipation skills 207
appropriateness of language see style, appropriate
assessment 13
 in listening comprehension 163
 in reading comprehension 185
 in speaking test 205, 214–16
 in writing test 233
 positive 205, 214
attitudes/opinions, identifying 165, 197

beginning of words 171, 173

cassette tapes for study 15, 167
checking piece of writing 220, 221–2
check-lists 24
 on accommodation 81–2
 on eating/drinking 92–3
 on health//welfare 122–3
 on holidays 72
 on home 39
 on identity 32
 on language 151
 on leisure 132
 on money 157
 on relations with others 138–9
 on school/career 145
 on services 111–12
 on shopping 100
 on surroundings 46
 on travel 62–3
class work 205
clues to meaning 163, 168, 188, 197
 background knowledge 171
 contextual 169, 173–4

grammatical 169–71
 in reading 195
 sound patterns 172
 word patterns 171–2, 173
communication, primary importance of 14, 214–15, 220–1, 232–3
concentration 212
context, clues from 169, 173–4
conversation, general 203, 204, 210–11, 215
criteria, national
 assessment of candidates 163, 185, 214–16, 233
 expectations from candidates 163, 185, 201, 219
 for listening comprehension 163
 for reading comprehension 185
 for speaking test 201
 for writing test 219
criterion referencing 13
cross referencing 15

descriptions of incidents based on pictures 229–32
dictionaries 15–16
differentiation in oral tasks 204–6
difficulties of speaking test 212–14
driving test 13

endings of words 170, 172–3
entry requirements for GCSE grades 12
examiners 203–4, 205, 210
expectations from candidates, in national criteria
 in listening comprehension 163
 in reading comprehension 185
 in speaking test 201
 in writing test 219

'faux amis' 173–4
fluency, oral 202

GCE O Level 9
GCSE (General Certificate of Secondary Education)
 assessment in 13; see also assessment
 benefits of 14
 effect on students 11–12
 fairness of 12–13
 grades 9, 11–12; see also higher tests
 introduction to 9–10
 syllabuses of 13
 thinking behind 11
 see also listening comprehension; reading comprehension; speaking test; writing test
gist, understanding 166, 169, 195–6, 197
grammar 15, 32, 221–2; see also verb tables
grammatical clues to meaning 169–71

handwriting 186, 192, 195, 223
higher tests 12, 201, 202, 204, 206, 207, 208, 211, 219, 220

initiative-taking 204–5
instructions, careful reading of 188, 195, 220, 229
irregular verbs 237–41

key points, extracting 186–7
knowledge, background 171, 176–7, 194, 195, 197

language tasks see check-lists

letters 186, 225–9
listening comprehension 161–81
 and national criteria 163
 clues to understanding 169–73
 points to bear in mind 163–4
 sample questions 174–81
 tackling examination, hints on 168–9
 two-stage approach 177
 types of skills in 165–8
 typical activities in 164–5
listening to examiner 207, 210, 212

memory 164
messages/notes/forms 222–4
mis-hearing 174
multiple-choice questions 163

narrative role-play 203, 211–12, 215
negotiating skills 206
nerves, examination 207, 212
Northern Examination Association 23
note-making 168–9
notices/signs, understanding 186

outlines, expansion of 230

partner, working with 25, 28–9, 105, 115, 134
phrases
 collecting 24, 25
 for beginning/ending letters 226
 for narrative 229–30
points to bear in mind
 in listening comprehension 163–4
 in reading comprehension 185–6
 in speaking test 201–2

# Indices

in writing test 219
positive assessment 205, 214
predictability/unpredictability 205–6
profile of competence 13
pronunciation *see* accent, French

radio, for study 167
range of topics, importance of 16
reading comprehension 16, 183–97
  and national criteria 185
  points to bear in mind 185–6
  sample questions 189–97
  tackling examination, hints on 188
  types of skills in 187–8
  typical activities in 186–7
realism of conversation 210
recording of oral test on cassette 203
reflexive verbs 237
regular verbs 236–7
revision 16, 17, 185, 202
role-play 17, 202, 204, 206–8, 211–12, 214–15

sample questions
  in listening comprehension 174–81
  in reading comprehension 189–97
scanning through text 187, 194–5, 197
SCE (Scottish Certificate of Education) 9
similarities between French and English 173–4

skills, types of *see* types of skills
skills practice 24, 25–6
  on accommodation 77–81
  on eating/drinking 87–92
  on health/welfare 116–22
  on holidays 66–72
  on home 35–9
  on identity 29–32
  on language 147–51
  on leisure 126–32
  on money 153–7
  on relations with others 135–8
  on school/career 141–5
  on services 106–11
  on shopping 96–100
  on surroundings 41–5
  on travel 53–62
skimming through text 187, 195–6, 197
sound patterns 172
speaking test 199–216
  and national criteria 201
  assessment of 205, 214–16
  conversation, general 210–11
  differentiation in oral tasks 204–6
  difficulties of 212–14
  points to bear in mind 201–2
  role-play 206–8, 211–12
  strategies in 213–14
  tackling examination, hints on 206–12
  typical activities in 202–4
  visual stimulus, questions on 208–9
speech, French, differences from written French 167–8

speed of French speech 167
stimulus material 23–4
  on accommodation 73–6
  on eating/drinking 83–6
  on health/welfare 113–16
  on holidays 64–6
  on home 33–5
  on identity 27–9
  on language 146–7
  on leisure 124–5
  on money 152–3
  on relations with others 133–4
  on school/career 140–1
  on services 101–6
  on shopping 94–6
  on surroundings 40–1
  on travel 47–53
strategies
  for speaking test 213–14
  for writing test 232–3
style, appropriate 207–8, 215, 220, 225, 226
syllabus 13, 23

tackling examination, hints on
  listening comprehension 168–9
  reading comprehension 188
  speaking test 206–12
  writing test 220–1
television, for study 167
tenses 205, 207, 208, 220, 229
timing in examinations 188, 222
two-stage approach to listening comprehension 177
types of skills
  in listening comprehension 165–8

  in reading comprehension 187–8
typical activities
  in listening comprehension 164–5
  in reading comprehension 186–7
  in speaking test 202–4
  in writing test 219–20

understanding, importance of 163–4, 185

verb tables 235–41
visual stimulus, questions on 203, 204, 208–9
vocabulary
  active role in developing 24–5
  importance of 15
  lists 23, 24–5
  range of 16

word patterns 171–2, 173
writing test 217–33
  and national criteria 219
  assessment of 233
  checking piece of writing 221–2
  descriptions of incidents based on pictures 229–32
  letters 225–9
  messages/notes/forms 222–4
  points to bear in mind 219
  strategies for 232–3
  tackling examination, hints on 220–1
  timing of 222
  typical activities in 219–20

*Index compiled by Peva Keane*